The German Greens: Challenging the Consensus

GERMAN STUDIES SERIES
General Editor: Eva Kolinsky

Volker R. Berghahn and Detlev Karsten, *Industrial Relations in West Germany* (cloth and paper editions available)
Eva Kolinsky (ed.), *The Greens in West Germany: Organisation and Policy Making*
Eva Kolinsky, *Women in West Germany: Life, Work and Politics*

In preparation

Eckhard Jesse, *Elections: The Federal Republic of Germany in Comparison*
Josef Esser, *The Politics of Industrial Policy in West Germany: Case Studies of Steel and Telecommunication*
Richard Stoess, *Right-wing Extremism in West Germany: Its Roots, Development and Organisation*
Alan Kramer, *West German Economy, 1945–1955*
Douglas Webber, *Health Policy in West Germany*
Michael Fichter, *Labour Unions in West Germany*
J.K.A. Thomaneck, *Workers and Trade Unions in the GDR*
Thomas Hummel, *International Marketing in West Germany*
Detlev Bald, *The Bundeswehr: Its Origins, Structure and Role in West German Society*

The German Greens:

Challenging the Consensus

Thomas Scharf

BERG

Oxford / Providence, USA

First published in 1994 by

Berg Publishers Limited

Editorial offices:
221 Waterman Road, Providence RI 02906, USA
150 Cowley Road, Oxford, OX4 1JJ, UK

© Thomas Scharf 1994

Library of Congress Cataloging-in-Publication Data
A catalogue record for this book is available from the
Library of Congress

British Library Cataloguing in Publication Data
A catalogue record for this book is available from the
British Library

ISBN 0–85496–777–X (hb)
0–85496–884–9 (pb)

Printed in the United Kingdom
by Short Run Press, Exeter.

To Jane

Contents

Contents

List of Tables

List of Figures

Acknowledgements

This study could not have been completed without the willing-ness of countless Green local political activists to respond to my questions and provide relevant information. The Mainz Greens deserve particular credit in this regard for granting access to all manner of documents, the confidentiality of which representa-tives of other parties would doubtless have wished to preserve. My thanks are due in particular to the three business managers of the Mainz Green *Fraktion*, Alla Bohn, Roland Graßhoff and Barbara Schneider, who endured my presence with patience and good humour between October 1987 and July 1988.

I am also indebted to the many institutions which provided the statistical data which were necessary for the completion of this study and to the Economic and Social Research Committee and the German Academic Exchange Service which funded the research on which the book is based. Colleagues at the Centre for Social Policy Research and Development, University of Wales, Bangor and subsequently at the University of Keele were kind enough to grant me sufficient time alongside my other responsi-bilities in which to complete the final stages of this work. Above all, however, this book owes much to the quiet encouragement and enduring support of three people. Eva Kolinsky guided the study from beginning to end and was always willing to provide constructive comments upon initial drafts. Claus Scharf's com-prehensive, inside knowledge of the local politics and history of Mainz was frequently called upon when other sources of infor-mation proved inadequate. Finally, this study owes a lot to my wife, Jane, to whom it is lovingly dedicated.

Thomas Scharf
January 1994

1
Introduction

The failure of the Greens – *Die Grünen* – to repeat their successes of the 1980s was undoubtedly one of the major surprises of the first elections held in post-unification Germany in December 1990. This electoral rebuke to what had until then been the most successful of Europe's ecological parties confirmed the existence of a growing crisis within the Greens. Indeed, crisis is a term which is often associated with the German Greens. For some commentators, the very emergence of the Greens in the late 1970s symbolised the presence of a crisis within the Federal Republic's established party system. The Greens developed at a time when the concentration of electoral support in western Germany's three established parties was at its most pronounced, with only 1 per cent of voters in the 1976 Federal Election voting for parties other than the SPD, CDU/CSU or FDP. For the Federal Republic's youngest age-groups in particular, raised in a favourable economic and social climate and already engaged in more active forms of political involvement in citizens' initiative groups, the Greens appeared to provide a credible alternative to the lacklustre policies and staid organisational structures of the country's traditional political parties. The inability of the established *Volksparteien* to respond adequately to the growing ecological, social and democratic challenges of the late twentieth century played into the hands of the fledgling political organisation. Germany's stable party system began to open up. When the Greens first secured representation in the *Bundestag* following the 1983 Federal Election, this was the first time since 1953 that a fourth political party had succeeded in breaking into the established party system and the first time since 1961 that there had been four parliamentary groups in the *Bundestag*.

To understand the appeal of the Greens in the late 1970s and early 1980s, it is important to emphasise the differences between this new political force and the established party system in western Germany. Electoral participation by the Greens represented the final stage of a process which saw the ecological movement

1

develop from being a force which was primarily based outside west Germany's parliaments to one essentially located within them. The Greens are a product of the protest movements which emerged in the Federal Republic in the wake of the student revolts of the late 1960s. A growing disenchantment with the established consensual processes of Germany's representative democracy among the younger and better-educated population groups facilitated the emergence of a series of new social movements whose aim was to provide citizens with a direct influence over decision-making structures. Rucht (1980) identifies three separate phases in the initial progression of the protest groups from movement to political party. In the first phase, which began in the second half of the 1960s and lasted until 1973, the individual citizens' initiative groups were still in their formative stages. A wide range of initiative groups existed across the Federal Republic, but although they addressed common issues they tended to view the topics in isolation from one another. This changed during a second phase of development. Between 1973 and 1976 a consolidation of the citizens' initiative groups occurred against the background of growing disillusionment with the slow pace of social and political reforms under the SPD–FDP government and a perceived worsening of the environmental crisis. At one level there was a thematic consolidation of the initiative groups, with the issues addressed by the groups being perceived within a broader context. With respect to environmental groups, for example, there was a heightened awareness of the global dimension of their locally based work deriving from a series of well-publicised scientific studies predicting an impending global environmental breakdown. At a second level, an organisational consolidation of the citizens' initiative groups took place, with individual groups beginning to collaborate on specific topics on a regional and occasionally on a national basis. For example, the *Bundesverband Bürgerinitiativen Umweltschutz* (BBU), formed in 1972, brought together almost 1,000 individual initiative groups who had almost 350,000 members between them in 1978 (Murphy 1979:53). The networking of the extra-parliamentary groups primarily occurred with regard to the mobilisation of protest against the construction of nuclear installations in several areas of Germany, in particular in the localities of Whyl, Brokdorf, Gorleben and Grohnde. A final phase of the progression of the Greens from movement to party began in 1977. Fuelled by public disquiet over questions of nuclear safety and possible military uses for nuclear by-products, the burgeoning anti-nuclear movement seized the opportunity to hit the politicians where it was likely to hurt them most; by taking votes away from them in elections.

The initial electoral successes of ecological lists in local elections in Lower Saxony (October 1977) and Schleswig-Holstein (March 1978) were soon followed by gains at elections to regional parliaments in Bremen, Baden-Württemberg, Hamburg and Hesse. Indeed, the role played by elections of all types in the organisational development of green lists is of the utmost importance. The prospect of competing as a single force in the European Elections of 1979 served to facilitate the programmatic and organisational consolidation of a host of green, alternative and rainbow groupings at national level. This process was accelerated by the imminence of the Federal Election of October 1980, which was preceded by the formal establishment of the Green Party in January 1980 at Karlsruhe. Electoral considerations served to force a degree of discipline upon factions vying for influence over and control of new political groups, which in turn promoted the process of consolidation and encouraged the achievement of at least temporary compromises on a host of divisive organisational and ideological questions. The major breakthrough for the Greens at national level came with the 1983 Federal Election, where they secured 5.6 per cent of the vote and gained 27 seats in the *Bundestag*. This was quickly followed by success at the 1984 European Elections and by the short-lived participation from the autumn of 1985 of Greens in an alliance with the SPD at regional level in Hesse. The Greens had become a significant factor in the German party system by the mid-1980s and were able to use their political platform to initiate debate on many of the so-called New Politics issues previously neglected by the established political parties, including ecological and peace issues, the rights of social minority groups and women's issues. Parliaments also became open to greater public scrutiny, with the Greens successfully calling the activities of the established parties to task in a series of public scandals.

However, success brought its own problems for the Greens. The shift towards electoral politics should not be perceived as an inevitable result of the organisational and thematic broadening of the new social movements in Germany. The motives behind participation in elections were most varied and it was clear that not all movement activists supported the electoral approach (Stöss 1987:293). Despite the belief consistently promoted by the Greens that they represented the parliamentary arm of the extra-parliamentary movement, for example, it soon became evident that a number of previously unrewarded political actors had been instrumental in the movement's ultimate shift into the parliamentary arena. Above all, members of failed Marxist groupings and unsuccessful conservative politicians acted as initiators in the formation of ecological parties, seeking to benefit from the expanding public interest in environmental issues (Klotzsch and Stöss 1986). Mez (1987) points out that movement activists opted for the parliamentary approach primarily as a means of safeguarding their interests and of preventing such opportunistic politicians from assuming the exclusive right to represent their cause. Consequently, there was a wide variation between the development of ecological parties in each of the Federal Republic's regions. The Greens spanned the whole political spectrum, from the communist-inspired groups which developed in certain urban areas (for example *Bunte Liste – Wehrt Euch* in Hamburg and its environs) to the rather conservative groups which formed in rural parts of west Germany (for example Grüne Liste Umweltschutz (GLU) in Lower Saxony). While it was possible for conflicting ideologies to coexist successfully at local level, once the various groups sought to establish themselves as regional or national bodies, underlying tensions inevitably came to the surface. The 'historic compromise' between neo-Marxist and conservative interests began to collapse almost as soon as the ink had dried on the Greens' programme adopted in 1980.

One of the many paradoxes of the Greens was that although they sought to provide a radical alternative to the established participative norms of western Germany and favoured the mechanisms of a grassroots democracy – *Basisdemokratie* – they rapidly became integrated into the parliamentary process. In contrast to the representational democratic structures of the established political actors in Germany, the Greens had set out to be an openly participative force, an 'anti-party party'. Based upon organisational forms adopted by the new social movements, the Greens aimed to implement grassroots democratic structures, with meetings being open to party members and non-members alike, party representatives being bound by members' decisions to a particular course of action (imperative mandate) and limits being placed upon the periods served by party and public office holders through a system of rotation. This strategy consistently attracted criticism both from members of the Greens and from beyond the party, with some conservative critics questioning the constitutional legality of the control mechanisms placed upon party representatives (Stöss 1984a,b). However, while it had been adopted as one of the Greens' four guiding principles ('ecological, social, grassroots democratic and non-violent'), the grassroots democratic strategy could not be successfully implemented. The desire of prominent party representatives to meet the professional requirements associated with parliamentary activity was increasingly called into question by party activists who felt that the link with the activists of the Greens' grassroots was being threatened. A series of highly publicised and acrimonious disputes between different sections of the Greens' organisation ensued. Some party members refused to be bound by the imperative mandate while others astutely rotated from one party position to another to avoid the condemnation of the grassroots. Above all, however, it proved difficult for the Greens to attract sufficient support either from their own membership or from their allies in the new social movements to sustain the desired system of checks and balances applied to their representatives. The avowedly amateur (unpaid) party organisation could no longer compete with the increasingly professional parliamentary groups, with their access to information and public funds.

There followed a period in which the Greens became bogged down in unproductive internal party squabbling. Programmatic, ideological, organisational and strategic considerations gave rise to bitter conflicts, with a bewildering number of new factions joining in the debate at successive party conferences. The realists, favouring reforms of the political process through making deals with established political forces, were pitted against a fundamentalist wing which rejected all forms of collusion with established parties. While eco-libertarians sought to promote individual responsibility and reduce the state's influence on individual rights, the eco-socialist wing adopted a leftist approach, seeking to forge an alliance between the new social movements and blue-collar workers in order to alter production processes which threatened the environment and the rights of social minority groups. Each faction had its own regional stronghold and was able to exercise its influence over some element of Green Party structures. Electoral victories or electoral reverses were employed by the competing factions as evidence to prove the legitimacy of their particular stance. Surprisingly perhaps, intra-party disputes did not appear to have a negative effect on the Greens' electoral performance during the initial years of their existence. No matter what they did, so it came to be seen, the Greens went from strength to strength. However, the Green vote finally began to stagnate after the party's strong showing in the 1987 Federal Election.

Given the heterogeneity of the Greens in their formative years, researchers experienced some difficultly in clearly identifying the social characteristics of the Greens' support. This led some commentators significantly to underestimate their potential level of support (for example Rönsch 1980a:426). Researchers still dispute the relative significance of social structural and attitudinal factors in explaining the emergence of the Greens. Yet while different means continue to be used to describe the Greens' core electorate, the party clearly derives the major part of its vote from the young, well-educated, more commonly male, members of the new middle class who are concentrated in Germany's towns and cities, where the Greens benefit from the existence of relatively stable social milieux (Veen 1987 and 1989). The fact that such milieux change only slowly over time lends support to the suggestion that the Greens will remain a decisive factor in German politics in years to come (Irving and Paterson 1991:370; Müller-Rommel 1989). From this perspective, recent electoral setbacks for the Greens might be interpreted as representing little more than a short-term hitch. However, the failure of the Greens at the 1990 Federal Election still came as something of shock, not least to the Greens themselves. For the first time at federal level, the crisis of the Greens was reflected in a decline in electoral support. Opinion polls conducted in the run-up to the first all-German elections had predicted a comfortable level of support for the Greens amounting to 7 or 8 per cent of the electorate. This electoral reverse was at least arguably of the Greens' own making. Disagreement between the Greens in the two parts of Germany over the vital issue of unification was reflected in a failure to present a single electoral list. The Greens in western Germany rejected the treaty stipulating the terms of unification, despite the support given to it by the Greens in the new federal states and by the overwhelming majority of their own supporters. While the east German *Bündnis 90*/Greens passed the 5 per cent hurdle (6.0 per cent), the western Greens fell just short (4.8 per cent). The fact that the SPD's candidate for the chancellorship, Oskar Lafontaine, had sound ecological credentials encouraged some potential Green voters to support the Social Democrats, while others simply failed to use their vote. Further reasons for the Greens' poor showing in the 1990 election are to be found in their organisational inadequacies and in the electorate's disenchantment with the internal party squabbling. The party's very existence has subsequently been called into question (Raschke 1991). To onlookers, the difficulty is in explaining not only what has happened to the erstwhile most successful of Europe's ecological parties, but also in predicting the future of the German Greens (Kaltefleiter 1991:30; Müller-Rommel 1991). Indeed, the question has to be posed whether the Greens are at all relevant in post-unification Germany. The participation of Greens in regional governments in Lower Saxony and Hesse and the success, at the third attempt, in securing seats in the *Landtag* of North Rhine Westphalia provide some firm indications that the Greens' star has yet to wane fully. Further encouragement can be found in the largely unpublicised activities of the Greens at local level.

In focusing upon the role of the Greens in Germany's local politics this study raises issues which have a direct bearing upon any wider assessment of the future chances of the Greens in Germany's party systems. The study looks into such questions as the relationship between the Greens and their supporters in the new social movements, the reaction of the established political parties to the Greens and the nature and scope of Green policy measures. An analysis of the Greens' role at local level lends itself particularly well to a discussion of such topics, since this is the arena in which the majority of Greens are actually politically active and in which the profile of the party has changed most rapidly during its relatively short lifetime. At local level there were estimated to be around 6,000 Green local councillors in the late 1980s (R. Roth 1988). The extent of Green local political involvement is much greater even than that implied by this figure, since there are countless further activities at local level throughout Germany in which Greens are engaged. For a party with a stagnating membership of around 40,000, local political involvement consumes a substantial proportion of the Greens' activists' time and resources. The widely debated 'parliamentarisation' (*Verparlamentarisierung*) of the Greens has evidently occurred less at the federal and regional levels than at the local level of the German party system. This fact alone would provide ample reason for conducting an analysis of the Greens' role at local level. Yet, apart from the work of Werle (1981) and Roland Roth (1988), there has been a marked absence of objective analyses of Green involvement at local level.

Two broad areas are considered in this examination of the Greens' role in Germany's local politics. Firstly, there is cause to look at the impact of the Greens upon established forms of local politics. The purpose is to establish whether the New Politics approach of the Greens at local level has contributed to a politicisation and parliamentarisation of a sphere of government which has traditionally been regarded as being 'unpolitical' in Germany. This provides a basis for assessing the extent to which any resulting conflict can be attributed to a divide between an emergent 'New Local Politics' and the traditional 'Old Local Politics'. Secondly, the study seeks to analyse the possible effects of local political involvement upon the Greens themselves. In particular, attention is paid to the degree to which the party's organisational structures affect the ability of the Greens to resist pressures which might lead to their integration into the 'established' political system. Although the focus for attention is necessarily directed towards the experience of the Greens in the western *Länder*, some comments can also be made about the possible future effects of Green participation in the local politics of Germany's five new regions. However, given that local government in the eastern *Länder* still awaits administrative and constitutional reform and that the local party systems are not yet well developed there, the study primarily concentrates on local political developments in Germany's western regions. In some ways, the Greens are perhaps best regarded as a 'western' phenomenon, reflecting specific processes of social, economic and political change in modern democratic states.

The study is divided into two parts, with a concluding summary. Part I provides an introduction to the role of the Greens in Germany's local politics. Chapter 2 details the traditional approach to local politics in Germany against the background of a description of Germany's local political structures. The Old Local Politics, with its administrative, unpolitical approach, is then contrasted in Chapter 3 with the emergence of a New Local Politics in the 1970s and 1980s. The transition to more overtly political and confrontational styles of local politics is discussed in the context of changes in party systems at all levels of Germany's political system brought about by the process of socio-economic modernisation. Building upon the theories of the New Politics, the extent to which variations in the rate of social and economic change across Germany can influence the development of its party systems is analysed. Chapters 4, 5 and 6 discuss general features of the Greens' role at local level, outlining the scale of Green local representation, the difficulties experienced by Greens active in local councils in organising their political activities and the manner in which the Greens' ideological approach to local politics sharply contrasts with the traditional Old Local Politics approaches of Germany's established political parties.

A case study of the Greens in one particular German city, Mainz, is undertaken in Part II. Reasons for the selection of Mainz are presented in Chapter 7, providing the basis for an analysis of the role of the Greens in the city's local party system between 1984 and 1987. In particular, events surrounding the failure of the city's SPD and Green council groups to agree upon a joint programme for the period under review are addressed in terms of their relevance to the New–Old Local Politics debate. The complementary Chapters 9 and 10 address the changing agenda of Mainz's local politics by examining the parliamentary initiatives (council motions) introduced by the four parties represented on the city council for the same three-year period. Potential strategic and programmatic differences between the parties are analysed using both quantitative and qualitative methods.

The purpose of these two chapters is to identify both the degree to which Mainz was characterised by a New Politics–Old Politics divide during the course of the analysis and the extent to which the Greens were responsible for introducing initiatives which resulted in conflict.

The study concludes with an assessment of the degree of importance to be accorded to the role played by the Greens in the changing nature and style of Germany's local politics. The extent to which the changes brought about by the Greens amount to the emergence of a New Local Politics dimension at local level is discussed and the influence of widespread participation in local politics upon the Greens examined.

Part I

The Greens in Germany's Local Politics

2
Germany's Old Local Politics

There are good reasons for undertaking a study of political change in Germany's local politics. In general, the Federal Republic's local level has been neglected in the standard works of English-speaking political scientists. At best, it warrants mention under the general heading of 'federalism'. Until recently, this criticism even applied to research undertaken within Germany itself (see Schacht 1985; Sontheimer 1979:206). Only in the 1970s did German political scientists begin to develop an active interest in local politics. Given that the Federal Constitution (*Grundgesetz*) apparently accords local authorities extensive rights to address all policy areas of relevance to its citizens (Article 28.2), the absence of research on the local level in Germany might at first appear rather surprising. The main reason for the slow development of research interest on the local level of the German party system is historical. Traditionally, the view has prevailed that this sphere of government is dominated by 'unpolitical' and 'consensual' practices. Local self-government in Germany has been perceived in terms of the need for objective decision-making, which transcends party political debate. Only relatively recently and in a limited number of western Germany's 8,500 localities (*Gemeinden*) has a gradual shift occurred towards the establishment of more parliamentary styles of debate.

Against this background, therefore, this chapter seeks to provide an overview of the duties, structures and established practices of local authorities and their political representatives in the Federal Republic. The aim is to provide a foundation for the discussion of changes in Germany's local politics, which in general are to be associated with the emergence of the New Politics and the success of the Greens in gaining a foothold at local level. However, when discussing political change, one must remain conscious of the danger of over-emphasising the points of change, whilst ignoring the persistence of existing structures and forms of activity. In this context, attention will also be drawn to those features at local level which have remained unchanged and which serve to stabilise local political activities in Germany. The elements of persistence in Germany's local politics – the 'Old Local Politics' – will provide a means by which the scale of local political change – the 'New Local Politics' – can be judged. Changes tend to occur against the background of long established and only gradually evolving local political structures in Germany.

Before discussing the mechanisms of local politics in the Federal Republic, it is first necessary to address the historical and constitutional framework under which local authorities operate. This requires a brief overview of the main elements of Germany's local self-government. The discussion is largely confined to Germany's western regions, given that sharp differences continue to exist between the structures and styles of local political activity in the two parts of the unified country. However, on the basis of developments in western Germany's local politics in the post-war period, it will still be possible to point to some likely and other potential changes which will affect the course of local politics in eastern Germany in the years ahead.

The Historical and Constitutional Framework

> Local authorities must be guaranteed the right to regulate under their own responsibility and within the framework of the law all matters pertaining to the local community

> (Article 28.2, Basic Law).

The concept of local self-government is securely located within Germany's constitution, representing a principal element of the country's federal structure. Tucked away in Article 28, which addresses the interrelationship of the federal and regional levels of the German state, the Basic Law (*Grundgesetz*) defines the function of local authorities in broad and rather unspecific terms. In doing so, the constitution formally places local authorities under the regulative competences of the Federal Republic's regional governments. In this respect, therefore, it is not possible to treat local authorities as a third tier of government in Germany. Whereas national and regional parliaments possess the right to issue laws of a general nature, local councils are only entitled to pass statutes affecting their particular locality. As a consequence, it is more correct to regard local authorities as a third tier of Germany's administration (Jesse 1986:67).

However, the loose formulation of Article 28.2 of the Basic Law can give rise to conflicting interpretations of the role of local decision-makers. According to an expansive, literal interpretation of the constitution, local authorities have the right to regulate *any* matter of direct relevance to the local population. To some this might even extend to the discussion of questions pertaining to national defence or foreign policy, if the issues concerned could be shown to have an immediate bearing upon the locality. This view sharply contrasts with a narrow interpretation of the constitution which would tend to limit the powers of local government. According to this view, local authorities are legally obliged to restrict themselves to matters of local relevance alone and have to operate within the framework of national and regional legislation. This second interpretation lies at the heart of the legalistic and unpolitical approach which has undoubtedly characterised local politics in western Germany for much of the post-war period.

By emphasising the new-found constitutional role of local authorities in the post-war Federal Republic, it is possible to lose sight of the historical tradition of local self-administration in Germany. A division of administrative responsibilities between the different layers of government was sought by the formulators of the 1949 Basic Law as a way of securing for regional governments and local authorities a number of key self-administrative powers (Stammen 1977). It is accepted that federalism represented a vital means of preventing any attempt to reintroduce the centralised governmental structures imposed upon Germany under National Socialist rule (von Beyme 1979:196; Jesse 1986:44; Kistler 1985:106; Smith 1986). However, it would be wrong to suggest that the development of local self-government in Germany was merely a post-war phenomenon. Nor should the adoption of decentralised forms of government simply be regarded as a post-war imposition of the Allies. Despite the obvious preference of the United States for the implementation of federal political structures, there is a long tradition of local self-government in Germany which reaches back into the Middle Ages (Wehling 1986:17). Indeed,[1] the more modern concept of local self-administration was introduced in Prussia's towns by Stein in the early nineteenth century (Kühr 1983; Naßmacher 1986; Wehling 1986:25). By encouraging and furthering the development of a strong form of local democracy, the Allies were simply using a single mechanism to achieve two key aims. Firstly, they sought to minimise the risks of a return to the powerful centralised system of government associated with National Socialism. Secondly, the Allies strove to exploit a long tradition of local self-administration, thereby enhancing the reforms' prospective degree of success and raising the level of their acceptability to the German people. As a result, the democratisation of German society in the immediate post-war period first occurred at local level (Gabriel 1989b:9).

Although the regional governments have the constitutional power independently to determine the details of local administrative structures within the area of their jurisdiction, in practice a rather uniform set of political structures has developed across Germany. This primarily stems from the nature of the tasks fulfilled by German local authorities and from the manner in which they are financed.

The Duties of Local Authorities

The relatively loose formulation of the German constitution with regard to the role of local authorities provides the local level, in theory at least, with a wide-ranging degree of control over the nature and scope of the activities to be performed. In practice, political and financial controls prevent local authorities from assuming certain tasks and restrict the latitude with which other responsibilities are undertaken.

Ever since the first steps were taken to implement forms of local self-administration in Germany, there has been a marked tendency for the scope and scale of the duties to be performed at local level to increase. Certain policy measures such as social security and health care provision and the satisfaction of housing needs were fulfilled by German local authorities in the nineteenth century, as localities sought to encourage the industrialisation process within their boundaries and thereby secure for themselves an independent economic base. Additional duties arose in the twentieth century, with public enterprises assuming control of tasks traditionally performed by the private sector (energy provision, water, transport), but also fulfilling duties which encouraged further economic expansion (street cleaning, waste disposal, drainage, road construction) (Naßmacher 1986:246). With the extension of the social state after the Second World War, further duties fell upon local authorities, including the establishment of schools, old people's homes and recreational and cultural facilities. In addition to providing services to their citizens and businesses, local authorities also play a major role in planning.

Figure 2.1 The Duties of Germany's Local Authorities

Voluntary Duties	Statutory Duties	Imposed Duties
Communities determine whether they wish to undertake these tasks	Communities are legally obliged to fulfil these duties	Duties which the community performs on behalf of the state
e.g. Culture Sport Transport Parks Clinics	e.g. Social security Youth welfare Fire prevention Policing Building supervision Schooling	e.g. Civil defence Financial compensation Federal and regional elections

Source: Based on Prinz 1984:17

Although it is most common to distinguish between two basic types of local authority duties in Germany, the tasks performed by them actually fall into one of three categories (Graf 1977:47; Prinz 1984:17; Schäfer and Stricker 1989; Sokol 1985; Wehling 1986:11f.). The three categories are illustrated in Figure 2.1. A first group of duties consisting of self-administrative tasks (*Selbstverwaltungsaufgaben*) can be subdivided according to whether such tasks are either of a voluntary or a statutory nature. Self-administrative tasks of a voluntary nature include the maintenance of the local infrastructure (water, sewerage, energy, transport system), the establishment of forms of social care provision for local citizens (youth centres, old people's homes), the provision of cultural and leisure facilities (theatres, libraries, parks, sport grounds) and planning and environmental protection measures. In this context, the 1960 *Bundesbaugesetz* granted local authorities the exclusive right to determine the economic and structural development of their communities by allowing them to specify the purpose for which all land within their boundaries was to be utilised. The manner in which such voluntary responsibilities are undertaken is determined by local authorities without reference to higher levels of administration. However, the extent to which an individual local authority performs such tasks depends upon its ability to secure funding for them (Schäfer and Stricker 1989:39f.). In this respect, the large, industrialised urban authorities have a distinct advantage over smaller rural authorities in terms of their financial status. Statutory self-administrative tasks include the provision of social assistance in all its forms and the operation of health and educational services. With the number of statutory duties constantly rising, ever fewer resources are available for the funding of voluntary duties. This severely restricts the ability of local authorities to provide for their local citizens and has led some commentators to question the continued applicability of the term 'local self-administration' (Jesse 1986:67).

A second broad group of duties fulfilled by German local authorities comprises duties placed upon them by higher levels of government as a result of federal or regional legislation (*Auftragsangelegenheiten*). Such tasks are performed by local authorities on behalf of the federal or regional governments according to strict guidelines which seek to ensure a maximum level of uniformity in their fulfilment across the Federal Republic. These duties include the administration of social security benefits, the operation of passport and citizen registration services, local policing and fire services and civil defence. Elections are also administered by local authorities on behalf of federal and regional governments, demonstrating the need to achieve uniformity in the implementation of such duties. Inevitably, it has been this second category of duties rather than the self-administrative tasks which has become increasingly important at local level in Germany in recent decades, particularly with regard to the extension of the welfare state and the enactment of new legislation governing such important areas as social and environmental policy.

The passing of new legislation at national and regional level tends to place additional burdens upon local authorities, given the key role played by these bodies in policy implementation. It has been estimated that about 80 per cent of local activities are taken up with statutory duties of one kind or another (Sokol 1985:31). Consequently, there is relatively little room free for local communities to fulfil their voluntary responsibilities. Added to this is a growing financial dependence of the local level upon state funding (Schäfer and Stricker 1989:47). The ability of local authorities to fulfil new duties adequately largely depends upon the provision of appropriate levels of funding by the competent legislating bodies (Voigt 1987).

Table 2.1 Structure of Local Authority Income, West Germany, 1956–1986 (in %)

Year	Taxation	State transfers	Charges, fees	Loans	Other sources
1956	34.2	20.7	15.2	8.5	21.4
1961	34.5	20.8	15.3	9.1	20.3
1966	28.2	26.2	16.0	10.6	19.0
1971	26.5	23.5	15.5	14.1	20.4
1976	30.0	25.4	19.6	8.6	16.4
1981	29.0	26.0	19.9	7.9	17.2
1986	31.9	24.3	20.9	6.3	16.6

Source: Based on Kunz 1989:66, Table 1

Local authorities in the Federal Republic receive income from several sources (Table 2.1). The largest proportion of local funding comes from central and regional government taxation, although local authorities are themselves allowed to raise their own local property and business taxes (*Grundsteuer* and *Gewerbesteuer*). In 1986, 31.9 per cent of local authority incomes were derived from taxation (Kunz 1989:66). A second major source of funding consists of the transfer payments which are made to local authorities by higher levels of government in order to meet the costs of implementing and administering national and regional legislation. The remaining sources of local funding are income derived from services provided by them and borrowings. Any reduction in the level of funding from these higher levels automatically reduces the financial manoeuvrability of local authorities, since they are legally obliged to balance their books each year and are prevented from operating with a deficit. For example, West Germany's brief economic crisis between 1966 and 1967 led to a reduction of central government funding for local government and forced many local authorities into debt. Additional financial difficulties for the Federal Republic's local authorities in the late 1960s resulted from the increased workload placed upon them by central and regional governments. Despite the regular demands made by professional bodies, local politicians and academics alike for more generous and stable forms of funding for local authorities (for example Richter 1987:74f.), it has proved difficult for federal and regional governments in Germany to agree upon an appropriate means by which this can be achieved.

The Organisation of German Local Government

The lowest level of political authority in Germany lies in the community (*Gemeinde*), of which there are just over 8,500 in the eight western regions and 7,500 in the five eastern regions (Table 2.2). The overwhelming majority of such communities, especially in the east, are too small to be able to fulfil all of the responsibilities placed upon them by higher levels of government and also belong to an administrative district (*Kreis*). The district authority tends to assume responsibility for undertaking those tasks which are beyond the financial reach of the communities of which it is composed. As a result, some 8,416 communities in the western Länder (so-called *kreisangehörige Gemeinden*) belong to 237 districts. In the former regions of East Germany, 7,537 communities belong to 189 districts. A smaller group of ninety-one communities in western and twenty-six in eastern Germany, comprising mainly the country's larger towns and cities, are sufficiently large to be able to fulfil both the duties of the smaller communities and the districts in their own right. Cities such as Munich, Cologne, Leipzig and Frankfurt are amongst the largest of these *kreisfreie Gemeinden*.

The local administrative structure of the five new regions of the Federal Republic is comparable to that of the western regions to the extent that there is a distinction between communities and districts. However, the eastern regions have not yet undergone an apparently necessary reform of their local government boundaries and are still characterised by a large number of very small administrative units (Henkel 1991). Until a decision is made about the desirability of such a reform, eastern Germany's pre-unification structures will persist, under which just under half (47.6 per cent) of the communities had less than 500 inhabitants (Städtetag 1991:517).

Table 2.2 Germany's Administrative Structure, 1992

Region	Dependent communities	Districts	Independent communities
Baden-Württemberg	1,102	35	9
Bavaria	2,026	71	25
Berlin	–	–	1
Bremen	–	–	2
Hamburg	–	–	1
Hesse	422	21	5
Lower Saxony	1,022	38	9
North Rhine Wesphalia	373	31	23
Rhineland Palatinate	2,291	24	12
Saarland	52	6	–
Schleswig-Holstein	1,127	11	4
Western regions	8,415	237	91
Brandenburg	1,769	38	6
Mecklenburg-Vorpommern	1,111	31	6
Sachsen-Anhalt	1,346	37	3
Saxony	1,617	48	6
Thuringia	1,694	35	5
Eastern regions	7,537	189	26

Source: Jesse 1986:68; Statistisches Amt der DDR

It is the responsibility of Germany's regional governments to determine the framework within which local councils under their jurisdiction operate. This is primarily done through the mechanism of the local constitution (*Gemeindeordnung*), which outlines the system of local government to be adopted and regulates the interrelationship of the three principal organs of local

21

government: the local council, the mayor or council leader, and the local administration. The local constitutions also specify how local authorities are to be supervised and the respective region's electoral law, the duration of the periods of office of the elected organs of local government and the nature of the local administration's leadership (Holtmann 1990:6).

Four basic systems of local self-government exist in the Federal Republic: the North German council constitution, the South German council constitution, the mayoral constitution and the collegial constitution (see Fabritius 1975; Gabriel 1979c; Holtmann 1990; Leder and Friedrich 1986; Schmidt-Eichstaedt 1989; Wehling 1986). Figure 2.2 illustrates the main elements of each and the areas in which they principally differ. Although the constitutions described below apply to the communities, similar regulations govern the operation of the respective regions' administrative districts (*Kreise*).

Figure 2.2 Germany's Local Council Constitutions

Region	Type of local constitution	Electoral period	Head of council executive	Executive elected by	Executive's period of office
Baden-Württemberg	South German council const.	5 years	Mayor	Electorate	8 years
Bavaria	South German council const.	6 years	Mayor	Electorate	6 years
Hesse	Collegial const.	4 years	Executive comm. with mayor	Council	6 years
Lower Saxony	North German council const.	5 years	Chief executive	Council	6 or 12 years
North Rhine Westphalia	North German council const.	5 years	Chief executive	Council	8 years
Rhineland Palatinate	Mayoral const.	5 years	Mayor	Council	10 years
Saarland	Mayoral const.	5 years	Mayor	Council	10 years
Schleswig-Holstein	Collegial const.	4 years	Executive comm. with mayor	Council	6-12 years

Source: Wehling 1986:70

The North German council constitution operates in the states of North Rhine Westphalia and Lower Saxony and accords the elected councils (*Gemeinderat* or *Stadtrat*) a central position in the decision-making process (Andersen 1984b; Leder and Friedrich 1986:38f.; Richter 1987). The adoption of this system of local government in the post-war period occurred under the influence of the regions' British occupiers. In these regions, the elected council acts both as a legislative and an executive body, assuming full responsibility for the formulation and implementation of policy decisions (Andersen 1984b:19). The council is presided over by an honorary rather than a professional mayor (*Bürgermeister*) who is elected by the members of the council for the duration of the legislative period only. A more influential role is fulfilled by the council's chief executive (*Gemeindedirektor*), whose function is to establish a basis upon which council decisions can be reached and then to implement the decisions according to the council's specifications. The council executive is elected by the members of the council for a period of eight years in North Rhine Westphalia, which extends beyond the five-year period of office of the council itself. In theory, this type of constitution can greatly enhance the role of the political parties in the council chamber, since the competences of the mayor and administration are subjugated to it.

The local electoral systems of Lower Saxony and North Rhine Westphalia are comparable in a number of ways and reflect the influence upon these regions of British electoral law. Although the systems are essentially proportional, half of all candidates are elected by a majority system in local electoral wards. This ensures that local elections possess a certain personality element, which can be missing from purely proportional systems (for example Hesse). Whereas a 5 per cent hurdle operates in North Rhine Westphalia, no such barrier to small parties exists in Lower Saxony.

The South German council constitution, operating in Bavaria and Baden-Württemberg, accords a similar leading role to the elected council (see Bockelt 1989; Ismayr and Kral 1990: 111; Schneider 1990:71f.; Wehling and Pfizer 1985). The most significant divergence from the North German system is to be found in the direct election of the local mayor, a feature which greatly enhances the status of the council's figurehead. In Bavaria the mayor is elected for a period of six years, in Baden-Württemberg for eight. The directly-elected mayor fulfils two roles, presiding over council affairs in addition to assuming control over the operation of the local administration. In both states, the mayor also maintains his or (rarely) her status as a member of the council and can participate with full voting rights in most council resolutions (Woyke and Steffens 1987:115). In Bavaria, the division of the competences between the council and mayor is clearly defined by the local constitution and works clearly in favour of the mayor (Bockelt 1989:21). The fact that the mayor is elected directly and that mayoral elections do not necessarily run concurrently with local council elections tends to further diminish the role of the parties in the southern states. Indeed, the local electoral systems of Bavaria and Baden-Württemberg also tend to reinforce the personality element, with a wide scope for electors to influence to composition of the lists put forward by parties for council elections (see Mann 1989). In Baden-Württemberg, for example, voters at local elections are entitled to cast as many votes as there are candidates to be elected, which means casting at least eight and possibly up to sixty votes (Gawatz and Petri 1989:144). Individual candidates can be given up to three votes by each elector (*kumulieren*) and votes can be cast across party lists (*panaschieren*). Once the overall number of seats gained by the respective parties and voting groups has been established on a proportional basis, the composition of the parties' council groups is determined by the number of personal votes gained (Woyke and Steffens 1990:114; Löffler and Rogg 1991). A similar system operates in Bavaria. In neither of these regions is there a clause which prevents parties or voting groups from gaining representation if they fail to secure a certain proportion of the vote.

One long-standing peculiarity of the Baden-Württemberg local constitution has been its openness towards elements of direct democracy (Wehling 1991). This arises with the opportunities for citizens or the local council itself to call for a plebiscite to be held once a number of basic criteria have been satisfied (Mattar 1983; Reidegeld 1985:49f.; Wehling 1986:73). The extension of similar rights to the citizens of other regions has long been a source of local political discussion in Germany, but has yet to occur in a way comparable to what is found in Baden-Württemberg.

In the Saarland, the Rhineland Palatinate and the majority of communities in Schleswig-Holstein a mayoral system operates. The principal difference to the Southern German council constitution results from the rather diminished role of the mayor. Although the mayor chairs council sessions and is formally responsible for the operation of the local administration and the execution of council decisions, he or (seldom) she is voted into office by the members of the council and not directly by the electorate (Hess and Hundertmark 1987:41). The mayor can also be removed from office in the Saarland and Rhineland Palatinate by a two-thirds majority of council members (Leder and Friedrich 1986:36). Despite these restrictions, the mayor still occupies a significant position in both states, if only by the duration of his term of office. In the large towns and cities of the Rhineland Palatinate and the Saarland, for example, the mayor is elected for a period of ten years (Hess and Hundertmark 1987; Plöhn and Barz 1990:400). In these regions the mayor must inevitably adopt a more cautious approach when dealing with the parties represented in the council, than would be necessary if he were directly elected as in the two South German states. This would tend to favour a more consensual approach to local government decision-making. In certain large towns and cities in the Rhineland Palatinate this approach has been augmented by the adoption of a system similar to the collegial system, described below (Hess 1986:28). In these cases the mayor chairs an executive committee (*Stadtvorstand*), composed of both honorary and professional administrators (*Beigeordneten* or *Dezernenten*) who are elected by the members of the council. The function of the executive committee is essentially to prepare council decisions and to smooth over potential sources of conflict before the start of full council sessions.

The electoral laws of the Saarland and Rhineland Palatinate are rather different. In the Saarland a simple proportional system operates, with parties requiring 5 per cent of the vote in order to gain council representation. Recent changes to the local electoral law of the Rhineland Palatinate have sought to bring the region closer to the South German model. Voters can cast as many votes as there are councillors to elect and can give individual candidates up to three votes, whilst being able to select candidates from more than one party list (Gabriel and Jann 1990:364). This serves to reinforce the personality element of local elections. The 5 per cent barrier in operation in the Rhineland Palatinate in the state's 1984 local elections was replaced by what is effectively a 3.03 per cent barrier in time for the 1989 elections (Unglaub 1988:3).

Finally, in Hesse and in the towns and cities of Schleswig-Holstein a collegial constitution (*Magistratsverfassung*) has been adopted (Schneider and Ramb 1988). Instead of a single person fulfilling the dual role of council leader and administrative head, this task is performed by an executive body (*Magistrat* or *Gemeindevorstand*) composed of the mayor and a number of professional administrators (*Beigeordneten*) (Lilge 1986). The administrators have specific authority in particular spheres of local government activity and are elected to the *Magistrat* by the members of the council for a period of six years in Hesse and between six and twelve years in Schleswig-Holstein (Wehling 1986:71). In Hesse, members of the council executive are limited to serving a maximum of two periods in office (Lilge 1986:56) and can be removed from the executive within six months of their election to it by a simple majority vote by the council (Schiller and von Winter 1990:250). In both Hesse and Schleswig-Holstein, the mayor's main function is to preside over the sessions of the executive committee, since the plenary council sessions are chaired by a secondary figure (in Hesse the *Stadtverordnetenvorsteher*), elected by the council for the duration of the legislative period only.

The electoral system in Hesse is a straightforward proportional system, with parties failing to gain 5 per cent of the votes being excluded from local council representation. In Schleswig-Holstein a system similar to that adopted in Federal Elections exists, by which candidates elected by a majority of voters in constituencies are supplemented by those elected from party lists on a proportional basis (see Woyke and Steffens 1990:124).

Although Germany's local constitutions appear to be quite different in their written forms, in practice the pressures towards the establishment of a degree of uniformity in local self-administration across the country means that the differences are not of such great significance. Each local constitution offers local authorities the potential to determine independently the type of policies that they can implement for the benefit of local citizens. In North Rhine Westphalia, for example, the constitution mirrors the wording of the Basic Law in allowing the council the power to address all issues it judges to be of local relevance: 'The local council is responsible for all matters of local administration ...' (Andersen 1984b:19). Similar rights are guaranteed within the local constitutions of all other regions (see for example Lilge 1986; Bockelt 1989; Leder and Friedrich 1986). In practice, local councils tend to use these rights in different ways. There are also unmistakable tendencies towards uniformity in Germany's local electoral systems. In recent years, the South German model, which emphasises the role of personalities, is becoming more popular elsewhere, with discussions about the direct election of local government officials under way in several states (for example Rhineland Palatinate, North Rhine Westphalia). This also applies to the extension to voters of greater powers to determine the composition of local councils by the adoption of electoral systems which allow for the modification of party lists and voting across party lists.

It appears likely that local administrative structures and patterns of activity similar to those long established in the western regions will be developed in Germany's five new regions, if only because of the manner in which the unification process has been managed. With the western regions having formed partnership arrangements with specific neighbouring regions in eastern Germany, the likelihood is that this support will also extend to the provision of appropriate local council constitutions and electoral systems. North Rhine Westphalia, for example, has assumed a responsibility for overseeing local governmental change in the two regions of Brandenburg and Mecklenburg-Vorpommern which entails more than simply transferring officials from the region's own communities to the eastern regions for a temporary period (Scheytt 1991:11f.).

Despite the differences noted above between Germany's local council constitutions, evidence suggests that the constitutions exert only a marginal effect upon local decision-making processes. This is important when it comes to determining reasons for the uneven spread of New Politics orientations at local level. Citing a comparative study by Derlien, Gürtler, Holler and Schreiner (1975), Gabriel (1979c) found that in practice a relatively uniform system of local decision-making exists across the communities of the Federal Republic. Any differences which do occur are attributed by Gabriel to other than constitutional factors (Gabriel 1979c:68). However, to a certain extent, the structure of the local constitutions can influence the degree to which conflict emerges between the various organs of local government. Where responsibilities are divided between the organs there would tend to be a greater opportunity for the appearance of conflict. Where a single person fulfils more than one role (Southern Germany, Rhineland Palatinate, Saarland), the likelihood of conflict arising is substantially less than in situations in which powers are separated between a range of bodies (as in for example North Rhine Westphalia) (see Richter 1987:54f.). However, as will be discussed in Chapter 3, factors other than the nature of local council constitutions are likely to be more important in determining the spread of the New Politics to local level. Such factors as the socio-economic structure of the relevant localities, the nature of the local parties and the composition of the local electorate are of most relevance in this context.

Before analysing processes of change in Germany's local politics, it is necessary to establish a picture of the nature of local politics before the emergence of the New Politics and the Greens. This will permit a more precise definition of what will be understood in this study to represent the 'Old Local Politics'.

The 'Old Local Politics' in Germany

Local politics in the first decades of the Federal Republic's existence was characterised by non-confrontational decision-making processes. This applied universally, irrespective of the nature of the relevant local council constitution or of the size, socio-economic structure or political complexion of the community in question. Several factors served to reinforce the 'unpolitical' label placed upon politics at local level in western Germany, of which the four most significant are to be highlighted in this study. These are, firstly, the traditional separation of the 'political' from the 'administrative' in German local politics, secondly, the nature of the tasks performed by local authorities in the post-war period, thirdly, the population's lack of interest in all aspects of politics in the wake of the Second World War and, fourthly, the absence in the overwhelming majority of Germany's communities of local organisations of the major political parties.

A strong German tradition seeks to draw a sharp distinction between political decision-making processes on the one hand and the successful running of a council administration on the other (K. Simon 1987:242). In many quarters these two features are seen to be incompatible, and in the academic literature there is still a tendency to over-emphasise the administrative nature of the activities of local councils (for example Pagenkopf 1975; Pappermann, Roters and Theisen 1981:32ff.; Schmidt-Eichstaedt 1989:31; Schmidt-Jortzig 1982:20ff.). Local officials, often educated in the legal profession, understood their role to be one which placed them above party politics and allegiance to particular social classes: '... the town halls were dominated by the type of local official who was educated in the legal profession and, rather than representing a party or his (bourgeois) social class, understood his role as leader of the local administration to be one which placed him above parties and classes' (Naßmacher 1986:245). This corresponds to a widely-held belief that the role of the elected council is simply one of rubber-stamping decisions made by the professional administration and of successfully fulfilling the requirements of legislation passed at higher system levels (Voigt 1986:4). Such an interpretation of the function of local councils and their executives seeks to emphasise the administrative rather than the political aspects of their tasks. The unpolitical idyll of local council activity even found its way into the political education of west Germans for much of the post-war period. The following quote from a school textbook shows the emphasis placed upon objective as opposed to politically motivated decision-making processes at local level: 'In the interest of the citizens, the work of all council representatives in the Federal Republic ... demands objective and expert decisions. Although decisions are influenced by party politics, they must not be made from the viewpoint of party politics alone' (Lilge 1966:154).

A seemingly unpolitical approach to local politics was also favoured by a majority of the German population at least until the 1970s. For example, in their study of a number of small communities in the Federal Republic Ilien and Jeggle (1978) identified public discontent with the term 'political' when it was applied to the running of local affairs. Politics was negatively associated by those questioned with their experience of party politics at higher levels of the west German party system (Ilien and Jeggle 1978:38ff., cited in Voigt 1986). Even studies carried out on local politicians (including members of political parties) tended to support the view that the holding of a seat on the local council was not an overtly political matter (Jakob 1975:26). Such

a belief is bolstered by the absence within the various local constitutions of specific reference to opposition groups. Paragraph
30 of the local constitution of the Rhineland Palatinate, for example, states that individual councillors are obliged to serve the
common good rather than party-political or sectional interests
(Hess and Hundertmark 1987:43). As a result, before the emergence of the New Politics, opposition at local level tended to
occur only in a loosely organised fashion, depending upon the
specific question under debate (Fabritius 1975:41).

A second factor underlying the unpolitical nature of Germany's local politics arose from the nature of the local councils'
duties. The problems facing local authorities in the immediate
post-war period were such that party-political conflicts simply
failed to develop. The rebuilding process and the requirement to
fulfil the local population's basic needs for food, housing and
fuel could count upon the support of all local groups, preventing
a sharp polarisation of public opinion. Grand coalitions of the
major parties or all-party executives became commonplace in the
Federal Republic's local councils in the 1950s and continue to
persist in many communities into the 1990s. Alliances of the
major political parties were and still are to be found on the councils of large and small communities alike. There was a general
consensus that the pursuit of economic growth would bring tan-
gible benefits to all. As Frey (1976:21) pointed out, there was no
controversy over town development issues in the 1950s and
1960s, since no town development plans were even in existence
at the time. The uncontroversial approach was a consequence of
the local councils' need to concentrate upon matters which could
be dealt with in an objective manner: 'What counted was the effi-
cient solving of a problem; the clarity of the decision being determined by the issue itself and the urgent need to resolve it. To
vote in unison on the matter resulted from the self-imposed
desire to minimize the political "costs" of a decision' (Beyer and
Holtmann 1987:152).

This consensus was carried largely intact from the rebuilding
period into the 1960s and still persists to a greater or lesser extent
in local politics in the Federal Republic today, especially in its
smaller communities (Kuschke and Cryns 1984:74). It forms the
basis of the political idyll held to exist at local level and
described by Pflaum in the following terms:

The local interest unites groups with conflicting world views; the problems which are decided at community level are of such a practical nature that basic questions of a global kind are only seldom touched upon and, since far-reaching social restructuring does not begin in the community, there is no opportunity here to discuss ideological differences and competing economic interests (Pflaum 1954:205, cited in A. Klein 1981:310).

The nature of the issues addressed by local councils also tended to reinforce the unpolitical and consensual approach to local affairs. As Lehmbruch noted in the mid-1970s, decisions on issues related to the building of kindergartens, the provision of drainage or the preparation of land for building purposes cannot be made according to the criteria of party politics (Lehmbruch 1975:5). In terms of the potential New Politics–Old Politics divide, the issues debated by local councils were very much of a materialistic nature, conforming to the agenda of the Old Politics.

A third factor which contributed to the unpolitical nature of German local politics for much of the post-war period was the pervasive lack of public interest in all political matters during this time. The general avoidance of confrontational politics has a long-standing tradition in Germany, but was significantly reinforced by the experience of National Socialist rule. The political polarisation which had done so much to undermine the stability of the Weimar democracy was to be resisted at all costs in Germany's second democratic republic. More consensual approaches to politics were regarded as a necessity, but also reflected the concentration of the attention of most German citizens upon the post-war rebuilding process. The necessity of satisfying basic survival needs left little time free for political activities or participation, which were in any case discouraged by the controls placed upon German society by the occupying powers (Beyer and Holtmann 1987:149). The lack of interest in politics was most clearly expressed in the low turnouts to elections at various levels of government (Ausschuß Wahlforschung 1987; Kuschke and Cryns 1984). Although political culture studies have consistently demonstrated that feelings of political efficacy are greatest at local level in Germany (for example Gabriel 1990), this does not tend to manifest itself in high turnouts at local elections. People still believe that they are able to influence the political process

31

most easily at local level, but are more inclined to vote at elections to parliaments with greater responsibilities. Almond and Verba (1963:140) found that 62 per cent of German citizens believed they could do something about unjustified measures implemented by the local administration, while only 38 per cent felt that they could exert similar influence over national policy measures. The same political culture studies have also indicated the existence of widespread political apathy amongst the German population in the post-war period (Conradt 1980; Gabriel 1986). At local level the lack of interest in politics was simply reinforced by the established working patterns developed by the local councils. Controversial political debate was rare in plenary council sessions, but tended to occur, if at all, in (closed) committee meetings. Agreements reached behind closed doors by the various organs of local government paved the way for the unanimous approval of the majority of proposals to the council in its open sessions. This in turn served to reinforce the consensual appearance of local decision-making in Germany (Frey and Naß-macher 1975:199).

Finally, the absence of political conflict at local level was facilitated in the Federal Republic by the fact that the major political parties were only organised in a small proportion of the country's local communities (Kaack 1971:489f; Kuschke and Cryns 1984:74). Although the parties tended to be present in the larger towns and cities, they were absent from the overwhelming majority of small localities. Kaack (1971:489) noted that the SPD, as the largest mass political party in western Germany, was only organised in one-third of local communities in 1967. This can be attributed to the large number of (mainly rural) local councils in the Federal Republic at that time. Until the universal reorganisation of local government boundaries in the late 1960s and early 1970s there were over 24,000 communities and a further 425 administrative districts in the Federal Republic (Gabriel 1979a:146). The majority of these communities were very small, with populations of less than 2,000 people, which served to make the establishment of an effective and comprehensive party organisation across the country very difficult.

The secondary role of the major political parties at local level was reinforced by the German population's previously described lack of interest in politics during the post-war period. In place of political parties, overtly unpolitical groups tended to dominate local political life in the majority of small localities, especially of Southern Germany. The appeal of the numerous independent voters' initiatives (*freie Wählergemeinschaften*) lay in their non-ideological approach to local affairs. These groups, largely composed of a cross-section of local dignitaries, continued to gain substantial support in local elections, particularly in Bavaria, Baden-Württemberg and the Rhineland Palatinate well into the 1970s. Table 2.3 shows the level of electoral support for free-voting initiative groups in local elections held in the Rhineland Palatinate between 1948 and 1989. Until the 1960s these groups gained almost one quarter of all votes cast in the region's local elections, and in 1989 they still secured 17.1 per cent of the vote in community elections (Rhineland Palatinate 1985 and 1990).

Table 2.3 Local Election Participation of Voters' Initiatives, Rhineland Palatinate, 1948–1989

Election year	% of vote	seats
1948	16.7	5,495
1952	33.6	12,147
1956	31.9	11,739
1960	25.9	9,863
1964	25.8	10,189
1969	25.9	9,111
1974	17.5	6,332
1979	15.7	5,317
1984	15.5	4,989
1989	17.1	5,281

Source: Rhineland Palatinate 1990

The significance of the independent electoral groups lies in the fact that they generally regard themselves as being 'anti-party parties'. They place great emphasis upon their unpolitical approach, and concentrate upon providing solutions to concrete local problems rather than formulating a coherent ideology: 'As a rule, local politics is regarded as an objective decision-making process and is disassociated from the value-oriented politics of the parties and interest groups' (Stöss 1986b:2398; also Voigt 1981:29).

'Single-party systems' are still relatively common in Germany's small rural communities (Wehling 1981:26). The predominance of such outwardly non-ideological groups has tended to reinforce the image of local politics being an unpolitical matter. Even in large cities, however, it was not uncommon in the first decades of the Federal Republic's existence for independent candidates to gain election to such important public posts as mayor (for example Lehmbruch 1975:4). In Stuttgart an independent mayor remained in office until 1974 (Frey and Naßmacher 1975:208), whilst Wehling's (1989) study of local mayors in the three regions of Bavaria, Baden-Württemberg and the Rhineland-Palatinate illustrates the abiding secondary role played by party membership in gaining public office. In Baden-Württemberg one mayor in two was not a party member in 1984, whilst in Bavaria in 1985 35 per cent of local mayors were initially proposed by free-voting initiatives (Wehling 1989:229). In addition, 60 per cent of mayors holding office in a series of larger towns and cities in the Rhineland Palatinate in 1987 were elected unopposed – a further indication of the persisting strength of consensus democracy at local level (Wehling 1989:230). As Schneider (1990:72) states, the direct election of the mayor and the personalised electoral systems of Southern Germany are major factors which contribute to the region's persisting consensual approach to local politics (see also Löffler and Rogg 1991:123). Where parties are present at local level they have traditionally tended to de-emphasise their political role: 'That decisions should be "objective", that prior discussions must have been "objectively" founded and that the debate in the town hall should not have "subjectively" been exposed to "party political conflict" – this basic conviction was fostered by the local parties themselves' (Beyer and Holtmann 1987:152). This also provides an explanation for the prevalence of collegial decision-making forms across the whole Federal Republic, regardless of the nature of the local constitution, the political complexion of the relevant local council or the balance of the parties and electoral groups within it. Given the emphasis placed upon the adoption of collegial techniques, Simon (1987:242) has described the political structure of German local councils in terms of their *'harmonische Proporz'*, with all council groups being represented to some extent within the council administration.

This is a feature which has been described as the *'Januskopf'* (two-facedness) of the political parties (Lehmbruch 1975:5). On the one hand the political role of the parties at local level is denied in order to conform to established patterns of local political behaviour. On the other hand the same parties act as local sub-organisations of national parties and seek to mobilise public support for their organisations in national and regional elections.

Summary: Germany's Unpolitical Local Politics

Traditionally, therefore, one can speak of local politics in Germany as being characterised by consensual decision-making and by a marked absence of party political conflict. This is the essence of what is to be treated in this study as the 'Old Local Politics'. This is a form of local politics which has prevailed in the overwhelming majority of Germany's local communities for much of the post-war period. Indeed, as will be discussed in subsequent chapters, there are still strong elements of the Old Local Politics in operation in most communities in the 1990s. Working within the strict bounds of Article 28.2 of the Basic Law, the Old Local Politics encompasses only those issues of direct local relevance, whilst long-established procedures exist which aim to minimise the risk of party-political conflict emerging. In the Inglehartian sense, the subjects of discussion are essentially materialistic. Topics for debate revolve around such issues as the provision of a modern local infrastructure, which incorporates the fulfilment of the locality's basic energy requirements (heating, lighting, water), the creation of new road and public transportation systems, and a concentration upon such basic public facilities as swimming-pools and libraries and a range of cultural activities.

In a number of ways, it is to be anticipated that the communities of eastern Germany will also be taken up with similar tasks in the years to come and that this will be reflected in a consensual approach to local political decision-making. The four factors, outlined above, which reinforced the unpolitical nature of west German local politics are currently to be witnessed to a greater or lesser extent in the eastern regions. Firstly, the separation of the political from the administrative tasks was a key feature of local government in the German Democratic Republic. Secondly, the tasks to be performed in the years ahead are also of a comparable nature to those of the early years of the Federal Republic. Thirdly, there are signs of a growing political indifference in eastern Germany. Finally, until a reform of east German local government occurs, it is also unlikely that the west's political parties will be able to organise themselves in many communities in the eastern regions, which will in turn reduce the potential for the development of party-political conflict at local level.

It is against the background of the Old Local Politics that the changes of the late 1960s, 1970s and 1980s, associated with the development of the New Politics in western Germany, must be addressed. This will provide the foundation for an examination of characteristics associated with the emergence of the German Greens at local level during the 1970s (Chapter 4). With the Greens developing as an overtly political and ideological force, initially becoming established at local level, there was a distinct likelihood that the harmonious balance which existed within Germany's consensual local party systems would receive a sharp jolt. The 'unpolitical' nature of local politics in the Federal Republic presents an ideal arena for an analysis of the Greens' contribution to local political change. As an openly political force, the Greens' ideology fails to differentiate substantially between administrative boundaries. Their motto is 'think globally, act locally'. The contention must be that this will influence the development of local party systems in some way. In particular, as a party of the New Politics, addressing new issues and favouring unconventional styles of parliamentary activity, the question arises of the extent to which the Greens have been responsible for the introduction of a new, conflictual element into the local politics of the Federal Republic.

3
German Local Politics in Transition: The Rise of the New Local Politics

Even before the Greens first appeared on Germany's political scene there were signs that local political practices in western Germany were changing. The first indications of a shift in the established consensual pattern of west German local politics came in the late 1960s and 1970s with a gradual politicisation of the work of local councils and an increasing parliamentarisation of their working patterns. The nature and extent of the transition at local level was symbolised in many ways by the political upheaval in Frankfurt in the mid-1970s (Arndt 1983; Schacht 1985), where for the first time in a major city one political party (the SPD) exploited its majority status to remove all members of· the major opposition party (the CDU) from the council executive committee. The precedent set by the Frankfurt SPD, in which the party's new left was dominant, was followed in many other large towns and cities in advance of the more universal and radical changes witnessed in the late 1970s and 1980s. In short, there was a growing awareness, in Germany's urban areas at least, that the idyll of objective and consensual decision-making was no longer appropriate at local level in the face of the rapidly changing demands placed by society upon Germany's local politicians and administrators (Gabriel 1984:149f.; Jesse 1986:67; K. Simon 1987:243). Indeed, more recent moves to reform Germany's local council constitutions are closely linked to perceived changes which have occurred in the country's local politics (for example Innenministerium des Landes Nordrhein-Westfalen 1989 and 1991).

There are good reasons for anticipating that any changes in Germany's local politics would occur first in a city such as Frankfurt, where shifting social structures and the forces of economic modernisation are highly pronounced. In the context of a wide-ranging process of socio-economic change affecting all levels of the German party system, this chapter addresses the three key factors which precipitated the decline in the salience of traditional approaches to local politics in the Federal Republic. Firstly, the changing macro-economic climate in western Germany re-emphasised the financial insecurity of the country's local authorities. Secondly, the changing political climate and political culture of the Federal Republic saw public expectations of local authorities grow and, under the influence of the Social–Liberal government and the new social movements, a greater degree of public interest in local political affairs. Thirdly, administrative reforms helped to ease the major political parties' difficulties in organising at local level. A combination of these three factors facilitated the spread of something resembling a 'New Local Politics' in German society. They also contributed to a greater or lesser extent to the emergence of the Greens themselves. In this sense, therefore, this chapter addresses reasons both for the shift in local political practices and for the rise of environmental politics in Germany. These developments are best viewed, however, within the broad context of more fundamental changes which have affected all levels of the German party system since the 1960s.

The Dynamics of Party System Change in Germany

Local party systems do not remain immune to the more general forces of change which affect party systems at higher levels of government. Party system change in western democracies is inextricably linked to fundamental changes in social structures and the emergence of new political value orientations amongst key social groups. The process of socio-economic modernisation, which has characterised the development of the Federal Republic during the post-war period, has reduced the relevance of traditional cleavages in the country's party systems and has contributed to the emergence of a New Politics dimension within them (Baker *et al.* 1981). However, given the fact that the pace of social and economic change has been rather uneven across the Federal Republic, it can be anticipated that the relevance of the New Politics dimension will vary depending upon a series of socio-economic and political factors. The changing nature of west German local politics during the 1970s and 1980s should, therefore, be viewed within the context of developments which have been shown to influence the operation of party systems at the federal and regional levels.

A cyclical pattern characterises the process of party system change in Germany. Müller-Rommel (1989) has suggested that major trends in electoral change are initially identifiable at regional level, progressing to the national level at a later stage. This argument is perhaps too straightforward in a federal system, since changes are liable to affect the three levels of the party system at different times and to varying degrees. For instance, a shifting balance of power between the political parties registered at the national and regional levels is commonly mirrored by subsequent changes within the Federal Republic's local party systems. Conversely, fluctuations in local party systems can also herald changes at the higher system levels, in the sense that regional and federal party system trends simply represent an aggregation of developments occurring at local level (see Cryns and Hembach 1987:131). This is particularly true when it comes to the growth of new political parties, such as the Greens, who began life at local rather than national level. Thus, the changing social structures and political values which are held to undermine the stability of German party systems at a national and regional level can also be expected to exert an impact upon local party systems. It can therefore be considered likely that local party systems will develop in different ways according to the extent of social change in the relevant locality.

Against the broad background of socio-economic and value change, conflicting interpretations have been made of the stability of Germany's federal party system. Some commentators choose to stress the persisting significance of traditional social cleavages and point towards the system's fundamental stability (for example Pappi 1984; Pappi and Terwey 1982; also Klingemann 1985). Indeed, before the events surrounding the unification of Germany, Schmitt (1989:130) referred to the 'almost perfect stability' of the west German party system. Other researchers prefer to draw attention to the forces of change, particularly to the emergence of new cross-cutting social cleavages in German society (Alber 1985; Baker *et al.* 1981; Bürklin 1981 and 1984). According to the approach and underlying concepts adopted, differing interpretations are made of the factors which lead to the emergence of new political parties such as the Greens or Republicans and of such parties' survival chances.

In their important work, Lipset and Rokkan (1967:54) suggested that the post-war party systems of the Western democracies were essentially founded upon the same underlying social cleavages present at their inception in the 1920s. If social cleavages are defined as enduring coalitions between population groups and political parties (Stinchcombe 1975), then the two principal cleavages underlying west Germany's 'stable' post-war party systems are based upon social class and religious affiliation (Berger, Gibowski, Jung, Roth and Schulte 1987:263; Klingemann 1985:244). The structural alliances of the blue-collar workers and trade unionists with the SPD and of the old middle class and religious sections of the population, especially the Catholics, with the CDU/CSU can still be regarded as the most enduring and stable features of the current German party system (Pappi 1984). Even more recent studies of Federal Election voting behaviour indicate the persisting strength of these cleavages (for example Berger *et al.* 1987; Bürklin and Kaltefleiter 1987; Kaltefleiter 1991; Klingemann 1985; Pappi 1984; Schultze 1987; Woyke and Steffens 1990:69f.). In Klingemann's (1985) analysis of the German party system, the clear dominance of the CDU/CSU among the Catholic and Protestant old middle class (the self-employed and farmers) and those groups involving religious Catholics is matched for a series of post-war elections by the SPD's superior position in the Protestant, unionised new middle class (*Angestellte* and *Beamte*) and the Protestant, non-unionised working class (Klingemann 1985:246f.; see also Veen and Gluchowski 1983 and 1988). The same structural cleavages have largely determined the composition and stability of the respective party systems at regional and local level. The CDU and CSU have traditionally performed well in areas in which the Catholic population has been in the majority, such as Baden-Württemberg, Bavaria and the Rhineland, and in the more rural areas with high proportions of the old middle class (Schultze 1987:13). The SPD on the other hand has tended to perform best in urban areas with large proportions of blue-collar workers, such as the Ruhr, Hamburg and Bremen.

However, whilst Pappi (1984) is correct to point out that the traditional social cleavages of class and religion still exert a significant influence upon the German party system, the party systems of the 1990s are much less stable than they were in the Federal Republic's first decades. This is not only a reflection of the uncertainty brought about by the unification process, but also a result of long-term shifts in German society. Party system stability relies to a great extent upon the maintenance of a balance between the relevant population groups and upon the ability of the established political parties successfully to absorb the vote of newly emerging social groups. This simply has not happened in Germany. Changing social structures, linked to the process of socio-economic modernisation, have reduced the size and importance of the very social groups upon which the stability of the country's party systems depends, whilst creating new population groups which are no longer bound by traditional social structural ties to particular political parties (Veen and Gluchowski 1988). In this respect, the non-aligned new middle class represents a principal source of electoral volatility in Germany (Conradt and Dalton 1988:26). Although differing definitions are adopted of this social group (Brinkmann 1988), in this study the new middle class is regarded as comprising higher-level civil servants (*Beamte*) and other civil servants and employees (*Angestellte*) engaged in the service sector of the German economy. There are pragmatic reasons for adopting such a broad definition of the new middle class, given that most official statistical sources are based on this interpretation (for example Datenreport 1989:85).

In general, the process of socio-economic modernisation is linked in the economic sphere to the expansion of service sector industries at the expense of traditional agricultural and heavy industries (Alber 1985:215). Other consequences of this process are to be found in changing employment patterns and rising education levels and in the disintegration of traditional social milieux. Although each of the components of the modernisation process can independently influence the composition and stability of Germany's party systems, when aggregated there can be little doubt that far-reaching social and economic changes fundamentally affect the relationship between political parties and voters. Thus, the movement towards a service-based economy is accompanied by a decline in the proportion of the electorate which is made up of blue-collar workers and the old middle class. Whilst a decline in the former social group will tend to diminish the core electoral support available to the SPD, a reduction in the latter affects the potential CDU/CSU and FDP vote. The CDU/CSU is also affected by the declining role of the Church, which stems from the secularisation process. However, the effects of socio-economic modernisation have not been balanced across Germany's two established *Volksparteien*. In Federal Elections at least, the CDU/CSU has had more success in winning over new, non-aligned voters than the SPD, which has consistently been less successful in adapting to the need for change (Feist and Krieger 1987:47). Germany's changing socio-economic base is of equal importance when it comes to explaining fluctuations in local political behaviour. It is to be anticipated that local party systems will be influenced in different ways by the modernisation process, depending upon the prevailing social and economic structures in the relevant locality.

In this analysis, two major aspects of the modernisation process will be addressed in order to illustrate the degree to which local communities often diverge from the national norm. Given the overriding significance of social class and religion in determining the composition of Germany's party systems, attention will be focused upon the areas of economic change (tertiarisation) and secularisation. Statistical data emanating from two levels of the federal system are to be used in this analysis. At national level, information is derived from publications of the Federal Statistical Office (Datenreport 1987 and 1989), whilst local data have been gathered from publications of a number of city statistical offices. Since not all localities provide electoral and social structural data in a form which can be utilised by researchers, there is an unavoidable tendency to concentrate attention upon political change in a number of urban areas in which relevant data are gathered. Although the limitations of such data are recognised (see Schacht 1985), the intention is simply to provide some illustrative information which can add weight to the argument that there is a need to differentiate between Germany's local party systems.

The Influence of Economic Change

The progression of the Federal Republic from a production-based towards a service-based economy is clearly demonstrated by an examination of the proportions of the country's workforce employed in the three sectors of the economy (Table 3.1). The most dramatic decline in employment has been witnessed in the agricultural sector. As a result of mechanisation and rising productivity levels, the share of the workforce engaged in the primary sector has fallen progressively from a level of 23.3 per cent in 1950 to only 4.2 per cent in 1988. The proportion of the workforce engaged in the secondary sector is also in decline. In the immediate post-war period, west Germany's economic growth was based upon the rapid expansion of industrial production. Between 1950 and 1960 the proportion of the workforce employed in the production sector increased from 43.1 per cent to 48 per cent. During the 1960s this sector's share of the working population began to stagnate, and since 1970 has fallen from a level of 48.4 per cent to just 41.1 per cent in 1988. During the same period the tertiary sector has experienced a rapid growth in its share of the workforce. In 1950 one-third of the workforce operated in the service sector of the west German economy (33.6 per cent). In 1988 this figure had increased to well over half (54.7 per cent) (Datenreport 1989:83).

Table 3.1 Employees by Economic Sector: West Germany, 1950–1988

Economic Sector	1950 %	1960 %	1970 %	1980 %	1988 %
Primary sector	23.3	13.4	9.0	5.3	4.2
Manufacturing	43.1	48.0	48.4	45.3	41.1
Service industries	53.6	38.6	42.6	49.4	54.7
All	100.0	100.0	100.0	100.0	100.0

Source: Datenreport 1989:83, Table 3

In certain German cities, predominantly the large urban areas of the South (Munich, Stuttgart, Frankfurt, Nuremberg), the movement towards a service-based economy has been even more rapid than that indicated by the aggregate data for the whole of the country. In Frankfurt, for example, the proportion of the workforce employed in the tertiary sector increased by 16.3 per cent between 1970 and 1987 from 59.6 per cent to 69.3 per cent. During the same period the proportion of the city's workforce engaged in the secondary sector declined by 24.4 per cent, accounting for just 30.1 per cent in 1987. In Frankfurt the agricultural sector plays no significant role, accounting for only 0.6 per cent of the workforce in both 1970 and 1987 (Frankfurt 1989a:44). Even within the city boundaries of Frankfurt, however, notable variations exist in the composition of the workforce. Whereas some city districts have profited from Frankfurt's expanding financial and commercial role, others remain economically dependent upon the production sector.[1]

Frankfurt typifies a growing dominance of the service sector in Germany's urban areas. In Cologne, for example, 53 per cent of the workforce was employed in the service sector in 1970, but by 1986 the proportion had increased to 64 per cent (Cologne 1987:125, Table 502). Over the same period, the proportion of the Neuss workforce employed in the tertiary sector increased by 38.3 per cent (Neuss 1989a:10). Even in such cities as Duisburg, in which the traditional industries of coal and steel production continue to play an important role, there has still been a long-term growth in the relevance of the tertiary sector. Between 1970 and 1985 the share of the Duisburg workforce employed in this sector rose from 41 per cent to 52 per cent (Duisburg 1988:26, Table P.2). In Bensch's (1985) comparative study of changing employment patterns between 1978 and 1983 in twelve west German cities, all cities witnessed varying levels of decline in the numbers engaged in the production sector. Whilst a general growth was registered in the service sector, in certain cities this applied more to the proportion of the workforce engaged than to the absolute numbers employed. In the Ruhr city of Bochum, for

---

[1] In the Höchst and Griesheim suburbs, for example, respectively 72.8% and 60.4% of employees were still engaged in the secondary sector at the time of the 1987 census. By contrast, a number of districts had over 90% of their workforce engaged in the tertiary sector (most notably in the central areas of Frankfurt and in the airport district) (Frankfurt 1989a:45; also Düsseldorf 1989:27; Heidelberg 1989:20).

example, there was a fall of nearly 10 per cent in the absolute number of employees engaged in the tertiary sector between 1978 and 1983 (Bensch 1985:24). The 1987 Census showed that the eleven largest cities of the Federal Republic (each with populations of over 500,000) had widely varying shares of the workforce engaged in the tertiary sector. The lowest proportion was found in Duisburg (56.8 per cent), the highest in Hamburg (78.4 per cent) (Frankfurt 1989a:45; also Deutscher Städtetag 1987). Even in the Ruhr conurbation, which has traditionally been associated with the production industries, it has been shown that the proportion of employees engaged in the service sector has increased to 59 per cent, with only 40 per cent still employed in secondary sector industries (Noll and Rechmann 1991:28).

Thus, despite the general trend towards an expansion of the service sector in Germany's cities, the movement has been rather more pronounced in some localities. Also, as the Frankfurt example has demonstrated, there can be further significant variations in the composition of the workforce within the boundaries of individual cities.

Table 3.2 Occupational Structure, West Germany, 1950–1988

Occupational group	1950 %	1961 %	1970 %	1980 %	1988 %
Self-employed	29.2	19.5	17.6	12.0	11.1
Beamte	4.0	7.1	5.5	8.4	8.7
Angestellte	16.0	22.4	29.5	37.2	42.1
Blue-collar workers	50.8	51.0	47.4	42.4	38.1
All	100.0	100.0	100.0	100.0	100.0

Source: Gabriel 1983b:79, Table 1–3b; Datenreport 1989:85

The movement of the west German economy from a production towards a service base lies at the heart of the growth of those social groups which are recognised as the principal source of electoral volatility. Changes in the country's economic structure are inevitably reflected in the occupational structure of the west German population (Table 3.2). Occupational structure lies at the heart of any analysis of the social-class cleavage upon which the stability of the German party system depends. Whereas blue-collar workers (*Arbeiter*) constituted over half the working population in the 1950s and 1960s, in 1988 they represented just 38.1 per cent. The decline of the old middle class has been even more dramatic. Between 1950 and 1988 this occupational group decreased as a proportion of the working population by over 60 per cent, falling from a level of 29.2 per cent to 11.2 per cent. The decline of both the traditional working class and the old middle class has been accompanied by a large rise in the proportion of people engaged in occupations associated with a service-based economy. The occupational groups which constitute the new middle class (*Angestellte* and *Beamte*) now account for the largest proportion of west Germany's working population. In 1950 only one-fifth of west Germans were employed in such professions, but by 1988 the figure had risen to over one half of all employed people (50.8 per cent) (Datenreport 1989:85).

Again, it must be pointed out that in a number of Germany's cities the rise of the new middle classes has been more rapid than the aggregate figures suggest. In Frankfurt, for example, over 59 per cent of the workforce belonged to the new middle class at the 1987 census, as opposed to the 55 per cent of 1970. Over the same period the proportion of the city's workforce made up of blue-collar workers fell from 36 per cent to 32 per cent (Frankfurt 1989a:97). Similar changes have occurred in other cities (Bielefeld 1990:32; Düsseldorf 1989:29; Lübeck 1989; Mannheim 1989:8; Neuss 1989a:12 and 1990:16).[2]

The growth of the new middle class, with its ambivalent position in the social structure, having attributes of both the old middle class and the working class (Baker *et al.* 1981:172), and its absence of 'voting norms which have grown out of historical experience' (Klingemann 1985:249) is a prime source of the

[2] In Neuss, for example, between 1970 and 1987 there was a decline of 15.6% in the city's working population belonging to the working class (39.9%), whilst an increase of 29.1% was recorded in the professions of the new middle class (54.3%) (Neuss 1989a:12). Even between boroughs of the same city there can be significant variations in occupational structure. The 1987 census returns for Neuss showed distinct variations in the proportion of the workforce belonging to the respective occupational groups across its twenty-eight boroughs. Thus membership of the new middle-class professions varied between 31.5% in the Erfttal borough and 65.3% in the Stadionviertel, whilst that of the working class varied between a low of 20.5% in Morgensternsheide and a high of 64.9% in Erfttal (Neuss 1990:16; also Mannheim 1989:8).

underlying electoral volatility in Germany (Conradt and Dalton 1988:26). It is also within this social group that the postmaterialist views associated with the New Politics are most widely held. Whilst it is important to emphasise the continuing strength of the social-class cleavage in German politics, therefore, it is also necessary to reassess its relative significance in the face of a shifting balance between the respective social classes. This is especially true at local level, where ongoing shifts in class-based social structure can have a great bearing upon the stability of party systems. Different forces will be in action in the modern, service-sector cities of southern Germany than in the traditional urban areas of the Ruhr and in the countryside. This applies equally to the effects of the process of secularisation.

Secularisation: The Declining Salience of the Religious Cleavage

The secularisation of German society is of equal importance in undermining the stability of the country's party systems. This process has two main features. Firstly, a growing proportion of the population belongs to no religious faith at all, and secondly, and perhaps more importantly, the links between Church members and their churches are becoming less pronounced.

Table 3.3 Church Attendance by Catholics, West Germany, 1960–1987

	1960	1970	1980	1987
Catholics (000s)	24,710	27,192	26,720	26,306
Church attenders (000s)	11,895	10,159	7,769	6,430
Church attenders (in %)	48.1	37.4	29.1	24.4

Source: Datenreport 1989:166, Table 9

   Congregation sizes in both the Catholic and Protestant Churches have sharply declined over the post-war decades. Whereas the overall number of Catholics living in the Federal Republic has remained relatively stable since 1960, there has been a significant drop in the proportion of Catholics regularly attending the Sunday mass. In 1960, 48 per cent of Catholics were regular attenders at the Sunday service, but the corresponding figure for 1987 was just 26 per cent (Table 3.3) (Daten-report 1989:166). Although directly comparable figures for the Protestant Church are not available, a survey conducted by the Federal Statistical Office established that only about 5 per cent of registered Protestants regularly attended church services in 1987 (Datenreport 1989:168). These findings are corroborated by studies of the strength of attachment of church members to their respective churches (Table 3.4). On the basis of surveys carried out by the *Forschungsgruppe Wahlen* following each Federal Election since 1953, the proportion of Catholics expressing a strong attachment to the church (calculated in terms of regular attendance at church services) progressively fell from 60 per cent in 1953 to 36 per cent in 1987. The attachment of Protestants to their church has traditionally been weaker than that of Catholics, but even in this case there are strong signs of a further loosening of ties. In 1987 only 7 per cent of Protestant respondents attended church frequently (Berger *et al.* 1987).

Table 3.4 Church Attachment, West Germany, 1953–1987 (in %)

	1953	1965	1969	1972	1976	1980	1983	1987
Catholics	47	47	48	48	43	46	43	46
Church attachment								
Strong	60	59	48	46	40	36	35	36
Moderate	20	24	30	27	26	29	27	31
None	20	16	21	27	34	35	37	33
Protestants	49	50	49	47	49	48	50	47
Church attachment								
Strong	19	8	7	6	6	7	9	7
Moderate	33	49	45	36	31	29	37	29
None	48	42	47	57	63	64	63	64
Other/no confession	4	3	3	5	8	6	7	7

Source: Berger et al *1987:264, Table 10*

In certain urban areas the secularisation process has occurred at a faster rate than that characteristic of the Federal Republic as a whole. In Frankfurt, for example, membership of the Protestant Church declined by 38.5 per cent between the censuses of 1970 and 1987, whilst the corresponding decline for the Catholic Church was 25 per cent. Although this absolute decrease can partially be explained in terms of a decrease in Frankfurt's population as a whole, the city's statistical office also points towards a large number of resignations (*Kirchenaustritte*) from the respective Churches (Frankfurt 1988:87). Church membership has also been in decline in most other German cities. In Duisburg membership of the Catholic Church fell by 17 per cent and that of the Protestant Church by 21 per cent between 1975 and 1986, whilst the population of the city as a whole fell by some 13 per cent. Over the same period the proportion of Duisburg's German population belonging to one of the other faiths or holding no church affiliation at all increased by 61.8 per cent, from 7.6 per cent to 12.3 per cent (Duisburg 1988:70, Table 5.2).

In terms of the frequency of church attendance, a survey undertaken in Hesse's Rhine–Main area (which includes the Frankfurt conurbation) showed that only 14 per cent of respondents regularly went to church in 1979; the figure for Roman Catholics was somewhat higher at 29 per cent (Schacht 1986). Significantly, a similar survey completed at the same time for the whole of Hesse indicated that 46 per cent of the region's Catholic population continued to attend church regularly (Schacht 1986:84). In urban areas, therefore, and most noticeably in the service-sector centres, there is clear evidence of a more marked shift away from regular church attendance than in the non-metropolitan areas of the Federal Republic. The alliance of the religious sections of the population with the CDU/CSU, regarded by Pappi (1984) as the main element of the country's 'stable' party system, appears less significant when placed into the context of the on-going process of secularisation evident in German society.

A brief analysis of the process of socio-economic modernisation serves to illustrate the degree to which the enduring stability of the German party systems is under threat. Not only are the dual processes of tertiarisation and secularisation weakening the power of traditional social cleavages to determine electoral behaviour, but they have also promoted the rise of new social groups which are no longer bound by historical traditions to support for particular political parties. By illustrating the variations in the socio-economic development of certain German cities, it is possible to suggest that some local party systems will be more stable than others. However, it must also be recognised that changes in Germany's social structures are just one element in the equation when it comes to assessing the relative stability of the Federal Republic's party systems. A further aspect which requires consideration is that brought about by a change in the basic value orientations of certain sections of German society, reflected in the rise of the New Politics.

The New Politics

Growing public interest in a series of new political issues has been a significant element of political change in the Federal Republic since the late 1960s. The development of a cluster of new issues, termed the New Politics, is not a feature confined to Germany alone, but has been identified in a number of other western Democracies (Inglehart 1983; Müller-Rommel 1982; Müller-Rommel and Wilke 1981; Poguntke 1987a,b). The inability of the established political parties to respond adequately to the New Politics was a prime factor underlying the emergence in Germany of the new social movements and the Greens.

New Politics theory essentially spans the three broad areas of ideology, party electorates and party organisation (Müller-Rommel 1989; Poguntke 1989). Firstly, the New Politics agenda is characterised by issues relating to the 'quality of life' (for example environmental protection; social equality; civil liberties) and by its emphasis upon the development of public participation in the decision-making process (Baker *et al.* 1981; Bürklin 1984; Poguntke 1989). This agenda is nurtured by the changing basic value orientations of certain population groups, whose members have in general been perceived as moving away from materialistic towards so-called postmaterialistic goals (Baker *et al.* 1981; Inglehart 1977). Although traditional materialistic issues linked to the maintenance of economic growth (for example control of inflation; provision of adequate pensions) and national security continued to be of overriding importance throughout the 1970s and 1980s (and into the 1990s) (Gibowski and Kaase 1986), the non-material aspirations of sections of the German electorate have increasingly been represented by new concerns. On the one hand, a growing awareness of the negative effects of industrial production led to expressions of support for measures to protect the environment and to demands to reduce further social and global inequality. On the other, there were calls for improved participatory rights, characterised by the increasing emphasis placed upon such issues as the freedom of expression (Baker *et al.* 1981; Chandler and Siaroff 1986; Dalton 1981; Hildebrandt and Dalton 1977). Secondly, with regard to adherents of the New Politics, the long-term significance of the new values emanates from the fact that supporters are most widely found within the new middle class, itself a product of the modernisation process. Thirdly, the New Politics influences the type of party structure adopted, with stress being laid upon non-hierarchical decision-making processes and informality (Poguntke 1987c and 1989).

The basis for New Politics theory is to be found in two broad lines of thought, each of which has in turn been utilised as a means of explaining the growth of Green parties across western Europe (Müller-Rommel and Poguntke 1989:20). The first school, based initially upon the work of Inglehart (1971, 1977 and 1981) and extended by Barnes and Kaase *et al.* (1979), emphasises the significance of changing political values at an individual level as reflected in the rise of a new postmaterialist generation. According to these authors, individuals socialised in periods of economic and political stability, such as occurred in the Federal Republic during the late 1950s and 1960s, tend to hold political values which accord traditional (materialist) economic and security goals less significance than the (postmaterialist) values associated with freedom of expression and increased opportunities to participate in the democratic process (Inglehart 1977). As a result, postmaterialistic values are most widespread amongst west Germany's younger generations, especially those with high levels of education and a social background in the new middle classes (Datenreport 1989:536). Such groups represent the very core of the Greens' electoral support in Germany (Betz 1991:66; Veen 1987 and 1989). The postmaterialist values are least common amongst blue-collar workers and members of the old middle class. As has been pointed out by Rüdig and Lowe (1986), the

51

narrow schema adopted by Inglehart to identify postmaterialist value orientations has been extended by other researchers to explain the emergence of a wide range of new issues in Western Democracies, including the subject of environmentalism (Cotgrove and Duff 1981). According to this line of thought, the Greens will continue to play a role in Europe's party systems for some years to come.

A similar approach is adopted by Bürklin (1984), although in this case greater emphasis is laid upon individual life cycle rather than early-life socialisation effects (see Dalton 1981). With regard to the expression of political support for the Greens, however, Bürklin (1984) suggests that the blocked professional aspirations of highly educated younger generations in the 1970s were the principal underlying factor. During the recession of the late 1970s and early 1980s the established political parties appeared unable to integrate the younger age-cohorts most acutely affected by the economic downturn. Thus, according to this approach the established parties should be able to recapture the Green vote in times of economic prosperity (Bürklin 1987). However, Inglehart (1983) suggests otherwise, and cites a growing proportion of postmaterialists in the west German electorate even during periods of recession as proof of the long-term relevance of the new values.

The second line of thought used to explain the emergence of the New Politics agenda lays particular emphasis upon the changing social structures of contemporary Germany (Alber 1985; Dalton 1984). Alber (1985) suggests that members of the new middle class are rather more aware of the negative effects of unlimited economic growth than members of those social groups intimately linked to the production process. This constitutes the possible cause of a new cleavage in the west German party system, with occupational groups intimately linked to the production process (blue-collar workers, the old middle class) competing with those groups which are largely alienated from it (the new middle class). The absence of a formal connection with the production process underlies the over-representation of the new middle class amongst adherents of the postmaterialistic, quality-of-life issues associated with the New Politics (Alber 1985:215).

However, as Chandler and Siaroff have pointed out, the two

schools of thought do not necessarily contradict one another: '... changes in social structure increase the probability of new and shifting alignments because new social classes produce their own distinctive set of values, preferences, and interests. As the 'new middle' classes ... emerge politically, they are less bound by bread and butter, materialist orientations or by the traditional values of prior political generations' (Chandler and Siaroff 1986:304). The principal difference between the socialisation and social structural approaches lies in the means by which New Politics issues have come to the fore. Whereas the socialisation approach emphasises the importance of individual level changes, the social structural approach stresses the role played by aggregated social changes. The fact that the two approaches are complementary suggests that New Politics value orientations will prevail where the social structural conditions upon which they are founded are present. Conversely, where the relevant social structures are absent, it can be assumed that New Politics orientations are not widely held. Generally, change can be expected to occur in urban areas more rapidly than in non-urban areas. However, one must also differentiate between cities with a modern economy based upon the service industries and cities which still have a high reliance upon the traditional production-based sector. This is an important point to make, since the analysis of variations in the progress of socio-economic modernisation across the communities of the Federal Republic would point to the existence of differences in the spread of the New Politics. Local party systems should therefore be characterised to varying degrees by the spread of the New Politics.

The New Politics approach also provides a means of interpreting variations in the success of the Greens across Germany's communities. Given the pace of social and economic change in the service-sector centres (Frankfurt, Munich, Stuttgart), it is to be expected that the party systems in these localities will be more susceptible to fluctuations in voting behaviour than party systems in localities in which the modernisation process has tended to lag behind, such as the cities of the Ruhr. The service-sector centres should also be at the forefront of the spread of New Politics issues and styles of politics to the local level of the Federal Republic.

The Changing Context of German Local Politics: The Rise of a New Local Politics?

The relevance of the New Politics at Germany's local level is to be discussed in greater detail with regard to the rise and consolidation of the Greens at this level of the party system. However, it is important to stress that even before the emergence of the Greens, a series of significant developments at local level in the Federal Republic indicated that a fundamental challenge to a number of the traditional interpretations of the function and scope of local politics was under way. A combination of the changing economic and political climates and a series of administrative measures facilitated the development of a more political and parliamentary style of local politics in Germany during the 1970s; a nascent 'New Local Politics'. Events described at the beginning of this chapter in Frankfurt were just one outward sign of an impending sea change in the conduct of local political affairs in Germany.

A first motor for change at local level was brought about by the declining economic status of Germany's local communities in the late 1960s. During the period of rapid economic growth in the 1950s and early 1960s, west Germany's local authorities could satisfactorily fulfil their legal obligation to cater to the needs of their inhabitants without being placed under undue financial pressure. This situation changed towards the end of the 1960s, when a worsening national economic climate coincided with a rapid expansion of the local authorities' duties. The financial reforms of 1969 (*Finanzreformgesetz*) did not fundamentally reduce the financial strains under which local authorities operated (Jesse 1986:67; Sontheimer 1979:209). Whilst the federal and regional governments sought to reduce their own expenditure in response to the economic downturn, they continued to expect that local authorities should independently meet the full brunt of rising social costs associated with the recession. As a result, local authorities were forced to increase their level of debt substantially. The ensuing financial crisis that affected Germany's local authorities served to politicise local council activities in its own right, since there was a growing awareness of the framework and limitations within which the councils operated. This in turn encouraged the development of conflict between local government on the one hand and regional and national governments on the other. Initially, the financial crisis at local level was treated as a problem irrespective of party-political allegiances, and all local parties sought to improve the collective financial situation of the local authorities. However, with the persistence of the crisis, the funding issue became increasingly controversial and the focus of local inter-party conflict.

A second element which facilitated a shift in the nature of local politics in the Federal Republic was the changing macropolitical climate of the late 1960s. In general terms, the significant developments affecting local politics related to changes in the political culture of western Germany. Signs of this change were a growing popular interest in local political affairs, the creation of the first Social–Liberal government in Bonn, and the emergence of the new social movements.

One of the main factors underlying the unpolitical nature of traditional local politics in Germany was essentially a throwback to the general lack of public interest which characterised all aspects of politics during the rebuilding period. The Almond and Verba (1963) study suggested that this lack of interest lay at the heart of western Germany's 'passive political culture'. At local level this was expressed in low turnout rates at local council elections and in the absence of public participation in local decision-making processes. Political culture studies conducted in the Federal Republic since the initial Civic Culture research have tended to illustrate Germany's rapid movement from a passive to a more active political culture, linking this to economic developments and to the emergence of the *Volkspartei* phenomenon (Baker *et al.* 1981; Berg-Schlosser and Schissler 1987; Conradt 1980; Gabriel 1986; Reichel 1981; Smith 1986). The most significant changes occurred in the second half of the 1960s (Baker *et al.* 1981; Conradt 1980). Although most political culture studies have concentrated upon transitions at the federal level, the local political repercussions were equally great. Even the first Almond and Verba (1963) study showed that feelings of political efficacy were greatest at local level, with more people feeling that they could influence the course of the local decision-making process than that at the federal level. With a universal willingness to participate more in political activities towards the end of the 1960s, there was inevitably a knock-on effect at local level (see J.J. Hesse

1982). One more immediate result of the developing interest in local political matters in western Germany was a gradual increase in participation rates in local elections during the 1970s, although these have never matched the rates recorded at elections to higher-level parliaments (Ausschuß Wahlforschung 1987:67f.; Kuschke and Cryns 1984:90).

The change of Federal Government in 1969 provided an additional focus for the improved status of local politics. The Brandt government's reform platform had a strong bias towards the local level, given that many of the reform proposals were to be implemented by local authorities. This applied in particular to planning legislation (for example reform of the *Bundesbaugesetz* 1976, *Städtebauförderungsgesetz* 1971), which sought to improve public access to local decision-making in the town-planning sphere. The fact that much of the impetus towards the reform and democratisation of western German society was blunted in the wake of the 1973 oil crisis did little to reduce public expectations of their local authorities. Above all, however, it was the SPD's youth wing, the *Jungsozialisten (Jusos)*, which adopted a leading role in efforts to upgrade the status of the local level. Adopting a neo-Marxist critique of the established pattern of local democracy, the *Jusos* chose to regard local politics as *Gesellschaftspolitik* (W. Roth 1972). During the course of the 1970s many new young members of the SPD were elected to Germany's local councils and injected a certain amount of conflict into council proceedings. However, the new left of the SPD experienced a great deal of frustration when it came to implementing their new strategy. The impetus for local reform was lost in the SPD's concentration on national topics and the SPD–FDP government's 'ignorance of local problems' (W. Roth and Edelhoff 1983:86). It was not until 1978, for example, that the SPD formally set up a forum in which local policies and practices could be coordinated. Despite the fact that Willy Brandt described the SPD's local councillors as the 'actual backbone of the party', the Social Democrats appeared to lose their way in local politics in the late 1970s and suffered a series of damaging electoral reverses in some of the Federal Republic's largest cities, including Munich and Frankfurt (Samtlebe 1983). Nevertheless, despite their inability to implement their radical strategy, it has been amongst the newer generation of SPD members that the Greens have been able to find their most powerful allies when seeking to change the face of German local politics. As will be discussed below, political alliances between the Greens and the SPD are most durable when there is a strong representation of the youth wing's ideals within the local party organisation of the SPD.

Perhaps the most important development in German local politics in the late 1960s within the context of this study was the emergence of the new social movements, particularly of the citizens' initiative movement. It is unnecessary to discuss in detail the origins, composition and characteristics of the various groups which belong to the new social movements since this has been done in detail elsewhere (for example Berg-Schlosser and Schissler 1987; Brand 1982; R. Roth and Rucht 1991; Rüdig 1980). Instead, attention is briefly to be drawn to the five factors identified by Pelinka (1986) that led to the rapid rise of the new social movements in the Federal Republic, each of which has a degree of relevance at local level.

Firstly, there was a growing popular dissatisfaction with a form of politics that appeared to be based merely upon objective rather than subjective decision-making process. This type of political behaviour (*Sachzwangpolitik*) lies at the very heart of the 'Old Local Politics' in the Federal Republic and is reflected in an emphasis placed upon the need for 'unpolitical' control of local affairs by council administrations. Secondly, there was a greater awareness of a series of new political issues, particularly those associated with the New Politics agenda. This applied in particular to the increasing salience of environmental matters, which lay at the heart of the rise of the citizens' initiative movement, but also to themes linked to the rights of social minorities, women's and peace issues and civil liberties. The failure of the established political parties to address the issues of the New Politics at local level was a fundamental factor behind the rise of new forms of political opposition in Germany. Thirdly, Pelinka (1986) refers to a renaissance of the normative definition of democracy, especially in the wake of the student protests of the late 1960s. Direct democratic decision-making structures were regarded as an attractive alternative by adherents of the emerging New Politics groups to the seemingly staid representative democratic organisational forms of the established political groupings. There was a desire on the part of politically active citizens to further their aims in a more direct, participative manner than that allowed by the *Volksparteien*. This helps to explain the evolution within the new social movements of non-hierarchical organisational structures, which were later to be reproduced within the Greens. A fourth factor underlying the rise of the new social movements was the developing interest in local politics itself, which was regarded as the least remote level of government and consequently as the best level at which such groups could achieve their aims. The local level effectively became the testing ground for those theories of the new social movements which were linked to the application of direct democratic procedures and the encouragement of mass participation in decision-making processes. Finally, Pelinka (1986) cites the declining loyalty of electorates in the traditional political parties, which had developed into catch-all parties and appeared unable to accommodate the specific interests of narrow-based interest groups, as a factor behind the emergence of the new social movements. This applied not only to the political parties operating at national level, but also to those present at local level. The fact that all-party coalitions existed in a significant proportion of Germany's local councils at the beginning of the 1970s only reinforced the prevailing impression that there was little to distinguish the traditional parties from one another.

Although estimates of the number of citizens' initiative groups in the Federal Republic varied considerably, depending upon the definitions adopted of such groups, Rüdig (1980) has suggested that there were at least as many members of such groups by 1980 as there were members of the major political parties in western Germany (see Arzberger 1980). However, of greater importance than the scale of membership of citizens' initiative groups was the fact that their universal appearance in both urban and rural settings placed local decision-makers under a greater degree of public scrutiny. Planning decisions in particular became the source of public debate, which in itself contributed towards a politicisation of the nature of the work undertaken by local councils. Given the level of expertise developed by citizens' initiative groups, it became increasingly difficult for council administrations to resolve planning issues behind closed committee doors.

Thus the Federal Republic's changing macropolitical climate

in the late 1960s and 1970s made local politics seem more important than had previously been the case. Not only was the local level the one at which much of the SPD–FDP reform legislation was to be implemented, but it was also the level by which adherents of the New Politics set great store, given its accessibility and the fact that many of their aims could be achieved by local means.

In addition to the economic and political factors, a final element which contributed to the politicisation and parliamentarisation of Germany's local politics was the effect of sweeping administrative changes upon the country's local organisational structures. One of the expressed aims of the boundary reforms (*Gebietsreform*) was to confirm the independence of local-level decision-makers (Jesse 1986:68). By creating larger units of local government, it was hoped that local authorities would find it easier to manage their resources, make planning decisions and provide funding for a range of public facilities. However, the principal political impact of the boundary reforms of the late 1960s and 1970s was that it became much easier for the established political parties to organise at local level. In the wake of the reforms, the overall number of communities in western Germany fell from over 24,000 to the current figure of around 8,500 (Table 3.5). In certain regions the reforms were more drastic than in others. In North Rhine Westphalia, for example, the number of communities was reduced from a figure of 2,362 in 1965 to only 396 in 1983; no community in this region currently has a population of less than 3,000 (Pappermann 1984:183). In Hesse between 1970 and 1980 the number of communities fell by 83.8 per cent, from 2,622 to 427, with the most significant decline again being experienced by the smallest communities (Stöss 1986b:2397). In 1984 Hesse had only eleven communities with less than 2,000 inhabitants, as opposed to the 2,209 which belonged to this category in 1970 (Lilge 1986:55). In the Rhineland Palatinate, however, the boundary reforms were altogether less dramatic, with the number of communities falling by just over one-fifth, from 2,903 in 1967 to 2,291 in 1979 (Kühr 1983:6). Measures were taken in some regions to compensate for the loss of independence of a large number of small communities and the resulting feelings of alienation on the part of their inhabitants. This primarily involved the establishment of neighbourhood councils (*Ortsbeiräte* or *Bezirksvertretungen*) with powers to influence council proposals affecting their locality. However, limited financial resources have tended to deprive neighbourhood councils of the chance to establish themselves as important political institutions in the Federal Republic.

Table 3.5 Administrative Structure: West Germany, 1968 and 1984

State	Communities 1968	1984	Independent towns 1968	1984	Districts 1968	1984
Schleswig-Holstein	1,378	1,131	4	4	17	11
Lower Saxony	4,231	1,031	15	9	60	38
North Rhine Westphalia	2,277	396	35	23	57	31
Hesse	2,684	427	9	5	39	21
Rhineland Palatinate	2,905	2,303	12	12	28	24
Baden-Württemberg	3,379	1,111	9	9	63	35
Bavaria	7,077	2,025	48	25	143	71
Saarland	347	52	1	0	7	6
City states	4	4	4	4	–	–
Federal Republic	24,282	8,507	137	91	414	237

Source: Jesse 1986:68, Table 23

The vast reduction in the number of local authorities – achieved by the fusion of many of the smaller communities into larger administrative units – made the possibility of gaining representation in a majority of the country's local councils a realistic aim for the major parties for the first time in the Federal Republic's history. The degree of success of the two catch-all parties in achieving this end was expressed in terms of the increasing number of local party organisations affiliated to each of the parties, and also from the parties' rising membership figures during the 1970s. An additional effect of the improvement of the major political parties' local organisational networks and their growing presence in local council chambers was the marked decline witnessed in the share of the vote gained by the apolitical free voters' associations. This development in itself tended to politicise local politics, since the diminishing role of the free voters' groups encouraged a shift away from the discussion of issues of a purely local nature by local councils. With the growing representation of the major political parties at local level, it was likely that a degree of confrontation would develop in local councils as national party-political divisions tended to be mirrored at the local level (Gabriel 1984). The administrative reforms had an additional impact upon the style of local politics in western Germany. Since councils were making decisions for greater numbers of people, it proved necessary for parties to professionalise their approach to local politics. With many more decisions being made and an increasing complexity in the subject-matter of topics under discussion, parliamentary decision-making procedures gradually began to find their way into local councils. One sign of this was the fact that decisions were increasingly deferred to council subcommittees, which in turn tended to be dominated by party experts. In effect, the patterns of decision-making adopted by federal and regional bodies became more common at local level (see Innenministerium des Landes Nordrhein-Westfalen:1989:77f.).

As a result of the economic, political and administrative changes, the traditional approach to local politics was experiencing a decline in the 1970s. Although the unpolitical and consensual approach still dominated, there were signs that the activities of local councils were becoming overtly more political and that the style of local politics was becoming more comparable to that of higher-level parliaments. This resulted in the emergence of something resembling a 'New Local Politics' in Germany. In order to illustrate the effects of this process on local council activities, and in particular of the role of the Greens at local level, this study will examine in Part II events in a particular west German city, Mainz, during the course of the 1980s.

Summary: New Local Politics in the 1970s

This chapter has sought to provide a foundation for the examination of the impact of the Greens upon Germany's local politics from the end of the 1970s. Within the broad context of changes affecting all levels of the German party system, it has been suggested that local party systems will be affected in different ways by the New Politics, depending upon the extent of the socio-economic change and subsequent value change experienced. Simply

61

stated, the New Politics is more likely to play a role in the party systems of those large towns and cities which have witnessed rapid social and economic change and less likely to be a factor in localities left behind by the modernisation process. Tentative signs of the impact of the New Politics upon local party systems were described in terms of the development of a 'New Local Politics', which was in stark contrast to the traditional 'Old Local Politics', discussed in Chapter 2. Even before the emergence of the Greens as a party of the New Politics towards the end of the 1970s, the first signs of a growing divide between adherents of the two styles of local politics could be discerned.

The Old Local Politics is characterised by consensual decision-making structures, symbolised in the all-party coalitions which governed and, in many cases, continue to govern a great proportion of the Federal Republic's communities. It strictly adheres to the narrow interpretation of the role of local authorities, as defined by Article 28.2 of the Basic Law, which seeks to restrict the scope of the issues addressed by the local council. Finally, the Old Local Politics is marked by an expressed preference for representative democratic decision-making forms, as opposed to participative structures.

The New Local Politics is fundamentally different. It is characterised above all by parliamentary styles of politics, which give rise to party-political confrontation. Adherents of the New Local Politics tend to adopt a broad definition of the powers of local decision-makers, which grants local councils the right to address all issues regardless of their appropriateness to the local level. This style of local politics strives for the implementation of open decision-making processes, which allow for a maximum level of public participation in council decisions.

The Old Local Politics clearly predominated in the Federal Republic prior to the emergence of the Greens. Such changes as occurred in the direction of the New Local Politics were confined to the country's major towns and cities, where the SPD's new left predominated. This was most clearly demonstrated by events in Frankfurt in the mid-1970s. The reforming zeal of the SPD's youth wing became blunted in the face of Germany's growing economic difficulties and pressures to follow the general party line on a series of important national issues. Only with the increased presence in Germany's local councils of the Greens, as a party of the New Politics, could the transition from the Old Local Politics to the New Local Politics occur in a greater number of local authorities of differing sizes and socio-economic types.

4

The Greens in Germany's Local Politics

This chapter provides an overview of Green local political involvement in western Germany, focusing upon three main areas. Firstly, some general characteristics applying to the origins of the Greens at local level are explored. Secondly, attention is paid to the scale of Green local council representation in the Federal Republic and to the characteristics of the Greens' representatives. Finally, drawing upon local electoral statistics from a number of German cities, the extent to which the Green electorate at local level is the same as that at other levels of Germany's federal system is assessed. This chapter provides a foundation for a more detailed discussion of the political role of the Greens in Germany's local politics in Chapters 5 and 6.

Characteristics of the Greens' Initial Local Successes

The electoral origins of the Green Party lie in the participation of citizens' initiative groups in local and regional elections in the Federal Republic during the latter part of the 1970s (Klotzsch and Stöss 1986; Rönsch 1983). These early electoral successes of the Greens have been well documented (Klotzsch and Stöss 1986; Kolinsky 1984:313f.; Murphy 1979; Papadakis 1984; Rönsch 1983). In the context of this study, however, it is useful to identify several key characteristics of the participation of ecological lists in local elections in the late 1970s and early 1980s. The most noticeable features were the influence of electoral deadlines upon the candidature of green lists, the political orientation and heterogeneity of the first lists and the often spectacular nature of their early electoral successes.

It is a point which might easily be overlooked, but a prime motivating factor behind the ecologists' decision to compete for votes across the regions of the Federal Republic was the timing of the relevant elections. Local elections provide new political parties with the opportunity to secure parliamentary representation at an early stage of their development. On the one hand voters appear to be more willing to experiment with their vote at local elections, while on the other the absence of exclusion clauses in certain regions for parties failing to secure at least 5 per cent of the vote means that new parties can gain seats with just a small level of support. Although the first green electoral successes in Lower Saxony (October 1977) and Schleswig-Holstein (March 1978) can largely be attributed to the existence in these regions of powerful citizens' initiative groups protesting against the construction of nuclear installations, it is unlikely that these groups would have made such a mark had they first competed in regional elections.[1] Success at local level made the Greens more ambitious. Hallensleben (1984:90) describes the process by which the local electoral successes of ecological lists in Schleswig-Holstein encouraged the *Grüne Liste Umweltschutz* (GLU) in Lower Saxony to contest the 1978 regional election. In other regions the Greens were obliged by election timetables to compete first in regional or national elections. In certain regions it was not until the Greens had already secured seats in the Federal Parliament that they were able to contest local elections as a unified force. In the Rhineland Palatinate, for instance, other than the *Alternative Liste Trier* no ecological group appears to have campaigned in the 1979 local elections. Thus the first opportunity for the Greens to compete on a widespread basis at local level in this region did not arise until the 1984 local elections.

At local level, despite a gradual convergence of ideologies, organisational structures and tactics, the Greens remain to a greater or lesser extent a heterogeneous force (see for example

---

[1] In local by-elections in Lower Saxony on 23 October 1977 the *Grüne Liste Umweltschutz* gained 1.2% in the Hildesheim district and, in the absence of a 5% barrier, one council seat. A *Wählergemeinschaft Atomkraft – Nein Danke* (WGA) won 2.3% of the vote in the Hameln-Pyrmont district and a council seat (Stöss 1986b:1515). Both groups developed out of citizens' initiative groups opposed to the construction of nuclear power plants in their vicinity. In Schleswig-Holstein two ecological electoral lists gained seats in local elections held on 15 March 1978. The *Grüne Liste Nordfriesland* secured two district council seats after gaining 6.0% of the vote, while the *Grüne Liste Unabhängiger Wähler* won three district council seats as a result of their 6.6% vote (Schleswig-Holstein 1978:113).

Wiesenthal 1985:151). Conservative and radical left-wing groups can still coexist successfully, since their action radius is limited to a particular locality. The Green Party itself helped to maintain the diversity of the local groups by declining to compete against alternative groups in local elections. The Green Party has nevertheless been able to establish itself as the principal ecological and alternative force in German local politics, despite the existence of a range of other green and alternative groupings in the country's local communities. In many cases this has happened simply because the alternative groups disintegrated or because the members of these groups transferred their allegiance to the Green Party.[2]

A third characteristic of the Greens' initial electoral involvement was the frequent competition at regional and national level of a plethora of green groupings for votes. It should be stressed, however, that this was most obviously a feature at the regional level (for example Hamburg, Bremen and Hesse). At local level it has been relatively uncommon for ecological groups to compete with one another at successive elections, given that there is rarely sufficient electoral support for more than one alternative group in a particular community. The 1982 local elections in Lübeck, for example, saw the conservative *Grüne Liste Schleswig-Holstein* compete with the more radical *Wählergemeinschaft der GRÜNEN Lübeck*, securing 3.3 per cent and 3.2 per cent of the vote respectively (Lübeck 1986). This electoral competition was enough to deprive either list of representation.[3] When alternative groups stood against official Green Party lists in Lower Saxony's local elections of 1981 they performed very badly (Rudnick and Goltermann 1981:59). Experiences of this type again

[2] Numerous examples exist of alternative and rainbow lists (*bunte Listen*) being succeeded by official Green Party lists in local elections. This includes the *Kölner Alternative* (Cologne), the *Alternative Grüne Liste* Bonn, the *Alternative Liste* Trier, the *Bunte Liste* Bielefeld and the *Wiesbadener Liste*, each of which competed in local elections between 1979 and 1981. However, in Oberhausen the reverse happened in the 1984 local election, with a *Bunte Liste* replacing the Green Party which had stood in 1979.

[3] Similar competitive candidatures of Green Party lists and alternative groups occurred in several communities in North Rhine Westphalia in the 1984 local elections. In Bad Honnef (Rhein-Sieg district), for example, the Green Party gained 4.8% of the vote, whilst a green voting group secured 8.3% and three council seats. Other conflicting candidatures occurred in Alsdorf (Aachen district) and in Kamen and Bergkamen (both Unna district).

impose a degree of discipline upon potential competitors for the green vote. Where lists purporting to be green or alternative have competed with one another in local elections in the second half of the 1980s, it has often been the case that only one of the opposing groups can claim to be truly green or alternative.[4] There have also been a number of cases in which radical right-wing and left-wing groups have assumed the guise of ecological or alternative lists in order to stand against 'official' green groups. Although the bogus groups are rarely successful themselves, they can gain sufficient votes to deprive the Greens of council seats. A radical right-wing group, the *Grünalternativen*, campaigned in the 1985 Hessian local elections in the Hersfeld-Rotenburg district, gaining only 0.3 per cent of the vote, but depriving the official Green Party, who won 4.97 per cent of the vote, of council representation (*Grüne Hessenzeitung* 4/85:44).

A final feature of the initial development of green and alternative lists in west German local politics was their often spectacular resonance amongst the electorate, with two factors playing a key role. The first was the expression of local protest against planning measures imposed upon the local community by either national or regional governments, against which the established local political parties were unable or unwilling to act. The second arose from the presence for the very first time in certain communities of an oppositional group in the local arena, thereby offering an element of political choice in local elections.

Where local citizens were protesting about specific planning measures in their region, oppositional ecological lists could become a decisive factor in the local party system. This was well illustrated in the Hessian local elections of 1981, which occurred against the backdrop of a proposed runway extension at Frankfurt airport (*Startbahn-West*) (Ernst 1982; Nessel and Nowack 1982) and the development of a contentious nuclear energy programme in the region. In the Groß-Gerau district, which was most immediately affected by the runway development, green

[4] Having declined to compete against the *Wählergemeinschaft Darmstadt* (WGD) in the 1981 local election, the Darmstadt Green Party decided to do so in 1985. Above all, the Greens appear to have objected to the authoritarian style of the WGD chairman (*Frankfurter Rundschau* 13.07.84). In the 1985 election the Green Party won 9.5% of the vote (seven seats), the WGD 4.5%.

lists gained seats in each of the communities in which they stood for election.[5] In the two towns of Büttelborn and Mörfelden-Walldorf ecologists gained 25.2 per cent of the vote, winning nine and eleven seats respectively. At the same time, North Hessian localities suggested as possible locations for a nuclear reprocessing plant recorded high levels of support for the greens. In Breuna, in the Kassel district, the Greens secured 37.7 per cent in the district elections. In Volksmarsen (Waldeck-Frankenberg district), the Green Party won 17.3 per cent of the vote in the district elections, but a newly formed local voting group did even better in the local community elections, gaining 41.7 per cent and thereby becoming the majority party in the local council (Hesse 1982). Comparatively high levels of green support were witnessed in local elections across the Federal Republic at the end of the 1970s (Kolinsky 1984:317; Müller 1979:150f.; Pridham 1978).

The high level of support for ecological lists in these communities was obviously motivated by opposition to large-scale projects imposed upon local citizens by higher levels of government (Brand 1982:181f.). However, in other communities the factors underlying green success were less obvious. Particularly in small rural communities characterised by an absence of local forms of political opposition, the candidature of a green list provided citizens with an element of choice in a local election for the first time. As a result, the Greens sometimes secured a large proportion of the vote in communities in which they might not have expected to succeed. This was the case in the 1984 local elections in the Rhineland Palatinate, for example, when the Green Party stood for the first time in the community of Isenburg, in the Neuwied district. The Greens won 41.3 per cent of the vote and four of the eleven seats in the local council (Table 4.1). A closer analysis of the local election results for this community suggests that this high showing resulted more from a protest about the absence of choice in the local council election than from any positive expression of support for the Greens and their programme. Whilst 163 voters supported the Greens in the local council election, 104 did so in the election to the community association

[5] On 22 March 1981, the Green Party won 14.2% of the vote in the Groß-Gerau district (twelve seats). Green lists campaigned in six of the fourteen communities which make up the district, gaining 11.0% of the overall vote and a further forty-four seats (Hesse 1982).

Table 4.1 Local Election Result, Isenburg (Neuwied District) Rhineland Palatinate, 17 June 1984

Election type	Turnout %	CDU No.	CDU %	SPD No.	SPD %	FDP No.	FDP %	GREENS No.	GREENS %	Others No.	Others %	All (n)
Local council	71.6	–	–	–	–	–	–	163	41.3	232	58.7	395
Community assocation	71.6	122	31.4	108	27.8	5	1.3	104	26.8	49	12.6	388
District council	71.2	158	40.8	143	37.0	7	1.8	61	4.7	18	4.7	387

Source: Rhineland Palatinate 1985:105

(*Verbandsgemeinderat*) and only sixty-one voted Green in the district council election which took place concurrently. In the latter two elections, voters could choose between each of the main political parties of the Federal Republic as well as local voting groups.

The diverse nature of the Greens' early electoral successes meant that it was often difficult for analysts to classify the Greens in the early stages of their parliamentary activities (see Klotzsch and Stöss 1986; Rönsch 1980a:420f.). Over time, however, the Greens have tended to become an increasingly distinctive force in German local politics. Green local politics have gradually become rather more homogenised, with independent and alternative ecological lists slowly giving way in local elections to official Green Party lists with their greater organisational and financial power. This in turn bolsters the trend towards uniformity in the nature and style of Green local politics. Furthermore, having been identified as a radical left-wing party by both the general electorate and their supporters alike, it is more difficult for the Green Party to secure the votes of a wide cross-section of the local population, even in areas in which planning measures threaten the local environment. As a result, spectacular electoral successes are less common than was once the case for green and alternative groups, and the Greens have become increasingly reliant upon a stable, core electorate. However, before identifying this electorate more precisely, it is necessary to establish a picture of the extent of Green local council representation in the Federal Republic.

The Scale of Green Representation at Local Level

The scale of Green representation at the national and regional levels of the German party system can be assessed relatively simply by examining the official electoral statistics published by the relevant regional statistical offices. However, this is not the case for Green local council representation for several reasons. Before addressing some of the difficulties associated with making such a calculation, it is useful to provide an indication of the speed with which the Greens progressed from being an extra-parliamentary to a parliamentary force. This can be derived from an

Table 4.2 Green Representation in Town Councils, West Germany, 1981–1991

Population size of community	Green Party 1981	All Greens 1981	Green Party 1986	All Greens 1986	Green Party 1991	All Greens 1991
500,000 and more						
No. of seats	22	26	62	102	95	141
% of all seats	2.1	2.5	5.8	9.6	8.2	12.2
200,000–500,000						
No. of seats	5	15	88	109	83	104
% of all seats	0.8	1.3	7.4	9.1	7.0	8.7
100,000–200,000						
No. of seats	29	40	151	168	173	197
% of all seats	1.5	2.1	8.2	9.2	8.3	9.5
50,000–100,000						
No. of seats	31	54	244	300	276	328
% of all seats	0.7	1.3	5.9	7.3	6.8	8.0
20,000–50,000						
No. of seats	104	162	692	833	710	869
% of all seats	0.8	1.2	5.1	6.2	5.2	6.4
All sizes						
No. of seats	191	297	1237	1512	1337	1639
% of all seats	0.9	1.4	5.7	7.0	6.0	7.4

Source: Der Städtetag 35, No. 6, 1982:429; 40, No. 6, 1987:369; 44, No. 8, 1991:593

analysis of the level of Green Party and green-alternative representation in west Germany's towns and cities with populations of more than 20,000 people between 1981 and 1991. Unfortunately, given persisting variations in the local political and party structures of east and west Germany, it is not possible to present comparable data for the Federal Republic's five new regions.

In 1981 only 1.4 per cent of all council seats (297 of 21,719) in German communities with over 20,000 inhabitants were held by representatives of the Green Party or of various green-alternative lists (Table 4.2). By 1986 this figure had increased fivefold to some 7 per cent (1,512 of 21,690 seats). The most dramatic increase in Green representation occurred between 1984 and 1986, with local elections taking place in each of the regions of the Federal Republic. With regard to the level of representation in towns of different size-categories, a clear pattern could be discerned by 1986. Although traditionally stronger in the larger towns and cities, by 1986 the proportion of council seats held by the Greens rose progressively through the various size-categories, from 6.1 per cent of seats in towns with populations of between 20,000 and 50,000 to 9.8 per cent in the three west German cities with populations of more than one million (Berlin, Hamburg and Munich).[6] Since 1986 there has been something of a consolidation of the level of Green representation in Germany's larger communities, which is the inevitable result of a stretching of the Green movement's limited membership resources. Also of note is the level of female council representation within the Greens. Whilst 40.8 per cent of official Green Party representatives in 1991 were women, the three traditional political parties had much lower proportions of female councillors. Just 15.5 per cent of CDU councillors, 23.2 per cent of SPD councillors and 19.4 per cent of FDP councillors were women (Der Städtetag, No. 8, 1991:593). Green representatives also tend to be younger than those of other parties, although this pattern is gradually changing. Green councillors elected in the 1984 local elections in the Ruhr had an average age of thirty-three years,

6 It should be noted that this calculation includes Green and Alternative representation in the Federal Republic's three city states (Berlin, Bremen and Hamburg), which are not otherwise regarded as units of local government.

but by 1989 this figure had risen to thirty-eight years (Kommunalverband Ruhrgebiet 1989:23; also Heidelberg 1990:62).

Given the rapid pace of their shift into the country's parliaments, an equally rapid saturation of the Greens' membership and organisational resources should have been anticipated. As will be discussed in Chapter 5, the fact that this process took place in an unplanned way caused particular problems for the organisationally weak Greens. Having shown the speed with which the parliamentarisation of the Greens occurred, it should be noted that it is much more difficult to establish the scale of Green representation in all local communities in the Federal Republic. The majority of German communities have populations significantly below 20,000. Consequently, estimates of the strength of Green local council representation are vague, although Roland Roth's (1988) figure of about 6,000 representatives seems most plausible. The two main factors which affect the reliability of such a calculation are the definition of green groups adopted and the type of local council covered. Whereas the Greens will tend to exaggerate their level of local council representation, it is common for electoral statistics to underestimate their strength.

Most official statistical sources publish only the local election results attributed to the official Green Party. This invariably leads to an understatement of Green strength, since those ecological and alternative electoral lists which compete independently of the Green Party are ignored. As was previously mentioned, the Green Party rarely stands for election in localities in which established alternative groupings have declared an interest in competing for votes. In certain regions, most notably in Baden-Württemberg and Bavaria, alternative lists are of particular significance, and often have a tradition which precedes the emergence of the Green Party by a number of years. Whilst it is relatively straightforward to identify the strength of the official Green Party, it is extremely difficult to establish the scale of representation of the alternative groupings. Generally, official statistics assign the share of the vote gained by such alternative groups to that of the independent voting groups (*Wählervereinigungen*), which predominate at local level in a number of regions. With these independent groups being so numerous, it is seldom possible for electoral offices to provide details of their composition, and even when statistical offices attempt to identify unofficial green lists separately, this is not always done accurately.[7] A second difficulty which marks attempts to calculate the scale of the Greens' local council representation stems from the disparate nature of Germany's local administrative structures. As was discussed in Chapter 2, the regions have varying types of local councils with differing levels of responsibility. It is necessary, therefore, to define clearly for this study what is to be regarded as local council representation. This can only be done on the basis of the councils of administrative units which are common to all of the regions of the Federal Republic, namely that of the community, the independent town and the district. Whilst it is possible to define electoral strength in terms of representation on a combination of the three types of administrative area, it is most common to treat the larger units of local government (the districts and independent towns) separately from the smaller units (the communities).[8] Generally, information pertaining to city and district elections is the most reliable, since the number of administrative units involved is relatively small. In the Rhineland Palatinate, for example, there are only twelve independent towns and twenty-four districts, as opposed to almost 2,300 communities (Rhineland Palatinate 1985). It should be recognised, therefore, that it easier to establish the strength of non-party green lists in the independent towns and districts than in the communities.

Problems arise when one addresses the level of Green representation in a range of additional councils in the Federal Republic of varying levels of importance. Such councils essentially fall into one of three types: neighbourhood councils, community association councils and supra-local councils. The most widespread supplementary council is the neighbourhood council, set

---

[7] Personal communications with the regional statistical offices of Lower Saxony (21.05.88) and Rhineland Palatinate (25.03.87) show that details of the titles of voting groups are not collected. Although an attempt was made in the latter case to list a number of 'possible' ecological and alternative lists which competed in the region's 1984 local elections, the list was inconsistent with data already gathered by the author.

[8] Baden-Württemberg's local election statistics distinguish between the district vote on the one hand and the vote gained in independent towns and local communities on the other. There are no independent towns in the Saarland. This should be taken into account when consulting Table 4.3.

up in the larger towns and cities of the Federal Republic in the wake of the administrative reforms of the late 1960s and 1970s.[9] Although limited in their competences by the financial restrictions imposed upon them, the neighbourhood councils are elected bodies in their own right. Indeed, neighbourhood councils in certain cities will have greater financial powers and represent significantly more people than some of the smaller rural communities. As yet, however, this level of local government is more often neglected in official election statistics than not, and it is not even clear how many neighbourhood councils exist in Germany. Consequently, estimates of party strength at this level of local government are bound to be unreliable. Nevertheless, the fact that the Greens are widely represented on neighbourhood councils and that a significant proportion of their time and resources are devoted to this level of government should not be overlooked. In North Rhine Westphalia, for example, 218 Green Party and green-alternative candidates were elected to the region's neighbourhood councils in the 1984 local elections, a figure which fell slightly to 207 councillors in 1989 (North Rhine Westphalia 1984 and 1989). In the 1989 local elections in Frankfurt alone, thirty-seven Greens were elected to the city's sixteen neighbourhood councils (Frankfurt 1989b).

A second group of supplementary councils, which exist only in the Rhineland Palatinate and Lower Saxony, represents associations of small communities.[10] These councils achieve a compromise between the need for larger planning units and the desire of citizens to maintain a degree of control over local policy-making. Whilst the Greens are liable to be absent from the councils of the administrative units which comprise the community association, it is relatively common for them to have representation in the council of the association. Thus, following local elections, the Green Party had thirty-five representatives on the Rhineland Palatinate's councils of the community associations in 1984 and seventy on those in Lower Saxony in 1986.

---

[9] Terminology varies across the Federal Republic. *Ortsbeiräte* exist in Hesse, Schleswig-Holstein and the Rhineland Palatinate; *Ortschaftsräte* in Baden-Württemberg; *Ortsräte* in Lower Saxony and the Saarland; *Bezirksausschüsse* in Bavaria; *Bezirksvertretungen* in North Rhine Westphalia (Bockelt 1989:208f.).

[10] In Lower Saxony community associations are termed *Samtgemeinden*, in the Rhineland Palatinate *Verbandsgemeinden*.

Finally, supra-local bodies should be taken into account. These are planning bodies of various types, assigned the task of coordinating specific duties which the individual component communities are unable to perform themselves. Communities belonging to the supra-local bodies can be, and often are, quite large urban units of government. This factor distinguishes them from the community associations, made up of small, rural communities. The supra-local bodies can be elected either directly by the voters or indirectly on the basis of an aggregation of the election results in their member constituencies. Examples of supra-local councils are to be found in the *Umlandverband* of Frankfurt, the *Bezirkstag Pfalz* of the Rhineland Palatinate and the two *Landschaftsversammlungen* of North Rhine Westphalia. The Bavarian *Bezirkstage* would also fall into this category, despite the fact that they are elected concurrently with the regional parliament rather than with other local councils (Bockelt 1989). Green representation in such bodies can be significant. For example, in 1985 the Green Party gained eleven seats on the *Umlandverband* Frankfurt and in North Rhine Westphalia they held twenty-two seats in the two *Landschaftsversammlungen* of the Rhineland and Westfalen-Lippe.

As a result of the widespread regional variations in the presence and function of the supplementary councils, the most meaningful calculation of the extent of Green local council strength should therefore take account only of those Greens elected to the councils of the three administrative units common to all German regions: communities, independent towns and districts. At the same time it should be recognised that the inadequacies of the statistical sources allow at best only an estimation of the level of local council representation of Green Party and alternative lists in the Federal Republic. This information is presented in Table 4.3 for 1991, thereby taking account of local elections which occurred in each region of the Federal Republic between 1986 and 1991.[11]

---

[11] City/district election results for Baden-Württemberg and the Saarland represent districts only; city election results in these regions are included in those at community level.

The figures given in Table 4.3 were compiled by the author from the following sources: Baden-Württemberg (1990); Bavaria (1990); Hesse (1990); North Rhine

Table 4.3 Green Local Council Representation, West Germany, 1991

Region	Election date	List type	City/district level		Community level		Total seats
			%	seats	%	seats	
Baden-Württemberg	22.10.89	Green Party	9.1	188	5.9	465	653
		All Greens	9.1	188	8.2	740	928
Bavaria	18.03.90	Green Party	5.4	239	1.7	243	482
		All Greens	6.5	305	2.3	345	650
Hesse	12.03.89	Green Party	9.1	190	5.8	619	809
		All Greens	9.1	190	6.9	777	967
Lower Saxony	02.03.86	Green Party	5.4	115	3.6	288	403
		All Greens	6.3	124	N.A.	N.A.	412
North Rhine Westphalia	01.10.89	Green Party	8.3	276	6.4	734	1,010
		All Greens	8.7	293	7.1	810	1,103
Rhineland Palatinate	18.06.89	Green Party	7.4	112	1.9	139	251
		All Greens	7.4	112	N.A.	N.A.	251
Saarland	18.06.89	Green Party	5.5	6	4.5	40	46
		All Greens	5.5	6	4.5	40	46
Schleswig Holstein	25.03.90	Green Party	6.0	31	0.6	79	110
		All Greens	6.0	31	N.A.	N.A.	110
West Germany		Green Party		1,157		2,607	3,764
		All Greens		1,249		3,218	4,467

Source: See note 11: N.A. – not available

In December 1991 there were at least 4,400 Green and Alternative local councillors in Germany's western regions. Given the difficulties outlined above, this is likely to be rather a conservative estimation of the Greens' local representation. Attention should also be paid in particular to the missing data from Lower Saxony. The 1981 local elections in this region provided Green and alternative lists with an estimated 2,000 local councillors (*Frankfurter Allgemeine Zeitung* 29.08.81; *Frankfurter Rundschau* 29.08.81). It is, therefore, to be anticipated that a slightly higher number of mandates will have been gained in 1986. This would bring us closer to Roth's (1988) estimation of 6,000 Green local politicians.

There is a large difference between the level of Green support at the city/district level and that at community level. This is largely a reflection of the weak organisational structure of the Greens at the lowest level of the German party system. The Greens, like other political parties, do not have the required resources to be able to compete in all communities in every region. In the Rhineland Palatinate, where there are over 2,000 local councils for which parties would need to put up lists, it is clearly beyond the organisational capacity of any party to campaign in each and every locality.[12] Although the percentage figures given in Table 4.3 refer to the vote gained by Green groups across the whole of the relevant region and therefore include communities in which Greens did not put up candidates, the Greens are noticeably more widely represented in certain regions than in others. In Baden-Württemberg and North Rhine Westphalia, for example, the Greens performed well in both the city/district elections and in elections to local communities. However, in Bavaria, the Rhineland Palatinate and Schleswig-Holstein Green representation at communal level is rather weak.

The data presented in Table 4.3 point to the degree to which the Greens are now primarily a parliamentary party. Whether by

Westphalia (1989); Rhineland Palatinate (1990); Saarland (1989); Schleswig-Holstein (1990); Thyerlei (1986).

[12] In 53.1% of local communities in the Rhineland Palatinate a majority vote was held in 1984, because no party put up a list of candidates. In the 1,081 communities in which a proportional vote took place the Green Party campaigned in just 61. This compares with a figure of 808 for the CDU, 835 for the SPD and 221 for the FDP.

default or design, it is apparent that the orientation of the Greens towards electoral politics now overrides any earlier preference for extra-parliamentary forms of politics. In certain regions the imbalance between party and parliamentary group is particularly stark. In Hesse, for example, it has been estimated that at least one in eight Green Party members was directly involved in local political activity in 1987 (Scharf 1989:173). By 1990, Veen and Hoffmann (1990:6) suggested that as many as four out of every ten of the Hesse's 5,000 Green Party members either represented the party in parliament or held a party function. The experience has been the same in other regions. In Schleswig-Holstein 150 of the party's estimated 1,700 members held council office in 1986 (Schomaker 1986:26). The 1984 local elections led to the election of one in five of all Green Party members in North Rhine Westphalia, which Wiesenthal (1985:154) suggests was one of the main causes of the party's poor showing in the state's regional election of the following year. When other parliamentary activities are taken into consideration, such as representation on other types of local and supra-local councils, membership of council executive bodies and the large number of personnel required for administrative tasks, it is evident that the active core of the Green Party is primarily engaged in local council activities.

The political repercussions of the parliamentarisation of the Greens will be discussed in more detail with regard to the organisational structures adopted by the Greens at local level. In this context, however, it must be stressed that the integration of the Greens into the established party system in Germany has occurred less at the national or regional level than at the local level. Regardless of events on the national level, this fact has a number of important implications for the Greens, given the nature of local political activity in the Federal Republic of Germany.

The Green Electorate at Local Level

Having examined the scale of representation of the Greens in west Germany's local councils, it is now necessary briefly to identify the Green electorate at local level in order to establish whether it is essentially the same as that at the national and

79

regional levels. In the absence of detailed studies of Green local electoral behaviour (see Schacht 1985), this issue is to be addressed on the basis of data provided by the statistical offices of a number of German towns and cities.

Despite differences in terminology, commentators have increasingly tended to agree that the core Green electorate at national level is younger and better-educated than supporters of other political parties (cf. Bürklin 1981; Fogt and Uttitz 1984; Klotzsch and Stöss 1986:1572f.; Kolinsky 1984:313f.; Mez' and Wolter 1980; Müller 1979; Müller-Rommel 1983a; ÖSS 1988; Rönsch 1983; Schultze 1980; Veen 1984 and 1987). For example, Veen's (1989) analysis of Green support at the 1987 Federal Election shows that 15.5 per cent of voters in the 18–24 age-group and 17.4 per cent of voters in the 25–34 age-group backed the Greens, while this applied to just 1.8 per cent of voters above the age of sixty. A study by the same author found that the proportion of Green supporters having a post-elementary level of education (*Abitur* and above, 39 per cent) was twice that of the population as a whole (18 per cent) (Veen 1987:80). Green support is further concentrated amongst people who are somewhat removed from the production process; people in education, members of the new middle class, the unemployed. In 1986 28 per cent of Green supporters were still in education, compared with 9 per cent of the German population aged eighteen and above. The Greens were also over-represented amongst white-collar workers; 31 per cent of supporters were either *Angestellte* or *Beamte*, compared with 25 per cent of the population. While 3 per cent of the electorate were unemployed in 1986, this applied to 6 per cent of Green supporters (Veen 1987:78). On this evidence, Green support corresponds largely to the New Politics electorate, described in Chapter 3 above, which tends to be concentrated in those urban areas of Germany which have experienced a rapid process of social and economic modernisation. It has variously been estimated that the stable core of Green Party support in the Federal Republic represents between 2 and 3 per cent (ÖSS 1988:3) and 5 and 6 per cent of the electorate (Veen 1987:67). This was in effect the level of support for the Greens in western Germany at the 1990 Federal Election. Over time the share of Green Party support coming from protest voters has progressively declined, as the party's ideological profile has become more focused. The notion that both conservative farmers in the rural areas of Lower Saxony and radical left-wingers in Hesse's university towns could vote for the same political force should be consigned to the past. Veen (1989:36) suggests that the protest element represents at most one-third of Green support.

What does the Green electorate look like at local level? The data presented in the official publications of the various city statistical offices allow conclusions to be drawn about the age and sex structure of Green supporters in local elections, as well as about the characteristics of the areas in which the party performs best.[13] Given the varying scope of the local statistics, some more interesting features of local Green support can also be addressed. However, at this point it is important to emphasise that caution should be used when attempting to generalise on the basis of these data. Notable variations from the norm can and regularly do occur.

Table 4.4 Party Support by Age Groups, Local Election, Duisburg, 1984 (in %)

Age group	SPD	CDU	GREENS	FDP	Others
18–24	55.1	20.8	21.2	2.2	0.7
25–34	58.8	18.2	20.6	2.1	0.3
35–44	55.7	32.3	8.5	2.4	1.1
45–59	60.7	29.9	5.3	3.0	1.1
60 and above	56.7	36.3	2.9	2.9	1.2
All ages	57.9	30.0	8.6	2.7	0.8

Source: Duisburg 1984:20, Table 3

Not surprisingly, the Greens' electorate at local level is much younger than that of the established political parties in the Federal Republic. Representative electoral statistics from most local communities illustrate this point (Bonn 1985:75; Frankfurt 1985;

---

[13] City statistical offices publish 'representative' electoral statistics, calculated on the basis of the ballots of a sample of the voters from representative electoral wards. This provides data for relatively small areas on the age and sex structure of the electorate and on the composition of the parties' electoral support (see Noeske 1985).

Krefeld 1984:12; Leverkusen 1985). Table 4.4 presents data from the 1984 local election in Duisburg. While there is no clear relationship between age-groups and support for the SPD, CDU or FDP, the level of support for the Greens falls progressively as the age-groups become more elderly. In the two youngest age-groups, the Greens were more popular than the CDU.

Table 4.5 Age Structure of Party Support, Local Election, Darmstadt, 1985 (in %)

Age group	SPD	CDU	GREENS	FDP	All voters
18–24	9.0	6.3	19.2	6.4	9.3
25–34	13.4	8.8	45.5	10.4	15.6
35–44	13.4	11.0	19.0	14.9	13.8
45–59	27.3	28.2	10.0	26.7	27.3
60 and above	36.9	45.6	6.2	41.7	36.9

Source: Darmstadt 1985:77

The imbalance of Green electoral support in the younger age-cohorts is well illustrated when the local election result in Darmstadt in 1985 is broken down according to the age-structure of the individual parties' supporters (Table 4.5). Almost two-thirds of Green voters (64.7 per cent) were younger than thirty-five, compared with only 24.9 per cent of all Darmstadt voters. In contrast, only 6.2 per cent of Green voters were aged sixty and above; a figure substantially lower than the proportion of elderly voters in the electorate as a whole or amongst the voters of the other political parties (see also Münster 1989:122).

Ecological analyses of local election data show that the Greens generally perform well where there is a concentration of younger voters (Wiesbaden 1983). In Frankfurt's electoral wards in which the proportion of young residents exceeds 30 per cent, the Green Party won 18.1 per cent of the vote in the 1989 local election. This contrasted markedly with the 6.6 per cent of the vote gained by the Greens in wards with less than 20 per cent of young residents and the party's vote for the city as a whole of 10.1 per cent (Frankfurt 1989c:13; also Cologne 1984). However, Neuss offers an exception in this case. In the 1984 local election, the Green Party performed least well in wards with a high concentration of young voters (Neuss 1984:25). This experience was repeated at the 1989 local election, with the Greens gaining 7.6 per cent of the vote in electoral wards with a very high proportion of first-time voters and 8.5 per cent of the vote in wards with a low proportion of first-time voters (Neuss 1989b:22). Such findings demonstrate the dangers of generalising about the Green electorate, and suggest that specific factors are at play in different localities.

Over time, whilst the growth of support for the Greens in the youngest age-group has tended to stagnate, the party has substantially increased its support in all but the eldest age-groups (see Bick 1985a; ÖSS 1988:8). In Kiel, for example, the most significant increase in support for the Greens between the two local elections of 1982 and 1986 occurred in the 25–34 and 34–44 age-groups (Table 4.6). In Oberhausen, 41.4 per cent of Green Party voters in the 1979 local election were younger than twenty-five. By 1984 the proportion of supporters of the Oberhausen *Bunte Liste* – which succeeded the Greens – in the 18–24 age-group had fallen to 26.7 per cent (Oberhausen 1985a:8). This pattern has also been reinforced in more recent local elections. In Cologne the Greens gained 29.2 per cent of the vote in the 25–34 age-group and 'just' 19.6 per cent in the 18–24 age group in the 1989 local elections (Ausschuß Wahlforschung 1989:23).

Table 4.6 Green Local Electoral Support by Age Groups, Local Elections, Kiel, 1982–1986 (in %)

Age group	1982	1986	Change in %
18–24	19.0	22.9	3.9
25–34	16.2	24.1	7.9
35–44	4.6	10.4	5.8
45–59	3.0	4.5	1.5
60 and above	0.6	1.9	1.3
All ages	5.4	9.1	3.7

Source: Based on Kiel 1987:21, Table 6a

The data from Kiel and Oberhausen clearly point towards the influence of generation upon support for the Greens. As the younger generations which supported the Greens in the late 1970s and early 1980s are ageing, so the level of Green Party support in the older age-groups increases. The level of support for the Greens in the youngest generations which have grown up under the influence of Green parliamentary participation is not as marked as it is amongst the generation immediately preceding it. Holtz (1985) has attempted to show the impact of generational change upon support for political parties in local and regional elections in the case of Münster (Table 4.7). Although the data on which Table 4.7 are based have their inadequacies (Holtz 1985:134f.), it is apparent that the most significant changes in party preference across generations have occurred in the youngest of the post-war generations – those with an average birth year of 1954. It is amongst this generation that the Greens have performed best in Münster. In the 1984 local election, 36.4 per cent of the 25–34 age-group voted for the Green Alternative List (GAL) in Münster, more than supported any other party. Evidence that this process is continuing can be found in the 1989 local election result for Münster. Overall the Greens' share of the vote fell by 3.3 per cent between 1984 and 1989, with the highest losses being recorded in the 18–24 age-group (–11.4 per cent) and the 25–34 age-group (–9.3 per cent). The only age group in which the GAL gained votes was the 35–44 group (+1.2 per cent) (Münster 1989:119). This suggests that the Greens have stabilised their support amongst the generation with an average birth year of 1954, but have failed to win over subsequent generations of young voters to the same extent.

A further interesting finding of the representative electoral statistics supports evidence from national and regional samples that there is a slight preponderance of men within the Green electorate (ÖSS 1988:11; Kolinsky 1988; Langguth 1984:39; Veen 1987:76). At local level the difference between the male and female vote for the Greens was commonly around 2 per cent during the mid-1980s (for example Bonn 1985:76; Frankfurt 1985; Krefeld 1984). Recently, the difference has become less marked. The difference in the Green vote for men and women in 1989 local elections was just 0.4 per cent in Münster and 1.3 per cent in Frankfurt (Frankfurt 1989c; Münster 1989). The 1989 local elections in Bielefeld and Bonn actually saw more women vote Green than men (Ausschuß Wahlforschung 1989:26). Furthermore, whilst the over-representation of men was once the case for all age-groups, more recent data show that more women than men in the youngest age-groups now support the Greens in local elections (for example Frankfurt 1989c; Leverkusen 1985:5; Münster 1989; Nuremberg 1991). In Bonn, 9.2 per cent more women than men in the 18–24 age-group voted Green in 1989 (Ausschuß Wahlforschung 1989:26).

Table 4.7 Local Elections 1979 and 1984 in Münster, Party Preference by Generational Groups (in %)

Average year of birth	Age Group	Election year	CDU	SPD	FDP	GAL
1954	22–28	1979	33.0	39.8	6.4	19.6
	25–34	1984	24.4	31.7	6.1	36.4
1945	29–38	1979	41.3	41.0	8.0	8.3
	35–44	1984	45.6	32.6	8.1	13.5
1935	39–48	1979	53.8	35.7	7.8	2.0
	45–59	1984	55.1	30.1	9.4	5.1
1915	49–63	1979	60.4	31.0	6.7	1.6
	60+	1984	60.3	30.7	6.2	2.6
All		1979	52.2	24.4	6.8	6.0
		1984	46.1	31.4	6.6	15.5

GAL = Grün-Alternative Liste
Source: Holtz 1985:143, Table 5

The nature of local electoral statistics allows no direct conclusions to be drawn about the links between socio-occupational status and party preference in local elections. However, social ecological analyses of local electoral data allow certain conclusions to be drawn in this respect. Such forms of analysis utilise varying types of social structural data to classify small administrative units (usually electoral wards) into specific categories (Engel 1984; Troitzsch 1976). It should be stressed that this type of analysis allows conclusions to be drawn about the social characteristics of an area in which a party performs well or badly, but not about individual-level voting behaviour.

Table 4.8 Party Support by Regional Types, Local Elections 1984, Ruhrgebiet (in %)

Regional Type	Turnout	SPD	CDU	FDP	Greens
Urban					
working class	60.3	60.1	27.7	1.9	8.2
mixed	63.8	53.7	32.1	2.7	9.4
middle class	65.7	47.1	37.7	3.5	10.8
Rural					
catholic	71.7	32.4	52.8	5.2	6.6
mixed	70.8	46.3	37.8	5.0	7.4
mining/and industry	68.3	53.7	33.2	3.5	7.2
Ruhrgebiet	63.6	53.2	33.1	3.0	9.3

Source: Kommunalverband Ruhrgebiet 1985:30

A study which divided the area of the *Kommunalverband Ruhrgebiet* (1985) into six distinct regional types indicates a concentration of Green support in the urban, middle-class areas (Table 4.8). Whereas only 6.6 per cent of voters in rural areas with a high proportion of Catholic inhabitants supported the Greens, in those urban areas characterised by a high level of middle-class voters the Greens gained 10.8 per cent of the vote. In Oberhausen, a differentiation between predominantly working-class and middle-class districts showed that the gains of the *Bunte Liste* between the local elections of 1984 and 1979 were concentrated in the second category (Oberhausen 1985b:6). However, in 1989 the *Bunte Liste* performed marginally better in the working-class districts of Oberhausen (Oberhausen 1989:33). An analysis of the 1984 and 1989 local election results in Duisburg illustrates a similar pattern of support for the Greens (Duisburg 1984:60f. and 1989:49f.). In districts with a high proportion of working-class inhabitants the Greens performed less well in 1984 than in those in which members of the new middle class (white-collar employees) were concentrated (Table 4.9). The data presented in Table 4.9 show that Green voters in Duisburg are more likely to be found in areas with above-average levels of support for both the CDU and FDP than in districts with high levels of support for the SPD. This also applies in other localities.

The Greens in Germany's Local Politics

In the SPD stronghold of Salzgitter in Lower Saxony, for example, the Greens were unable to increase their overall share of the vote between the local elections of 1981 and 1986, despite the general trend in their favour (Salzgitter 1987).

Table 4.9 Party Preference and Social Status, Duisburg, Local Election 1984 (in %)

Area type	SPD	CDU	FDP	GREENS
Proportion of blue collar workers				
low (<49%)	51.1	34.5	6.1	9.6
average	56.6	31.2	5.9	8.7
high (>58%)	65.5	24.1	3.9	7.3
Proportion of white collar workers				
low (<12.5%)	64.5	24.8	2.1	7.3
average	57.8	30.6	2.7	8.1
high (>18.8%)	51.4	34.7	3.1	10.1
Duisburg	57.9	30.0	2.7	8.6

Source: Based on Duisburg 1985:61, Table 24

Over time, the Green Party has tended to perform least well in the socially deprived urban strongholds of the SPD, with high proportions of working-class inhabitants. This is a feature which is backed up by a number of other social ecological analyses of German local elections (for example Neuss 1984:29; Wiesbaden 1983 and 1984). In Frankfurt, the Green Party failed in 1985 to improve on the 3.9 per cent of the vote won in wards classed as SPD strongholds on the basis of 1981 local election results, and by 1989 could still only secure 5.8 per cent of the vote in such wards compared with an overall result of 10.1 per cent (Table 4.10). However, in wards with changing or CDU majorities, the Greens gained 11.1 per cent and 10.7 per cent of the vote respectively in the 1989 local election (Frankfurt 1986:19 and 1989b:13). Similar findings stem from electoral data collated by the Ausschuß Wahlforschung (1984) (see also Krefeld 1984:31; Munich 1984:108).

87

Table 4.10 Green Party Support in Party Strongholds, Frankfurt, Local Elections 1981–1989 (in %)

Party stronghold	Green vote 1989	Green vote 1985	Green vote 1981	Change 1989–1981
SPD stronghold	5.8	3.9	3.9	1.9
SPD majority	8.2	6.5	5.4	2.8
Changing majority	11.1	8.8	6.8	4.3
CDU majority	10.7	8.9	7.0	3.7
CDU stronghold	8.5	6.5	6.2	2.3
Frankfurt	10.1	7.9	6.4	3.7

Source: Frankfurt 1986:19 and 1989b:13

Obviously, factors such as housing costs can also play an important role in locating Green support. Given the relative youthfulness of the Green electorate and the fact that many Green voters are not yet in full-time employment, it is likely that they will tend to occupy poorer-quality housing stock which is traditionally found in the inner cities (see for example Wiesbaden 1983). This shows up in a commonly-found link between Green support in electoral ward categories and the proportion of immigrants living in those areas (see for example Cologne 1984; Frankfurt 1989b:13).

Summary

On the basis of local election statistics, it is possible to establish a picture of the structure of the Green electorate and of the social environment in which Green voters live. With regard to the social composition of Green support, the similarities between national and local voting patterns are evident. The findings tend to support suggestions that local electoral behaviour is largely similar to that witnessed at regional and national elections, with the Green electorate differing only slightly from one type of election to another. The early successes of ecological lists, which could gain the support of a broad cross-section of the local population, have rarely been repeated in the 1980s and 1990s. Instead, Green support has stabilised and, despite reservations about generalising, has tended to become concentrated amongst the young members of the new middle class who live in relatively affluent parts of the Federal Republic's cities. Recent shifts in the composition of their electorate suggest that the Greens are increasing their support amongst women, particularly amongst younger women, and that their core support is shifting from the youngest to older age-groups. Evidence derived from local electoral statistics also tends to support the notion of the existence of a specific, relatively stable green–alternative milieu in the Federal Republic's urban areas, noted at an early stage by Müller (1979:146) and developed further by Veen (1986 and 1989; see also R. Roth 1988:12; and Schacht 1987 for Frankfurt). The existence of this milieu has a certain significance in determining the electoral future of the Greens. When one considers the contrasting social environments from which the Greens and SPD recruit their support, for example, it is difficult to imagine how the SPD will achieve their stated aim of regaining voters lost to the Greens in local elections since the late 1970s (Güllner and Löffler 1981; Klein and Clauditz 1983; Klein and Kirchner 1983). The Greens, however, must succeed as a small party in mobilising their potential support at successive elections. Rather than immediately switching their allegiance to another party, people living in the green–alternative milieu might be more likely to abstain from voting. This not only fundamentally threatens the position of the Greens in Germany's party systems, but also poses a more general problem for democracy in the Federal Republic by generating a substantial population group who are politically interested yet disenchanted with the parties on offer.

5

The Organisation of the Greens: The Failure of the Grassroots Democratic Model at Local Level

Having discussed the scale of Green representation in Germany's local councils and pointed to the existence of a core New Politics electorate for the Greens, it is now necessary to address the manner in which the Greens are organised at local level. There is no need in this study to repeat the analysis of the origins of the strategy of grassroots democracy (*Basisdemokratie*) or indeed to generalise about its principal shortcomings. Both Zeuner (1983) and Fogt (1984) treat this topic in detail, albeit it from differing perspectives, with regard to the operation of the Greens at the national and regional levels of the German party system (see also Ismayr 1985; Kolinsky 1984:306f.; Scharping and Hoffmann-Göttig 1982:405f.; Weinberger 1984:127f.). The purpose of this chapter is to illustrate the inherent weakness of this strategy at the level of the German party system at which it should be most readily implemented; the local level at which the Greens are arguably closest to their grassroots.

The Grassroots Democratic Strategy

Müller-Rommel and Poguntke (1989) identify two structural characteristics of a New Politics party, which lie at the heart of the strategy of grassroots democracy favoured by Germany's Greens. The first guarantees the political autonomy of the 'grassroots', whilst the second places emphasis upon unconventional forms of political action (Müller-Rommel and Poguntke 1989:22; also Poguntke 1987b:80f.). The intention is to ensure representation for party supporters (the *Basis*), to counteract tendencies towards a hierarchisation of decision-making and to avoid pressures which might lead to an institutionalisation of Green politicians. In this respect, it was the intention of the Greens to be an 'anti-party party' (Hoplitschek 1982:82). Such was the emphasis placed by the Greens upon the grassroots democratic strategy, that it became one of the four unifying tenets of the federal party organisation at its Saarbrücken programme conference in 1980 (Bolaffi and Kallscheuer 1983). The principal characteristics of the concept require party meetings to be open to the public, ensure that certain controls are placed upon party office-holders and elected representatives (for example office-rotation; voting by representatives mandated in advance – the so-called imperative mandate; a ban on holding multiple offices) and seek to guarantee full participatory rights for members in all party activities.

Despite formal attempts to implement New Politics structures at local level, the grassroots democratic strategy has been of limited long-term significance in Green local politics. In practice, such organisational forms tend to undermine attempts to participate in local decision-making processes successfully, and have gradually given way to more traditional forms of political behaviour at local level. In many ways this development mirrors the experience with *Basisdemokratie* at the regional and federal levels. While it is acknowledged that this organisational strategy has enabled groups previously excluded from or under-represented in the political process to participate in decision-making (for example social minority groups, women, peace groups, civil rights groups, Third World groups), the manner in which this participation occurred has been recognised as being largely counter-productive. Huber (1983:77) describes a process in which 'whoever wants to comes along, simply joins in the discussions and votes – without responsibility for the consequences and thus mostly without effect'. The pressures towards the integration of the Greens into more established representational styles could not be resisted. The office-rotation question became especially contentious at national level. Adopted primarily as a mechanism for achieving a balance between realist and fundamentalist factions (Weinberger 1984:117), the application of the rotation principle resulted in a series of unseemly conflicts within the Green parliamentary group and between this group and the party organisation. Similar conflicts occurred at regional level (for example in Hesse and Baden-Württemberg). In the end

the rotation principle was effectively dropped as party supporters became more aware of the necessity to maintain a degree of
continuity in Green parliamentary representation.

Nevertheless, the formal elements of grassroots democracy
can be identified within the statutes of local Green parties
throughout the Federal Republic, irrespective of the size or
socio-economic type of the relevant community. The manifesto
of the Pulheim Greens for the 1984 local elections in North Rhine
Westphalia neatly summarises the main elements of the strategy:

> The substantive decisions of the Greens in Pulheim's council will be
> discussed and resolved at the general meeting of the party. The
> Greens' councillors see themselves only as the body which imple-
> ments these grassroots democratic decisions.
>
> Given the negative experience of the parliamentary system, the
> Greens will rotate their councillors half-way through the legislative
> period, unless the Greens' grassroots decide otherwise.
>
> General meetings of the party are held in public and grant every
> citizen the right to express a viewpoint.
>
> One of the Greens' basic principles is to make local problems
> transparent to the individual citizen and to the public as a whole
> (*Pulheim* 1984).

An additional feature of the grassroots democratic approach
is the tendency for the Greens to campaign in local elections with
'open' party lists which grant non-members of the party the
opportunity of gaining council representation. This policy, followed by the Greens during the course of the 1980s in cities such
as Bonn, Krefeld, Cologne, Bochum and Munich, is used as a
means of ensuring that the views of the new social movements
are adequately represented in Germany's local councils.

Despite continued ideological support for the concept, evidence suggests that the strategy of *Basisdemokratie* has failed to
operate successfully at local level. Although several problems
relating to the attempted implementation of the grassroots
democratic structure can be discerned, the most fundamental
weakness of Green and alternative groups at local level is their
inadequate membership levels and the overwhelming lack of
interest in local political affairs amongst Green activists. This lies
at the heart of almost all of the problems to be raised in subsequent sections of this chapter. The swiftness with which the
Greens have essentially become a parliamentary force at local

level has already been shown. With a concentration of activists' attention on council work, there is a marked absence of people willing to assume the controlling functions required for the successful working of the grassroots democratic concept. This is a problem aggravated by the prevailing uninterest of party supporters in local political matters. Whilst political culture studies have demonstrated that Green Party supporters have a higher degree of general political interest than adherents of other parties (for example Veen 1987:109), this does not appear to apply at local level. Signs of the lack of interest in local politics are evident not only in low attendances at regular meetings of Green council groups (see for example *Bonn* 1985:6), but even in the lack of activists willing to assume public office.

The lack of interest in local political matters can partially be explained by the banal nature of much that goes on in Germany's local politics, despite the Greens' attempts to liven up debate. This is the principal reason cited by Güllner (1986:36) to support his contention that the Greens offer little long-term hope for an improvement of local authority competences in Germany. Confrontational styles and the discussion of 'political' issues have not yet become the universal norm in German local politics. Instead, the type of New Politics issues which interest Green supporters tend to have a national or international focus. Whilst the Greens seek to bring such issues into local councils at every opportunity, there is not much that their elected representatives can do to combat the lack of interest of party supporters in their activities. This was reflected in a report of the Green *Fraktion* in Bonn's city council:

> We have been engaged in parliamentary politics for a year now. This is the context in which we operate and which we can only criticise but not overcome. We use every possible opportunity available in local politics to prioritise the questions of war and peace. However, we do not debate the reasoning (?) or lack of reasoning behind NATO. Nor do we stand at the microphone to state that capitalism is to blame for everything ... Instead, we vote against the privatisation of public landholdings. ... But we do not introduce any council resolution which states that Pinochet is a pig (*Bonn* 1985:7).

The limited scope of local council activity ensures that local politics is treated as being of only secondary importance by the majority of Green Party members (see Metzger 1987; Swatzina

1987). Attempts by councillors to raise issues of local political relevance in party meetings are seemingly predestined to fail. As a result, only highly controversial issues which may crop up just once or twice a year, such as the annual budget debate or the question of whether or not the Greens should form an alliance with the SPD in the local council, can arouse the interest of the majority of party members. Once these issues are resolved, membership interest once again wanes and the council group is left to its own devices. Swatzina (1987) sums this situation up with a quote from a member of the Cologne Green *Fraktion*: 'When it comes to council politics, we can totally dispense with the party' (see also *Bonn* 1988:2).

This is the background against which Green local politics occurs. Inadequate membership levels and widespread apathy characterise all areas of the party's local political activities, making it difficult to implement an effective grassroots democratic structure. The problems which result for Green council groups will be illustrated below with regard to three key issues. Firstly, difficulties regarding the identification of the Greens' grassroots will be addressed. Secondly attention will be paid to the failure of the control mechanisms adopted by Green groups at local level. Finally, the often difficult relationship between the Greens and their grassroots will be depicted.

The Identification of the Greens' Grassroots

Local Green groups find themselves in a unique position within the structure of the Green Party, since they fulfil two roles. Firstly, they are treated by Greens operating at higher levels as a *Basis* in their own right, being assigned certain control functions. The participation of the local grassroots in important party meetings is regarded as imposing discipline upon competing national party factions. One telling example of the contribution of local activists to the strategy debate within the federal Green Party came in an open letter sent by a body representing Green and alternative local councillors in Bavaria (*Grüne und Alternative in den Räten Bayern*) to the belligerent Federal Executive Committee and Federal Parliamentary Group on the occasion of a crisis meeting in Bonn in December 1987: 'we have just about had enough of hearing about your latest conflicts from our newspapers and television sets. Our rage is well justified: we can see our first, arduously won victories at the much-cited grassroots – in the communities – being endangered' (*Pantheon* 1987: no page number).

The second role fulfilled by local Green groups is to interact with their own grassroots. It is the second aspect which is of prime importance in this analysis. However, the Greens' grassroots effectively vary from locality to locality, depending upon the nature of existing local oppositional groups, the strength of electoral support for the Greens and the political composition of the Greens. In general, three different types of grassroots can be discerned (see Huber 1983). In some localities the Greens regard party members as the *Basis* to which they are accountable. In other communities more emphasis is placed upon links with the new social movements. Evidence suggests that it is the third type of grassroots, the electorate, which is increasingly treated as the Greens' *Basis* in German local politics. In this respect the Greens are becoming less distinguishable from the established political parties in terms of their organisational structures. It is useful at this point to differentiate between Green groups which operate in urban and rural areas. Although the variations between the different groups are no longer quite as marked as was once the case, certain characteristics of Green and alternative groups in both regional types need to be addressed.

It is easiest to begin with the identification of the Greens' grassroots in Germany's non-metropolitan areas. In rural areas, the Greens seldom have the choice of which group constitutes their grassroots (see Metzger 1987:5; Wiesenthal 1985:153). Under such circumstances examples exist of Green groups seeking to co-opt unaffiliated groups to act as their grassroots. This appears to be the result of desperation on the part of rural Green groups, who are often condemned to act without an identifiable grassroots. In Königstein in Hesse's Hochtaunus district, for example, the rather conservative *Aktionsgemeinschaft Lebenswertes Königstein* (ALK) strongly objected to attempts by the Green Party to treat its members as part of its *Basis*:

> The relationship with the Greens in the district is difficult. Shortly after the local election they invited all the local voting groups to a meeting at which they declared that they regarded the voting groups

95

as their basis, given that their contact to the real grassroots, the people, was very difficult in the large Hochtaunus district. These 'grassroots democratic' views ... were criticised by ALK members and an exchange of information and experiences was offered instead. We have never been invited to such a meeting again (*ALK* 1985:67).

Active forms of local opposition, such as citizens' initiative groups, are less common in rural Germany than in its urban areas. Under such circumstances it is simply impossible for the Greens to claim to be the parliamentary arm of an extra-parliamentary movement. Where initiative groups exist in rural areas, they tend in any case to be keen to preserve their independence from political parties. Voigt (1986:12) acknowledges that this is the only way in which they can hope to secure broad support for their aims. The sparsity of local initiative groups is compounded in rural areas by low membership figures for the Greens. In many rural localities the council group and the local Green Party are one and the same (Weiß 1986:38). The parliamentarisation of the Greens appears to be most acute in the small rural communities of the Federal Republic: 'The difficulties for councillors are especially marked in communities with less than 8,000 inhabitants. Here Green lists were often formed just before the respective elections. ... In many cases the Green/alternative councillors sit as lone fighters in the council, which increases the danger either of becoming totally isolated or of being forced into the role of the patronised outsider' (T. Simon 1986:32). In a small community such as Bad Schwalbach in Hesse, for example, the Greens found it difficult to maintain their supra-local profile once two of the party's six local members had become councillors after the 1985 local election (Novy-Huy 1988:6). However, Nippkau (1986:30) suggests that the absence of a rural grassroots can also have its more positive features: '"One gets used to being one's own grassroots." These complaints are typical of Green local politics as a whole. ... However, the sparse coverage in terms of personnel also has its advantages in the countryside. "Because we unfortunately have too few activists, the relationship between the council group and the grassroots is unproblematic."'

In this context, the only grassroots relevant to the Greens can be the citizens of the relevant locality. This corresponds to traditional forms of local political control, which stem from the everyday social contacts between councillors and citizens. Such contacts are also held to inhibit excessive displays of radicalism on the part of local Green politicians (Nippkau 1986). If Green councillors want to be successful in rural areas, they need to ensure a healthy rapport with local citizens, which leads them to adopt pragmatic viewpoints on most local issues: 'above all it is the personal relationships which determine to a greater or lesser extent the behaviour in the council' (Henning 1986:35).

Established forms of political behaviour also increasingly mark the activities of urban Green groups, in their keenness to escape the restrictions placed upon their council activities by the constantly changing composition of the other types of grassroots support, namely of party members and the new social movements. Whilst the latter sources of support are in a permanent state of change, the electorate can be relied upon to remain relatively stable.

The Green Party's membership changed radically during the 1980s, as was to be expected for a party which was still in its formative years. Changes in the composition of the membership served to create unanticipated difficulties for local party organisation, which adhered strictly to the grassroots democratic concept. In Bielefeld, for example, Boch *et al.* (1982) attributed the development of competing factions within the *Bunte Liste* (*BuLi*) to changes in its membership. Whilst the founder members of the *BuLi* in 1979 shared a common social and political background, enabling the implementation of a consensual decision-making model, the structure of the group's support altered in the period which succeeded their initial election to council office: 'All in all we have to contend with a situation in which, on the one hand, the previous fund of common political interests has basically proved itself irrelevant to practice and, on the other, a new consensus to guide our actions has yet to be formulated' (Boch *et al.* 1982:41).

Local initiative groups are subject to an even greater degree of fluctuation than Green Party membership (see R. Roth 1988:14). At one level, initiative groups have a restricted life cycle. The only thing which binds their members together is the single-issue cause they follow. If this cause is taken away, then the groups tend to disintegrate. Numerous examples exist of local initiative groups abandoning their activities once the

Greens were elected to the local council, feeling that they have achieved their aim in gaining representation for their wishes (for example *Krefeld* 1988). In one (unnamed) Hessian community, a Green representative reported the decline of five local citizens' initiative groups, following the 'parliamentarisation' of the Greens: '... now and again I get the impression that the people who were most critical of the parliament were the ones who entered the parliament, whilst the grassroots in the citizens' initiatives now display full trust in the parliament because we sit on it' (Anon. 1985:99).

At another level, the initiative groups are limited in their action radius. Despite the tendency for Green council groups to foster the illusion that they are the parliamentary arm of an extra-parliamentary movement, the extra-parliamentary movement has never existed in a single, recognisable form (Brand 1987:41f.; Rucht 1987). Instead, the heterogeneous nature of the new social movements necessitates a differentiation on the part of the Greens, who are often required to accommodate the conflicting and contradictory aims of local initiative groups. The difficulties associated with the maintenance of links with extra-parliamentary groups have been addressed, for example, in two detailed reports prepared by the Greens in Bonn city council (*Bonn* 1985 and 1988). It took the Greens only one year of council representation to be able to establish in 1985 that they could not successfully aggregate the wishes of their *Basis*: 'there are unrealistic expectations of us. ... different grassroots' representatives expect different things of us' (*Bonn* 1985:7).

Contradictions arise most readily when the Greens attempt to represent the demands of all initiative groups at the same time. In one instance the Bonn *Fraktion* and an unemployed workers' initiative found themselves in conflict with other initiative groups on the question of whether or not they should make use of a government employment scheme (*Arbeitsbeschaffungsmaßnahmen – ABMs*). Whilst the Greens and the unemployed workers' initiative objected to the measures, on the grounds that the employment opportunities which arose were both poorly paid and temporary, the other groups supported the scheme, since it offered them a subsidised source of labour. In order to avoid alienating either source of support, the Greens were obliged to adopt the following contradictory position: 'So as not to annoy the project movement and because we represent their demands, we opt for a split in which we politically fight against *ABM*, but do not let the survival of a project fail on account of our vote' (*Bonn* 1985:7).

Initiative groups whose survival depends upon local authority finance, such as cultural groups, social initiatives or alternative businesses, fundamentally differ from those groups which follow more general political aims (see R. Roth 1988:19f.). The former do not want the Greens to use the parliament as a platform for making radical statements (*Standbein-Spielbein* theory), but simply require 'rooms and money' (*Bonn* 1985:7). The latter can afford to be more radical and critical of the Greens, since their aims are not to be achieved at local level. In practice, the degree of cooperation between the elected Greens and the local initiative groups is most straightforward when specific local demands are placed before the Greens and the council group can use its influence to represent the demands by way of parliamentary questions or motions (*Bonn* 1985:8).

It has been as a result of their unstable membership base and the *ad hoc* nature of initiative group support, that the Greens in urban areas have tended to seek a more representative basis for their council activities. These grassroots can only be found in the local population. Even people who would not normally vote for the party appear to regard the Greens as a party willing at least to listen to their cause. This stems from the absence of precisely defined forms of opposition in most localities (Gabriel *et al.* 1984). The Dortmund experience is typical. Following their election to the city council in 1984, the Green council group in Dortmund became another contact point for citizens seeking to resolve problems arising from dealings with the city authorities or wishing to draw attention to local environmental problems (see also *Bochum* 1987). Although such people do not belong to the Greens' grassroots in any formal sense, the representation of their views by the Greens occupies much of the Green council group's time: 'As a council group, we have an enormous head start in "informational power". What a citizen might only learn after trailing about and with great effort, if at all, is clarified for us (as a rule) within a short time without especially great effort. The saying "knowledge is power" is proven in our everyday work' (*Dortmund* 1987:3f.).

In the increasing number of communities in which the Greens have assumed executive responsibilities for certain aspects of local politics, it is no longer possible for them to adopt a narrow view of who they are to represent. In Leverkusen, for example, where the city environment office (*Umweltbüro*) was headed by a Green nominee between 1984 and 1989, as a result of an agreement reached with the SPD, the Green council group was obliged to hold public meetings as a means of involving local citizens in the decision-making process and of explaining policy measures: 'The council group was prepared to listen to the citizens again and again, but without putting itself at the mercy of a citizens' vote' (*Leverkusen* 1988:12). Given that such red–green coalitions have become more widespread in Germany since the mid-1980s, with Green representatives assuming executive positions in local councils (Scharf 1989), the Greens are obliged to broaden the scope of their *Basis*, increasingly representing the population as a whole.

The obvious question which arises at this point is whether the Greens are actually very different from the established political parties in terms of the people they aim to represent. Evidence suggests that they are not. When one talks of *Basisdemokratie*, it is apparent that this concept has applied only to Green groups active in Germany's urban areas. As has been shown, however, even the Greens in the metropolitan areas appear to be becoming less distinctive. Although the majority of local Green Party organisations adopt the formal structures of a New Politics party, this is in many ways simply a façade.

The Absence of Control Mechanisms at Local Level

A second area of difficulty arising from the Greens' attempts to operationalise a grassroots democratic organisational model corresponds to the situation, identified by Fogt (1984) for the national and regional levels, that the Greens soon become dominated by an activist clique (see also Langguth 1984:86). Owing to the demands placed upon the time of unpaid party workers and elected representatives, only certain social groups are available to participate in Green politics. In this study it is necessary to establish the relevance of Fogt's critique at local level.

Elected Green groups originally seek to organise their local council activities in a manner which encourages the participation of a maximum number of supporters in the party's internal decision-making processes. In Bonn, for example, all council group meetings are open to members of the public, and non-hierarchical structures have been implemented. The Green *Fraktionsgruppe*, which determines the party's policy in council, comprised during the 1984–9 legislative period the party's eight councillors, their successors (*Nachrücker*), members elected to the Bonn neighbourhood councils and their successors, appointed committee members (*sachkundige Bürger*) and five part-time business managers. In all, forty people helped determine the Greens' local political strategy. However, the size of the group was not deemed to have reduced the efficiency of the Bonn *Fraktion*: 'Despite the occasional major conflict over individual policy questions, we have not required to date standing orders to serve as a formal crutch in muddled situations' (*Bonn* 1988:7).

In other cities, such as Cologne, Munich and Marburg, local political strategies are determined by specialist working groups (*kommunalpolitische Arbeitskreise*) of varying sizes, composed of elected councillors, party activists and interested persons. However, the existence of these large steering groups has failed to resist the institutional pressures towards the adoption of forms of hierarchisation, which has occurred at two levels. At one level, important administrative and coordinative tasks are increasingly carried out by appointed business managers. The criteria for their appointment are not always clear to outsiders, but previous service in the Green movement is essential. It is these individuals who are in charge of the everyday management of local council affairs rather than the Greens' elected representatives, who are prevented from holding multiple positions in the party. Further decisions are made by elected spokespersons. The second level at which hierarchisation has occurred is in the policy-making process itself. As the Greens become involved in the intricacies of local politics, a need for specialist advice on specific policy areas develops. This presents acute problems for a party with low levels of active membership and a general lack of interest in local political matters. Although working groups exist in the majority of cities, the size and composition of these groups varies quite markedly. In practice, a highly motivated activist core can exert great influence over the strategy to be adopted by the council group. In areas of limited interest to the majority of local activists, it is common for just one or two people to represent the views of the entire party.

The tendency towards the concentration of decision-making in the hands of a few activists is made more serious by the absence of suitable forms of control over their actions. The control of elected representatives appears to be of little relevance in the great majority of local party organisations. This again derives from low membership figures, which result in an absence of candidates willing to assume elected office. This feature can be illustrated with regard to the history of the rotation issue at local level.

In some communities rotation was not adopted for reasons of principle, whilst in others it was not instituted on more pragmatic grounds. Commenting on the inappropriateness of a two-year rotation period at local level, for example, Helga Boldt, a former councillor of the *Bunte Liste* in Bielefeld, felt that 'you need a certain amount of time to get used to your new job, before you can be at all politically effective. There has to be a rotation, but even after three or four years a councillor doesn't normally become a career politician' (*AKP* 6/86:66). However in a number of communities, despite the general acceptance of the need for a change of personnel, the rotation principle could still not be implemented owing to the lack of party members willing to succeed rotating councillors. This has applied to rural areas in particular, in which Green activists are still relatively thin on the ground. Titus Simon (1986) illustrates the point in the context of rural communities in Baden-Württemberg with a weak infrastructure of citizens' initiatives and in which other potential sources of Green support are absent. In the communities of this region, with its flexible voting system which emphasises the element of personality (Woyke and Steffens 1987; Wehling 1986), rotation could be interpreted as a contravention of the electorate's wishes. Similarly, the electoral system also encourages Green councillors to stand at successive elections, in order to benefit from any impression they have made upon voters during their first period in office (Metzger 1987:5). Even in communities in which rotation was held to be desirable, the policy has been undermined by the absence of people willing to succeed serving councillors: 'If I, as a town councillor, talk about rotation to one of the people occupying a lower position on the electoral list, then they simply get the creeps and say no. They have learnt by now that a council seat uses up an awful lot of one's free time, is not very interesting and is often very frustrating' (Anon. 1985:98). Despite the fact that the local alternative group in one Hessian community had a reserve electoral list with some seventy-five names on it and the desire of a number of its elected councillors to leave office, there were no people keen to 'rotate' into their positions (*ALK* 1985:75; also T. Simon 1984:54). Even in urban areas, in which radical democratic structures were most whole-heartedly adopted by the Greens in their formative years, rotation of officials has seldom been a salient issue. A study by the *Grüne und Alternative in den Räten Nordrhein-Westfalen* (1988) discovered instead a 'natural rotation' of Green councillors, which occurred irrespective of any formal decisions supporting such a policy (see also Rohr and Hau 1985:41). In Bonn, the decision to rotate half-way through the 1984–9 council term could not be fulfilled since three people had already left the council group before the designated change-over point, and the rotation principle could no longer be fairly applied to remaining group members (*Bonn* 1988:7f.).

In practice, therefore, the issue of rotation has never played a major role at the local level of the Green Party organisation (*AKP* 4/84). This also applies to other elements of grassroots democratic control adopted in local party statutes. While the imperative mandate was formally applied in a number of cities, the relevance of this measure to everyday internal party decision-making processes must be called into question. In Cologne, for example, the imperative mandate operated in the context of two public meetings each year with between seventy and 150 people present; Green city councillors agreed to abide by the decisions of these meetings, although only Green party members were allowed to vote on measures to be adopted. The imperative mandate did not extend in Cologne to automatically adopting decisions made by local initiative groups (Swatzina 1987:52). Similar limitations applied in Bochum: 'The resolutions of the party general meeting are upheld even against one's "better judgement". However, in cases of doubt the rule is that the councillor has to abide by his conscience. Should the worst come to the worst, this includes giving up his mandate' (Swatzina 1987:45). The problems associated with operating under an imperative mandate are most acute when there is a passive grassroots. Even in a city the size of Munich, with 1,200 party members in the mid-1980s, only between fifty and one hundred members normally attended party meetings (Swatzina 1987:61). The policy which seeks to limit the holding of multiple offices by Green representatives is also increasingly falling into disuse at local level. The shortage of local political activists means that some people are (often unwillingly) obliged to assume office in different councils at the same time. In the Rhineland Palatinate, for example, between 1984 and 1989 one Green Party member held office in the district council and in the supra-local council (*Bezirkstag-Pfalz*) simultaneously, having also submitted an application for the office of mayor of the district town (Rohrbacher-List 1984:10). Particularly in rural areas of Germany, it is becoming more common for Greens to hold party office in conjunction with public office. This again serves to emphasise the pace with which the Greens are becoming more and more like the established political parties, in which the holding of multiple offices is regarded as a positive feature.

However, the problem which results from the creeping hierarchisation of the Greens and the absence of formal controls upon party representatives is that they support the continued dominance of activists in local council decision-making. In this context, there appears ample evidence to suggest therefore that Fogt's (1984) hypotheses also apply at local level. Given that the Greens have failed to attract sufficient members from a broad social spectrum, they are necessarily dominated by an activist clique composed of hard-pressed and unpaid party workers and elected representatives.

The Strained Relationship Between the Greens and their Grassroots

A third problem which characterises the Greens' grassroots democratic structures at all levels of the political system in Germany is the poor level of coordination between the party's elected representatives and their grassroots (Heidger 1987). Although this applies to links within the Green Party itself (*Bonn* 1988:11;

Weiß 1986:58; *LWL* 1987:18; Swatzina 1987:14), the area to be addressed in this section regards the relationship between the Greens and the new social movements at local level.

As has previously been discussed, it is difficult for the Greens to represent the views of the highly disparate initiative groups without contradictions emerging in their policies. Even in seemingly clear-cut cases in which the views of the relevant initiative groups do not conflict with those of the Greens, the links can become highly strained. An example of such a case comes from Tübingen in Baden-Württemberg. An initiative group was formed in 1983 to press for the introduction by the town council of a night taxi service for the exclusive use of women. The initiative's overriding aim was to draw attention to the issue of violence against women, which the group felt was being ignored by both the police and the local council. The women of the initiative group regarded the *Alternative Liste* (AL) in Tübingen as their natural allies, but were disappointed by the lukewarm support expressed by the AL for their proposal. Only one woman in the AL council group apparently displayed an interest in the project: 'Both the demand in the AL manifesto and the motion to the council for the approval of a budget heading for the women's taxi were formulated by us, with all of the time-consuming, detailed work which that requires. Even so, the project was still ranked by the AL as an also-ran' (*Taxi* 1985:37).

Supporters of the initiative group were particularly dismayed when, having secured some financial support for the project, it was the AL which became the focus of media attention from throughout the Federal Republic rather than them. Criticism was expressed that the AL failed to inform initiative group supporters of vital decisions affecting their project. When funding for the taxi-project was ultimately withdrawn by the council, the initiative group still believed that the AL's lack of interest was instrumental:

> In the end the persisting lack of interest of the AL in the feminist political perspective of the women's taxi was shown in the behaviour of their representative in the decisive committee meeting. She gave the impression of being unprepared, she argued poorly in parts and was sometimes not forceful enough. The women's taxi initiative was no longer able to offer her help with the basis of her argument, since we were not informed about the course of events (*Taxi* 1985:40).

Although there are inherent dangers in attempting to generalise about Green local politics on the basis of a single example, the Tübingen case is typical of the often strained relationship between the Greens and initiative groups purporting to be their Basis. The initiatives' principal criticism of the Greens is that their councillors often fail to consult with them or fail to inform them immediately of developments which may affect the initiative's success (see also Schulz and Schmitz 1985): 'Our central criticism of the AL's cooperation with us remains that the AL completely failed to inform us of internal administrative processes' (*Taxi* 1985:40). At the same time, it should be recognised that the underlying cause of such criticism is the desire of the majority of local initiative groups to secure funding for their projects. The Greens are often regarded as the best means of securing such funding, particularly in localities in which the party has assumed executive office as a result of an arrangement with the SPD (see for example Henkeborg 1987:108). In this sense, the relationship between the Greens and the initiative groups largely appears to be a one-way affair.

Summary: Grassroots Democracy in Practice

The experience of the relationship between the parliamentary and extra-parliamentary wings of the ecological movement sums up the contradictory nature of the Greens' organisation at Germany's local level. Although the principal tenets of the grassroots democratic model are widely adopted in local party programmes, the reality appears to be rather different when the day-to-day organisation of Green local council affairs is analysed. Against a background of inadequate membership levels and the absence of widespread grassroots support, the majority of Green adherents display a complete lack of interest in local politics and local council work. This stems from a growing (and realistic) recognition by movement activists that the local level is simply not the sphere in which the 'system' is to be changed. In reality, a hierarchisation marks the Greens' local organisation in Germany, in much the same way as it affects the organisation of the council activities of the established political parties. The danger which can result from the continued espousal of the strategy of *Basisdemokratie* for the Greens is that behind the formal façade of checks and balances placed upon their parliamentarians, a situation exists in which party representatives are in practice accountable to no one in their everyday work. The almost universal desire of Green councillors to see more grassroots activity does nothing to alleviate this fundamental weakness of Green local politics.

Parallels are therefore to be drawn between the operation of the grassroots democratic strategy at local and supra-local level. Fogt's (1984:104) finding that only 10 per cent of Green supporters in Baden-Württemberg were willing to play an active role in the party's affairs and the experience of the *Alternative Liste* in the Wilmersdorf district of Berlin who went on strike to motivate the *Basis* into greater activity (Weinberger 1984:121) support the view that this organisational strategy in unsuited to a party which has such a low level of membership. There is little evidence to suggest that Green party members are more likely to participate in the party's internal affairs than members of the traditional parties are likely to be active. Instead, the grassroots democratic model tends to encourage conflict within the party at all levels; conflict between party factions, within parliamentary groups and between parliamentary groups and their respective 'grassroots'.

6

The Disappearing Consensus: Green Ideology and the Old Local Politics

'The Green councillors' wild days are over. The conversion of the Ford works to the manufacture of bicycles has not been debated for a long time now'

(*Cologne* 1989:133).

Given the heterogeneous origins of the Greens and the sheer multiplicity of Green and alternative lists at local level in Germany, it might appear at first inappropriate to talk in terms of a Green local political 'ideology'. On the one hand, this would imply a certain degree of uniformity in the type of issues addressed by the Greens in local politics. On the other, it would run counter to the historical interpretation of the role of local politics in the Federal Republic, which treats this area of government as being essentially non-ideological. A first aim of this chapter is to demonstrate that there is indeed a distinctive Green local political ideology. This will allow the identification of potential sources of conflict which might result from the Greens' attempts to introduce their ideology into the local arena. The Greens' distinctive approach to local politics is reflected not only in the New Politics issues raised by them at local level, but also in the manner in which they seek to participate in the Federal Republic's local party systems. It is not within the scope of this study to enter into great detail about all individual aspects of Green local policies. The function of this chapter is simply to provide a broad overview of Green local ideology, whilst recognising the inadequacies of the source documentation. The case study of the Mainz Greens which follows in Part II will give a more objective analysis of Green local politics in practice.

Green Local Ideology: The New Local Politics in Practice

The Greens' approach to local politics is best summed up in the slogan *global denken, vor Ort handeln*. The concept of thinking globally and acting locally motivated sections of the new social movements to enter into parliamentary politics in the first place (see Brand 1982:181f.; Mez 1987; Rucht 1980). It forms the basis for the Greens' highly ideological approach to local politics in the Federal Republic, providing a justification for the introduction of new issues and new styles of politics into the local arena. As was discussed in Chapter 3, the New Politics approach at local level corresponds to more than simply the treatment of new issues, such as ecology and the rights of social minority groups. Also relevant is the manner in which the issues are addressed by the Greens and other local political actors.

In general, the Greens aim to avoid the highly compartmentalised way of thinking which has dominated west German local policy-making in the post-war period. Instead they seek to transgress the narrow confines of arbitrarily placed administrative boundaries by emphasising the interconnection of local, regional, national and international issues (Spretnak and Capra 1985:28f.; Maren-Grisebach 1982). In the local context, when 'global' issues are mentioned, all issues of relevance beyond the boundaries of the relevant local council are included. The interconnection between local and global or supra-local issues can be demonstrated in two ways at local level. Firstly, local issues can simply be perceived as being the effect of a more universal, global phenomenon. Secondly, global issues of no immediate local relevance can be transported into the local context under a real or contrived pretext. Examples of both forms of global issue can be illustrated in terms of actual Green behaviour in German local councils.

A wide range of local issues have the potential to be regarded as having a 'global' dimension. This applies most obviously to the area of environmental policy. One need only consider the powers of Germany's local authorities in the fields of energy provision, transport policy and waste management to recognise the potential for the Greens to introduce proposals which are of supra-local relevance. The areas of social policy and town planning can also have a strong global orientation, given the increasingly complex nature of the links between international (European Community), national, regional and local laws and statutes. Even by acting within the established constraints of local authorities, the Greens are able to introduce proposals which will address the local repercussions of problems which essentially lie beyond the scope of local government. In this manner it is deemed possible to play some part in solving the more global problem (see for example *Marburg* 1985:7). This applies, for example, to the major environmental problems of acid rain and ozone depletion. Despite the fact that solutions to these global questions will require concerted long-term action in the international arena, the Greens feel that limited measures taken at local level are necessary in the short term. In this context, Green groups have proposed a host of measures to cut down on the localised production of the harmful emissions which create acid rain and which lead to a depletion of the ozone layer. Amongst the many measures suggested have been the following:

(1) The fitting of filtration systems to locally-owned power stations, to reduce the emissions of carbon dioxide (the major cause of ozone depletion) and sulphur dioxide, which is one of the main sources of acid rain (*Leverkusen* 1988:7; *Munich* 1984:4; *Kassel* 1985:19).

(2) Energy-saving devices to reduce demand for electricity, increase energy efficiency and thereby reduce emissions (*Leverkusen* 1988:6). The Kassel Greens suggested that a 30 per cent energy saving was possible between 1985 and the turn of the century (*Kassel* 1985:19). In the local context this can entail anything from improved insulation of official buildings and the use of alternative sources of energy to the construction of new, energy-efficient heat and light power stations and price increases for large-scale electricity users in industry.

(3) Greater emphasis on public transport, to reduce the level of emissions from car exhausts. This is variously to be achieved by reducing public transport fares (see for example *Dortmund* 1987:22), by instituting a park-and-ride system on the edge of the city centre (for example *Marburg* 1985) or by lowering speed limits in built-up areas (for example *Wiesbaden* 1985:17). The aim of such measures is to make car usage in built-up areas unattractive, which in turn has great repercussions in the planning policy field, resulting in reduced demand for new roads and car-parking facilities.

This brief catalogue of proposals serves to exemplify the first manner in which the Greens think globally and act locally. In these instances, the Greens are clearly exploiting the long-established rights of German local authorities under Article 28.2 of the Basic Law to address all issues of direct relevance to the locality. The second way in which the Greens rise above the narrow confines of local government is to raise international issues at local level. In these cases, a more expansive interpretation of the Basic Law is adopted. The chances of failure are high if this is done without any attempt to disguise the issue in a form which would make it acceptable in the local context. Instead, Greens tend to adopt a more sophisticated approach, by establishing a definite, if sometimes contrived, local framework within which the international issue can at least be discussed in a council session (see Kanitz 1988:41). This more radical approach can be exemplified in terms of two specific topics which gave rise to much local council debate in the Federal Republic during the 1980s. These are the questions of military affairs and local council partnership arrangements.

The most controversial military matter to be raised by the Greens was that of a nuclear-free zone. The concept of the nuclear-free zone became the focal point for wide debate in local councils in the early 1980s as a result of the NATO twin-track decision of 1979, which sought to deploy new strategic nuclear weapons on West German soil. One of the first examples of a successful initiative to establish a nuclear-free zone arose in the Groß-Gerau district of Hesse, where an SPD–Green alliance operated between 1981 and 1985 (*Kommunalpolitische Blätter* 5/1983:381f.). On this specific policy area, the Greens could often rely on the more measured support of some left-wing SPD party organisations. Whilst the issue of nuclear-free zones tended to represent a one-off for the SPD, often keen to reach back to the party's opposition to rearmament in the 1950s, for the Greens the nuclear-free zone merely represented one element of a much wider attempt to debate issues of world peace in local councils. The aim is summed up in the electoral programme of the Greens in the Munich district in 1984: 'Our aim is to change the consciousness of the individual citizen in order to achieve a peaceful society' (*Munich* 1984:26).

A host of other military issues have been raised by the Greens in Germany's local council chambers. For example, in aiming to heighten public awareness of military issues, questions arising from military manoeuvres and low-flying aircraft are often raised. Between 1981 and 1984 the Frankfurt Greens introduced ten motions relating to peace issues, covering the topics of nuclear-free zones, local (US) military installations, US troop manoeuvres and the civil rights of conscientious objectors (*Römerfraktion* 1984). In Paderborn, the Greens aroused controversy by sending a resolution to the British Queen, demanding that low flying by Royal Air Force aircraft be stopped. Even the naming of warships after towns and cities has become a contentious issue in German local politics under the influence of the Greens (see for example *Paderborn* 1988; *Cologne* 1989:3).

A further controversial issue in German local politics of recent years has been the question of town partnerships. Traditionally such partnerships have been regarded as means of rebuilding bridges destroyed during two world wars. The Greens treat this established area of local politics in a less conventional manner, seeking to exploit town partnerships as a means of drawing attention to regional conflicts and of expressing solidarity with 'oppressed' peoples in the developing world. This applies in particular to links between German and Nicaraguan towns and regions. Links have been sought by Greens in most communities, including Nuremberg, Wiesbaden, Munich, Bielefeld, Frankfurt and Bonn (see *Nuremberg* 1985). In the formulation of their initiatives, however, it is possible to ascertain the international orientation of the Greens' proposals: 'We believe that Nicaragua in particular desperately needs our help, since the people there are fighting and working for political self-determination against the violently imposed hegemony and exploitation by the imperialism of the USA – with our FRG at its side!' (*Munich* undated:76). While the best chances of success for such links again arise in communities in which the Greens share political control with the SPD, in Aachen even the CDU was able to support a proposed partnership with a Nicaraguan town in 1986 (Scheffler 1987:19). A more recent development in the partnership arena has been the attempt to establish links with East European towns and cities. Such initiatives are again intended to reduce the level of conflict within Europe by establishing common bonds between communities on either side of the former East–West divide.

The Greens' desire to improve the status of the local level in Germany through a greater degree of decentralisation inevitably brings them into conflict with the restrictions placed upon local authorities by Article 28.2 of the Basic Law and by financial limitations affecting the work of local decision-making bodies. The Greens' desire to debate their global measures in the local context goes hand-in-hand with their ideological support for a radical shift in the balance of power in the Federal Republic away from the national and regional levels towards the local level. The preference for decentralised forms of decision-making underpins the manner in which the Greens seek to achieve their local political aims and encourages a tendency to disregard traditional forms of political behaviour in local councils. Here it is possible to discern the existence of a growing divide between the traditional Old Local Politics of the established political parties in Germany and the emergence New Local Politics of the Greens. In the opinion of Rieß (1985), the Greens should aim to breach the restrictions placed upon the activities of local councils: 'The Greens should consciously break through the traditional division of competences and reclaim a maximum of responsibilities for the local community' (Rieß 1985:38).

Traunsberger and Klemisch (1986) have suggested that the development of a general perspective of the role of local self-government is the only means by which the Greens can avoid being overwhelmed by the mound of papers placed before them by council administrations. In recognition of the limits of local councils, therefore, proposals to decentralise decision-making are widely found in the local election programmes of the German Greens (for example *Marburg* 1985; *Lippstadt* 1984; *Geseke* 1984; *Bonn* 1984). Examples from North Rhine Westphalia, Wiesbaden and Augsburg serve to illustrate the point:

> We Greens see it as one of our most important duties not only to stop the increasing centralisation in the Federal Republic, but to introduce a comprehensive process of decentralisation (*Erklärung* 1984).

> To strengthen decentralised, self-administering units and counteract centralisation is a tenet of green politics. This especially applies to the sphere of local self-administration (*Wiesbaden* 1985).

> We know that local political problems are difficult to solve, that their causes often lie beyond the direct influence of the community or

their solutions cannot be financed. For this reason we stand for an extension of the political and financial leeway of the communities (*Augsburg* 1984).

This global aspect of the New Local Politics is just one element of the Greens' involvement in local debate. Of course, not all issues raised by the Greens in local council chambers are global in their orientation. The New Politics agenda is not confined to areas beyond the competences of local authorities. A brief examination of just some of the specialist topics covered in issues of the periodical *Alternative Kommunalpolitik* illustrates the broad spectrum of themes to which Greens have addressed themselves in recent years. These include health matters (AKP 5/88), Third World politics (AKP 3/88), privatisation (AKP 5/87), local cultural politics (AKP 1/88), children's issues (AKP 1/87) and even sport themes (AKP 1/86). What such topics tend to share in common with the global issues is their ideological base and often controversial nature and the conflictual manner in which the Greens seek to portray them. Whilst the established parties aim to avoid confrontation, the Greens thrive upon the publicity caused by conflict in an arena normally regarded as unpolitical. Again, an examination of just three specific areas of Green local politics serves to illustrate the potentially contentious nature of their initiatives.

One important area of Green local activity is the creation of public awareness of the country's National Socialist past and the fight against radical right-wing tendencies in German society. At local level this involves portraying the role played by National Socialism in an individual local community as well as encouraging debate upon its legacy (see for example *Geseke* 1987:12; *Krefeld* 1988). This can be done in a number of ways. Exhibitions are encouraged on the National Socialist period, with particular emphasis placed upon the persecution of the local Jewish population and the use of forced labour in local factories; guided tours are arranged of local landmarks; events are organised to commemorate significant local anniversaries (for example *Lippstadt* 1988:2).

A second area of Green local council activity concerns social issues, such as women's rights and the role of social minority groups. With regard to women's issues Meyer-Ullrich (1988) has identified three main focal points of Green attention. Firstly,

Greens seek to initiate and stabilise the women's subculture by securing financial support for autonomous women's projects. Secondly, they actively support institutional projects with a feminist orientation. Thirdly, they try to expose discrimination in all local political spheres (Meyer-Ullrich 1988:37). Policies linked to these goals can include the adoption of quota statutes which aim to grant half of all jobs in the local authority administration to women (*Bonn* 1984:8f.) or the provision of crèche facilities in public offices as a means of encouraging economic activity by women (*Dortmund* 1987:13). In addition, policies which seek to draw attention to the question of violence against women have aroused much debate in local councils since the Greens became active in local politics. Schemes such as women's refuges, special car parks reserved for women and night-taxis for women have received widespread media attention. Night-taxi schemes have been proposed, for example, by Greens in most large towns and cities, including Cologne, Heidelberg, Bielefeld, Tübingen and Dortmund (for details see Meyer-Ullrich 1988). With regard to social minority groups, the Greens propose measures to reduce discrimination in all its forms. Symbolic actions, such as the nomination of a Spanish citizen to head the local election list in Nuremberg, are complemented by concrete measures to improve the rights of minorities. In Munich district, for example, the Greens proposed that foreigners be given the right to vote in local elections after a two-year residence period (*Munich* 1984:18; also *Cologne* 1989:13; *Dortmund* 1987:10f.). Further proposals were introduced to protect asylum seekers from deportation in a number of communities.

A final issue which requires attention in the context of the Greens' role in local politics arises from the manner in which they address administrative matters. Generally, the Greens have an ambivalent attitude towards council administrations and established representative practices of council officials. At one level, the Greens occupy a conservative role, seeking to control council expenditure on seemingly unnecessary items. This can involve calls for the withdrawal of official cars for members of the council executive and their replacement with official bicycles (*Römerfraktion* 1983) or attempts to limit increases in expense allowances for attendance at council meetings. At a second level, the Greens seek to politicise the procedure by which council officials are appointed. Traditionally, in the absence of party-political debate in local councils, the most significant decisions to be made by councillors were linked to the appointment of council officers and administrators (Naßmacher 1989:179). In order to demonstrate the existence of a consensus in local councils, the tradition has been for all parties to be represented in either the council executive or in the local administration, regardless of the parties' respective strengths in the council chamber. This behaviour is depicted in a study by Gabriel *et al.* (1984) of CDU oppositional activities in ten cities in North Rhine Westphalia, with the election of an SPD mayor being opposed on only one occasion by the minority CDU group (Gabriel 1984:116f.). Decisions regarding the election of local mayors or chief executives have also traditionally been made unanimously (Wehling 1989). The Greens have introduced an element of conflict into the appointment procedure, either by putting up opposing candidates for key council offices or by voting against the candidate supported by the established parties. Increasingly, however, the Greens have started to recognise the importance of having party adherents in key council departments. This applies especially in communities with red–green alliances. Loreck's (1987:16) comment that the Greens can be regarded as more suitable alliance partners for the SPD than either the CDU or FDP in local councils because they are not '*Postenjäger*' (post-hunters) no longer seems to hold true.

The Greens' ideological approach to local politics lies at the heart of the extension of the New Politics agenda and its confrontational styles of debate to the local councils of the Federal Republic. Despite difficulties associated with generalising about Green local politics, it is apparent that to date issues have played a more important role for the Greens than those established areas of local political debate which are related to administrative and personnel matters. The potential sources of conflict which emerge from this process will be addressed below.

New Sources of Conflict at Local Level

It has already been demonstrated that traditional interpretations of the function of local politics in Germany seek to limit the scope of local council activities to the self-administrative duties laid down in Article 28.2 of the Basic Law (see Gabriel 1979a and 1983b). Although the SPD Left, acting under the influence of the party's youth wing (the *Jungsozialisten*), sought to broaden the horizons of local decision-makers at the beginning of the 1970s (W. Roth 1972), their results were rather modest (W. Roth and Edelhoff 1983). The full parliamentarisation of local politics (Gabriel 1984; R. Roth 1988) has only occurred widely with the entry of the Greens into local councils. Since the Greens are not obliged to operate within the narrow constraints of responsible political behaviour at local level, they can be regarded as the only political party in the Federal Republic to have consistently and systematically challenged the limitations placed upon the role of local government. By no means all commentators support such a confrontational strategy. Opposition has come from a number of political sources (for example Strauß 1984; Schuster *et al.* 1985; Kanitz 1988; Borchmann 1982), with a publication of the *Konrad-Adenauer-Stiftung* summing up the general perception of the Greens' local political role: 'Local self-administration is not regarded in first place as being the right to regulate matters of the local community under its own responsibility (Art. 28.2 of the Basic Law). It appears much more to be a means to the end of overcoming the social and political order, of fundamentally changing it' (Schuster *et al.* 1985:46).

Evidence suggests that the introduction of globally-based issues into local councils has increased the level of conflict within them by a quite considerable degree. Güllner (1986:33) even suggests that this is a possible reason for declining turnouts in local elections, since most citizens are judged to prefer consensus politics at local level. Werle's (1981) study of the political orientations of candidates for local council office in Baden-Württemberg demonstrated the existence of a potential gulf between the Greens on the one side and all other local parties on the other. In the context of this study, it will be necessary to examine in greater detail the nature of this conflict, and in particular the extent to which the Greens' New Local Politics approach meets with opposition from across the political spectrum, thereby indicating the emergence of a new cross-cutting cleavage at local level.

A second potential source of conflict arising from the Greens' role in local politics, which also derives to a certain extent from the growth of new global issues, is the scant regard paid by them to the traditional legalistic practices at local level. This question has been debated widely in the specialist press with regard to specific issues raised by the Greens (see Kimminich 1983:223; Stober 1986). The constraints placed upon local councils by Article 28.2 of the Basic Law, which states that local authorities have the right to regulate matters of relevance to their localities as long as they do not transgress higher-level legislation, are generally disregarded by the Greens. The fact that the New Politics Left of the SPD occasionally supports such practices by the Greens gives cause for conservative concern: 'The degree to which the SPD tolerates or encourages the flouting by the Greens of the limits to local self-determination does not preclude the possible weakening and undermining of local self-determination' (Kanitz 1988:73). Whether or not such fears are justifiable will be the focus for further attention in Part II.

The Greens' Strategy in Local Politics

Having outlined the nature of the issues raised by the Greens, it is now necessary to address a further key element of the party's participation in local politics – the strategy adopted by Green and alternative groups in local party systems in order to achieve their aims. It should be recognised that whilst the strategy debate has often led to an impasse in the operation of the Green Party at regional and national level, the main questions involved in the debate either did not arise or were solved relatively early on at local level. A realist majority only emerged gradually in the federal Green Party, belatedly reflecting the views of the majority of Green voters. However, there has been less scope for damaging factionalism to develop at local level. In local party organisations, where inner-party conflicts did emerge, the pragmatists tended to gain the upper hand relatively quickly, largely as a result of the nature of German local politics. It tended to be only the large towns and cities in which disputes mirroring those of the national and regional party organisations developed, and this can be attributed to the compromises which were made in the formative stages of the disparate groupings by activists of differing political orientations.

Given that the Greens have yet to gain majority-party status in any German council chamber, it has been necessary to adopt some form of strategy in order to achieve any degree of success. In this context, it is worth examining briefly the conflicting approaches of two key local council groups in the 1980s. Greens in Frankfurt and Bielefeld have played an important historical role in influencing the course of the strategy debate in the whole Green Movement at local level.

The stance of the first Green representatives in Frankfurt's city council (the so-called *Römerfraktion*) is of particular relevance. Between 1981 and 1985 this group adopted a strategy of fundamental opposition, becoming the model for other Green groups with similar political outlooks. In a series of publications, the *Römerfraktion* sought to present their political aims, influencing Green local politicians throughout the Federal Republic (*Römerfraktion* 1983, 1984 and 1985). During the 1980s Frankfurt effectively became the political battleground of the competing fundamentalist and realist factions within the Green Party, with the main protagonists in the local debate, Joschka Fischer and Jutta Ditfurth, carrying the conflict into the organs of the federal party organisation. Whilst Ditfurth, a prominent fundamentalist, was chairperson of the Federal Green Party for a number of years, Fischer became Hessian Environment Minister in the Federal Republic's first ever red–green coalition at regional level (1985–87) and again in the wake of the 1991 regional elections in Hesse.

Acting upon the belief that Green parliamentary work had less to do with holding power than with heightening public awareness of the basic questions of survival, members of the first *Römerfraktion* regarded the purpose of their council activities as being to encourage citizens to become active on issues of concern to them. The emphasis was placed distinctly upon extra-parliamentary forms of protest. In this respect they played down the decision-making function of representative institutions, treating them as bodies designed to maintain the status quo. The task the *Römerfraktion* set itself was to make local citizens aware of the inadequacies of representative democracy and thereby engender the dissatisfaction necessary to create the right conditions for the overturning of the established system: 'To create these conditions also means operating in a consciously disillusionary man-

119

ner with regard to the actual function of the parliament, continually questioning our own representative role and by means of a process of classic disillusionment reaching the point at which the citizens no longer allow themselves to be administered, but rather increasingly represent their interests themselves' (*Römerfraktion* 1983:1).

The *Römerfraktion* sought to publicise their ideals by repeatedly exposing the 'failings' of Frankfurt's established political parties. The fundamentalist strategy involved the concentration by Green councillors on technical details which could be used in plenary debates to support their radical assertions. Meticulously worded motions on all conceivable policy areas were introduced with a view to creating the long-term potential for change: 'Small changes can only be meaningful if they contain the essence of utopia within them or, at least, if they do not obscure the path which leads to the concrete utopia' (*Römerfraktion* 1983:1). The principal flaw in such an approach lies in the failure of Green fundamentalists to establish a positive perspective of the future which could be of electoral appeal. During the course of the 1981–5 legislative period, Frankfurt's fundamentalists became involved in a bitter inner-party dispute with the city's strong realist faction. The difference between the apocalyptic vision of the radical ecologists and the pragmatic approach of the realists can be discerned in their views on water policy in Frankfurt. The fundamentalists openly favoured the adoption of radical, long-term measures:

> We stand today before the alternative of either continuing with the prevailing poisoning policy or of starting a radical ecological water policy. There is no third choice. Even a small amount of poisoning ultimately leads to death ... Since the consequences are radical, we should not be afraid of seeking radical solutions. Nevertheless, small steps can also bring about an improvement. However, they must be conceived under a perspective which will lead to a radical change ... (*Römerfraktion* 1985:134).

The realist faction, on the other hand, chose to emphasise the importance of undertaking short-term measures to improve water supply:

> ... we also want to act, rebuild, reorganise, use the many opportunities in Frankfurt to create an ecological city – preferably today rather

than tomorrow. – Of course, the Main is already polluted when it reaches Frankfurt. Nevertheless, the largest polluter of the Main is currently still the city of Frankfurt itself, larger even than the Hoechst corporation. That is why the city is for me the first level at which to act (Koenigs 1988:5).

Green party realists in Frankfurt obviously held a long-term vision of the city in which they would like to live, but it was a vision which they sought to achieve through concrete reforms. Party realists were very much aware of the inherent limitations associated with being a small political party, at best a junior coalition partner (Nimsch 1989:21). The nascent realism within the Frankfurt Greens was helped along by political events during the 1980s. In 1985, for the first time, the fundamentalist strategy was overwhelmingly rejected by both the local Green Party in Frankfurt and, more significantly, the electorate. The Greens' share of the vote in local council elections in Frankfurt in 1985 increased at a rate well below that of the Green Party in Hesse as a whole, and in elections to neighbourhood councils, which took part concurrently within the same geographical area, the Greens secured an additional 2 per cent of the vote (Frankfurt 1986:50). As a result, the realist faction was able to gain the upper hand in the Frankfurt party between 1985 and 1989, mirroring events in the Hessian Green Party (Johnsen 1988; Scharf 1989). Only in 1989, with the adoption of clear strategy in favour of a coalition with the SPD, did the pragmatists finally establish control over the local party organisation in Frankfurt. In this regard, the Frankfurt Greens regarded themselves as leading the way in the strategic debate within the entire Green Party. For Joschka Fischer the strategic choice facing Frankfurt Greens was not between realism and fundamentalism but between the continued dominance in the city of the CDU under their mayoral candidate Walter Wallmann and a new red–green administration: 'The conflict was not fundi–realo or Fischer–Ditfurth, rather the alternative was red–green or Wallmann' (Fischer 1989:27). In the 1989 election which followed these remarks, the city's seemingly impregnable CDU absolute majority was broken and an SPD–Green administration was formed.

A rather different strategy has been adopted in Bielefeld by the alternative *Bunte Liste* (*BuLi*) and the Greens since 1979. The *BuLi* was established in 1979 as a distinctly left-wing list to contest the local elections of the same year in North Rhine West-phalia. Drawing upon the established protest tradition of the university city, the view of the *BuLi's* members was that the par-liamentary and extra-parliamentary activities of the Green Movement should complement one another, without either aspect's being of overriding significance. The *BuLi* is of particu-lar relevance to the development of a coherent Green local poli-tics in Germany, since it has been instrumental in efforts to coor-dinate policy-making, acting as a motive force behind the foun-dation of the *Alternative Kommunalpolitik* periodical, whose head-quarters are still in the city. The *BuLi* also played a significant role in organising a first national conference in 1980 of Green local politicians from thirty-three Green and fifteen rainbow lists. The aim of the conference was to clarify the Greens' role in Ger-many's local and regional parliaments (*Frankfurter Rundschau* 18.11.80).

Having gained election to the local council in 1979, the *BuLi* recognised the limitations of what could be achieved with only four councillors and adopted a pragmatic view of their council activities, welcoming compromises in certain areas since: 'the experience of success and proof of the principled realism and practicability of one's own ideas can inspires the extra-parlia-mentary struggle, which in turn improves the prerequisites in parliament' (Krämer and Winter 1982:160). Although often in conflict with the SPD council group, the *BuLi* passed the city budget three times with the Social Democrats in the 1979–84 leg-islative period, without ever formally entering into an alliance with the party (AKP 4/84:18). Such a strategy was rewarded in 1984 with a greatly increased share of the vote and subsequent participation in the local administration as part of a full red–green coalition.

In effect, the approach of the *BuLi* in Bielefeld represented a compromise between the competing strategies of the Frankfurt fundamentalists and realists. Council representation was not viewed as an end in itself, nor was it regarded as being of sec-ondary importance to extra-parliamentary activities. Perhaps the most significant difference, however, lay in the differing party constellations of the two cities. Where the *BuLi Fraktion* in Biele-feld was obliged to come to terms with a situation in which they could support a minority SPD administration as early as 1979

(Krämer and Winter 1982:174), the *Römerfraktion* in Frankfurt was able to develop its fundamentalist concept in a city with a seemingly impregnable CDU absolute majority. Under such circumstances it was perhaps rather academic what stance the Greens adopted to various issues, since their influence over council decisions was severely restricted. However, the adoption of a more pragmatic approach does not always result in increased electoral support. The 1989 local elections in Bielefeld saw the Greens lose 3.5 per cent of their percentage vote and the alliance of the SPD and *Bunte Liste* lose their overall majority (Bielefeld 1989).

Although individual local party systems vary considerably across the Federal Republic, it is increasingly the Bielefeld model which has been adopted, albeit unconsciously, by the majority of local Green party organisations. Fundamentalist strategies have rapidly given way to more active participation in local council affairs, in the form of alliances with the SPD (see Bullmann 1985 and 1987; Henkeborg 1987; Kanitz 1988; Loreck 1987; Scharf 1989; Tolmein 1986:8f.). In some cases alliances have even been forged with the CDU, such as that in the Hessian community of Mainhausen between 1985 and 1989, which served as the location for a disputed waste disposal site (Behr, Breit, Lilge and Schissler 1986:48). The fact that such forms of cooperation are now relatively commonplace at local level, yet still present difficulties for Greens at national and regional level says something about the nature of local political involvement. Despite their openly ideological approach to local politics, the Greens have rapidly become aware that the local level is not the level at which the 'system' is to be changed. This has been neatly summed up as follows in a report produced by the Greens in the Soest district in North Rhine Westphalia: 'In essence, the term "local politics" is also to be understood as a shortened form of the ... "realism of taking small steps"' (*Soest* 1988: no page number).

Summary: An Emergent New Local Political Cleavage?

During the late 1970s and 1980s, the Greens sought to redefine the function and scope of local politics in Germany. With their growing level of representation across the communities of the

Federal Republic, the issues of the New Local Politics were to be seen on the agendas of councils in both urban and rural settings. This chapter has sought to draw attention to the divide which exists, in theory at least, between the Greens' espousal of a conflict-oriented, ideologically based local politics and the traditional, non-political structures of local politics. The continued discussion of distinctly non-local issues, for example, would tend to encourage the development of conflict. This also applies to the politicisation by the Greens of traditionally uncontroversial administrative matters, such as the appointment of council officials or the espousal of new town partnership arrangements. In this respect, there already appears ample evidence to suggest that a new conflict line is emerging in Germany's local parliaments. Although the traditional left–right cleavage is still important at local level, the signs are that a New Local Politics–Old Local Politics cleavage now exists, which sets the Greens against Germany's established local political actors.

Signs of the potential relevance and implications of the New Local Politics–Old Local Politics cleavage can already be discerned in the often conflictual alliances between the Greens and the SPD at local level. Whereas agreement can readily be reached over policy matters, it is often less straightforward reaching consensus on administrative and personnel questions. In many cases, it has simply been easier for the SPD to form an alliance with the CDU than with the Greens. Although Kanitz (1988) has suggested that red–green alliances are most successful when the SPD is dominated by its left wing, it is more likely that the success of such alliances depends upon the strength of the SPD's New Politics Left in the relevant community. On the contrary, the traditional left wing of the SPD has little in common with the Greens, and appears to experience difficulties in coming to terms at all levels of the German party system with the unconventional approach of the Greens.

Part II

The Greens and the Mainz Party System

7

The Selection of Mainz as a Case-Study Community

In Part I of this study, the role played by the Greens in the changing nature of the Federal Republic's local politics was discussed, by necessity, in rather general terms. Evidence gathered from a range of sources suggests not only that the German Greens are a heterogeneous force at local level, but also that they themselves have experienced a significant amount of internal change during the course of their period of local council representation. This highlights the difficulties associated with generalising about the Greens' activities at local level, especially when one considers the absence of objective or comprehensive source materials on many aspects of Green local politics. In Part II, therefore, a case-study analysis is to be undertaken in order to provide a more detailed picture of the Greens' contribution to the changes which have characterised Germany's local party systems since the late 1970s. In particular, attention is to be paid to the role of the Greens in conveying New Politics agendas and styles of political activity to the local level.

Before commencing the analysis of the Greens' impact upon the party system of the city of Mainz over a three-year period, it is necessary to demonstrate the extent to which this locality can be regarded as representing a typical community in terms of the issues under debate. In this chapter, the principal criteria for the selection of a suitable case-study location will be outlined, and the extent to which the city of Mainz satisfies the criteria identified. This chapter ends with a short section which indicates the manner in which the analysis is to be completed.

Criteria for the Selection of the Case-Study Locality

One main aim of this study has been to demonstrate the extent to which the changes evident in the local politics of the Federal

127

Republic are linked in general to the emergence of the New Politics and in particular to the rise of the Greens. Given this aim, three key criteria present themselves for the selection of a suitable case-study community for the purposes of the analysis. These pertain to the level of socio-economic modernisation witnessed by the community, the existence of an 'established' local party system and the availability of and degree of access to relevant source documentation.

In Chapter 3, the emergence of the New Politics was discussed in terms of the disparate rates of socio-economic modernisation experienced by communities across the Federal Republic. The key indicators judged to be representative of the varying pace of the modernisation process were the relevance of the service sector to the local economy and a growing degree of secularisation. Consequently, it was suggested that the impact of the New Politics upon local party systems would be greatest in those urban localities in which the rate of socio-economic change, measured in terms of the level of employment in and income generated by the service sector, has been most marked. The first selection criterion, therefore, sought to identify a study community with a modern, service-sector economy.

A second important criterion for the selection of a case-study locality was the existence of an 'established' local party system prior to the emergence of the Greens. As previously explained, the activities of German local councils for much of the post-war period have been characterised by consensual forms of decision-making (Gabriel 1979a; Gabriel 1984). In place of party political conflict, council chambers have tended to become dominated by administrative decision-making procedures (Lehmbruch 1975). It has already been suggested that the Greens' 'New Local Politics' approach represents a prime factor underlying increased levels of dissent in local councils and the development of more parliamentary styles of local politics during the 1970s and 1980s. By selecting a community in which party-political debate had largely been absent in the years preceding the election of the Greens, it would be possible to assess the full impact of the Greens' unique approach to local politics. For this reason, communities at the forefront of tendencies towards parliamentarisation, primarily large cities such as Frankfurt, Cologne or Munich, were to be avoided. Similarly, communities in which the Greens had played an important role in local affairs before the commencement of the fieldwork stages of research were also excluded from consideration. Given the amount of change experienced by local Green groups within a relatively short time-period in terms of their membership levels and the extent of their grassroots support, any attempts to reconstruct the events of the late 1970s and early 1980s would have been extremely difficult. This criterion further reduced the number of potentially suitable study communities, since the initial local electoral successes of Green and alternative lists primarily occurred in the service-sector centres of the Federal Republic.

The final selection criterion regarded the accessibility of relevant source materials necessary for the completion of a case-study analysis. Two basic types of data were required for the proposed analysis. Firstly, it was necessary to gain access to the internal, often confidential, party papers of the relevant Green Party council groups. This would allow conclusions to be drawn about the manner in which the party's key decision-making bodies operate at local level. Secondly, it was necessary to gain access to documentation provided by local council administrations. The minutes of local council and council committee meetings and a complete register of the parliamentary initiatives (motions) of the various local council groups were to be utilised as a means of illustrating the role played by the Greens and the New Politics in changing the established patterns of local council activity. While no real difficulty in gaining access to the first type of data was anticipated, since the Greens operate as a highly accessible and open political force, the second requirement was less straightforward. Not only does the quality of the minutes of council sessions vary from community to community, but in some communities there can be lengthy delays between the completion of a council session and the production of the relevant minutes. In Wiesbaden, for example, minutes of the relevant council meetings were not yet available for the 1985–7 period when fieldwork began in October 1987. Since the council administration in Wiesbaden could only provide limited details of council resolutions, it was impossible to ascertain how individual council groups in the city voted on particular issues. Without access to both data sources, therefore, it would prove extremely difficult to analyse in detail the impact of the Greens upon the local party system.

In this study the city of Mainz was selected as a focus for research into the role of the Greens in Germany's local politics. In the following sections, the extent to which Mainz satisfies the relevant selection criteria will be assessed. To this end it is necessary to discuss briefly the socio-economic structure of the city, the key characteristics of its party system prior to the election of the Greens to the local council and the nature of the data made available for the completion of the analysis.

Mainz as a Typical Service-Sector City

Mainz is a medium-sized university and cathedral city, located in the centre of the Federal Republic, where the River Main joins the River Rhine. With a resident population of 180,422 at the 1987 census, it occupies thirty-second place in a list of west Germany's most populous cities. As the capital of the Rhineland Palatine, Mainz is the seat of the regional government, fulfilling important functions both as an administrative centre and as a regional centre for the Rhinehesse area. Being on the edge of the Rhine–Main area, Mainz is also greatly influenced by the rapid pace of social and economic change which has characterised this expanding region during recent decades (see Weber 1987).

In a comparison drawn between seventeen west German cities of a similar population size, Mainz occupies an average position with regard to a series of social structural characteristics (Mainz 1987a:4f.). With immigrants representing a proportion of 10.5 per cent of the population, for example, the city is only slightly above the national average, and typical of communities on the periphery of a large conurbation (Mainz 1987a:4). The principal features which distinguish Mainz from most other cities included in the cited comparison are its above-average population density, its high proportion of population of working age (74.3 per cent in the 15–64 age-group), its correspondingly high levels of economic activity and its relatively high tax income (Mainz 1987a). Although Mainz has also been afflicted by a number of the social problems which have accompanied Germany's fluctuating economic performance since the first Oil Crises of the 1970s (see for example Sozialbericht 1987(1988); Sozialbericht 1988(1989)), it has been less badly affected than other towns and cities (Köth and Kolmer 1983:41). In 1987, for example, an unemployment rate of 7.0 per cent in Mainz compared favourably with an average rate of 12.6 per cent for the seventeen cities included in the analysis cited above (Mainz 1987a).

Table 7.1 Mainz: Employees by Economic Sector, 1975–1985 (in %)

Year	Primary sector	Secondary sector	Tertiary sector	All sectors (n)
1975	0.3	40.0	59.6	84,067
1980	0.3	36.8	63.0	89,722
1985	0.3	35.8	63.9	91,035
Change 1975–85	0.0	–4.2	4.3	6,968

Source: Mainz 1987b:26; calculations by author

In this study particular interest is accorded to the role played by the tertiary sector in the Mainz economy. Table 7.1 depicts the growing significance of employment in this sector of the Mainz economy. Whilst the proportion of the workforce engaged in agriculture has remained static since the mid-1970s, there has been a marked decline in the proportion of employees engaged in the manufacturing sector (Köth and Kolmer 1983:41f.). Between 1975 and 1985, the period which marked the rise of the Greens, the proportion of the Mainz workforce employed in service industries rose by 7.2 per cent, to a level of 63.9 per cent (Mainz 1987b:26). With regard to the proportion of the workforce engaged in the tertiary sector in similarly sized cities, Mainz again occupies an average position. Only other university cities, such as Oldenburg (74.0 per cent), Freiburg (69.2 per cent), Göttingen (68.4 per cent) and Heidelberg (67.4 per cent), have a significantly higher proportion of employees engaged in service industries (Mainz 1987a:18). A comparison of the contribution of the service sector to the economies of Mainz and west Germany as a whole clearly demonstrates that the economy of Mainz has shifted much more rapidly towards the service sector than the national economy (Table 7.2).

Despite the general growth in the income derived from the service sector in the Federal Republic, the rate of growth has been much faster in certain service-industry centres. This feature

131

also pertains to Mainz. Between 1970 and 1984 the tertiary sector in Mainz increased its contribution to the gross national product by 17.4 per cent, compared with a national average increase of 10.8 per cent (Mainz 1987b:30).

Table 7.2 Gross National Product by Economic Sectors, Mainz and West Germany, 1970–1984 (in %)

Economic sector	Year	Mainz	West Germany
Primary	1970	0.5	3.8
	1984	0.2	2.4
	Change 1970–84	–0.3	–1.4
Secondary	1970	48.4	58.2
	1984	31.3	48.8
	Change 1970–84	–17.1	–9.4
Tertiary	1970	51.1	38.0
	1984	68.5	48.8
	Change 1970–84	17.4	10.8

Source: Mainz 1987b:30

Table 7.3 Mainz: Student Population, 1975–1985

Year	Students	Population	Students per 1,000 inhabitants
1975	20,777	185,304	112
1980	24,676	188,076	132
1985	26,681	185,840	143

Source: Mainz 1987b:3 and 22; calculations by author

In terms of its changing economic structure, therefore, Mainz can be regarded as being a typical service-sector city. Linked to this is the presence of a highly educated population. As has previously been discussed, New Politics values are most widely found within the young, highly educated members of the new middle class; the group which corresponds to the Green Party's core electoral support. As a university city, it can be anticipated that Mainz will have a high proportion of citizens with an above-average level of education. One means of demonstrating this feature is to depict the development of the ratio of students to the population of Mainz as a whole (Table 7.3). Whilst there were only 112 students for every 1000 inhabitants of Mainz in 1975, in the ten years which followed this figure increased by some 27.7 per cent to 143 in 1985. In 1985 there was one student for every seven Mainz inhabitants (Mainz 1987b:22).

In terms of its economic structure and its education status, Mainz can be regarded as representing a typical medium-sized university town. In this respect, therefore, Mainz was judged to satisfy the first relevant criterion for the selection of a suitable case-study locality.

The Established Party System in Mainz

The second criterion for the selection of a case-study community was the existence of an 'established' local party system. The absence of notable forms of party-political conflict was judged to present an ideal backdrop for an analysis of the full impact of the Greens' New Local Politics approach at local level.

Somewhat unusually for a relatively large city, Mainz had succeeded in maintaining a traditional party system for much of the post-war period. In the most important areas of local self-administration, such as budgetary and personnel matters, consensual decision-making practices were the norm in this community. Despite signs of parliamentarisation in similar cities in the late 1970s and early 1980s, Mainz remained seemingly immune to the various pressures for change prior to the election of the Greens to the local council in June 1984. The presence of an active youth wing in the SPD from the mid-1970s onwards could apparently do little to change this situation. The consensual decision-making patterns adopted by the three parties represented in the city council lie at the heart of the so-called Mainz model (*Mainzer Modell*). In the absence of a stable majority for either the SPD or CDU for much of the post-war period, and with local party élites unwilling to become dependent upon a smaller alliance partner (the FDP), Mainz was governed by a Grand Coalition of both major parties. Whereas the SPD has always

133

occupied the strategically dominant position of city mayor, both the CDU and FDP were represented in key posts on the council executive committee (*Stadtvorstand*). The political complexion of Mainz in the late 1950s, described by Chaput de Saintoigne (1961:199), essentially persisted into the mid-1980s. The five council subcommittees of 1959 comprised nine members each, with five belonging to the SPD, three to the CDU and one to the FDP. Significantly, two of the committees were chaired by SPD councillors, two by CDU councillors and one by an FDP councillor. Moreover, the council executive was composed of members of each of the parties, with the first deputy of the SPD city mayor belonging to the CDU (Chaput de Saintoigne 1961:201). Needless to say, this form of power-sharing bore little relation to the political constellation of the city council chamber, as had been determined by the Mainz electorate.

Attempts in the 1970s by the youth wing of the Mainz SPD to dissolve the Mainz Model or even reduce the degree to which the Social Democrats relied upon the CDU, in line with the dual strategy adopted by the *Jungsozialisten* at their 1971 conference (W. Roth 1972), foundered when confronted by a structural right-wing majority in both the council group and the local party organisation. Before the emergence of the Greens in Mainz, therefore, the major decisions in the city council were made in unison between the established political parties. This absence of any significant form of local opposition made Mainz an ideal subject for the analysis of the influence of the Greens' unique approach to local politics.

A further factor which lent itself to a study of the impact of the Greens on the local politics of Mainz was the fact that the Green Party developed relatively late in this city. In the Rhineland Palatinate as a whole, the Greens stood in regional elections for the first time in 1983, failing to overcome the 5 per cent hurdle with just 4.5 per cent of the vote. In this region the Greens have remained relatively weak (Mez 1987:275), given a socio-economic structure and religious profile which tends to favour support for the Christian Democrats (Sarcinelli 1984; see also Heidger 1987). Only with the burgeoning of the Peace Movement in the early 1980s in the wake of the NATO twin-track decision did the Greens in the Rhineland Palatinate gain a strong foundation of support amongst certain sections of the regional population. In Mainz itself, the Greens stood in the local elections for the first time in 1984. At the previous local elections of 1979 there was no Green organisation capable of competing for the vote. With the Greens acting as a new element in a traditional local party system, the potential for addressing the full effect of their New Local Politics approach upon established consensual practices was great. In particular, the 1984 local election presented the possibility of an alliance between the Greens and the SPD in the city council. The outcome of the red–green debate in Mainz could be regarded as providing an ideal means of analysing the effect of the Greens' New Politics upon an SPD divided between a New Politics left wing and an Old Politics right wing. In terms of its established party system and the potential for change, Mainz represented a suitable choice as a case-study community.

Access to Source Materials in Mainz

The final criterion of importance in the selection of a case-study community was the degree of accessibility to relevant source materials. Such access was made possible during the course of an extended period of fieldwork in Mainz.[1] It proved possible to make use of a unique range of papers, private correspondence and other documents, which for the main part have remained unpublished.[2] The willingness of the Greens in Mainz to make important data available greatly facilitated the completion of the case-study analysis. Although it was not possible to gain direct access to similar source materials from the other council groups in Mainz, the comprehensive nature of the Greens' own archive largely obviated the necessity of gaining information from alternative sources.

---

[1] The author held a scholarship from the German Academic Exchange Service between October 1987 and July 1988. During this period much of the fieldwork for this study was completed.

[2] The principal sources which were made available were: the minutes of meetings and internal discussion documents of the Green *Fraktionsgruppe*; the archive of the Green *Fraktionsgruppe*; personal correspondence between the Greens and other council groups and extra-parliamentary initiatives; the accounts books of the Green *Fraktionsgruppe* and a range of publications of the Mainz Greens.

In addition to the accessibility of important internal party source documents, recourse was had to the published minutes of Mainz city council sessions for the period of the proposed analysis. The fact that the parliamentary initiatives of the four parties represented on the Mainz city council between 1984 and 1987 were held in a central database ensured that a full analysis of the nature of the various parties' motions would be possible (see Chapter 9 for details).

Summary: Mainz as a Focus for Study

Mainz fully satisfied each of the three criteria judged important for the selection of a suitable focus for study. Firstly, it is a modern, service-sector city with a social structure amenable to the values and issues of the New Politics. Secondly, it operated a traditional party system characterised by consensual decision-making patterns before the emergence of the Greens in the mid-1980s. Finally, the selection of Mainz was simplified by the accessibility of relevant source materials for the completion of a detailed analysis.

The purpose of the case-study analysis is to address general questions relating to aspects of Green involvement in Germany's local politics on the basis of an interpretation of developments in Mainz in the period which followed the Greens' initial election to local council office. The questions arise from the analysis of general trends in Green local politics identified in Part I of this study, and pertain to the following areas: the ideological (New Politics) and confrontational orientation of Green local politics, the openly parliamentary styles adopted by Green local political activists, and tendencies towards an institutionalisation of the Greens at local level. By examining the experience of Green participation in the politics of a particular locality, the intention is to cast new light upon the general changes which have affected local politics in the Federal Republic since the late 1970s.

The case-study analysis is divided into three chapters. In Chapter 8, the role of the Greens in the Mainz party system between 1984 and 1987 is investigated. In examining the course of political events in Mainz during this period, in particular the controversy surrounding the question of a possible alliance between the Greens and the SPD on the city council, questions relating to the ideological nature of Green local politics and their confrontational approach to council activity will be examined. While this analysis is essentially to be founded upon the source documentation outlined above, a number of other means of establishing a picture of the impact of the Greens in Mainz's local politics were utilised. During the course of fieldwork, a number of interviews were conducted with key participants in the city's local politics, belonging to the Greens, SPD and CDU. By attending the regular meetings of the Green council group, vital background information was gathered.[3] A number of sessions of the Mainz city council were also observed, with the aim of identifying differences in styles adopted by the representatives of the four parties with seats in the council chamber.

Chapters 9 and 10 address the parliamentary initiatives of the four parties represented on the Mainz city council during the period of analysis (July 1984–June 1987). By utilising both quantitative and more qualitative techniques, comparisons are to be drawn between the council motions of the Greens and those of the other parties represented on the council. Whether any differences which emerge from such an analysis correspond to the existence of a New Local Politics–Old Local Politics dimension in the Mainz party system will be the focus for further discussion.

---

[3] The author attended the regular weekly meetings of the Green *Fraktions-gruppe* and participated in a number of additional party activities during the course of fieldwork. It was also possible to present some preliminary research findings from this study to members of the Mainz council group. The ensuing debate proved useful in clarifying certain aspects of the research.

8

The Greens and the Mainz Party System 1984–1987

In this chapter attention is to be focused upon the strategic role adopted by the Greens in the Mainz city council between 1984 and 1987. The chapter is divided into two sections. Firstly, a brief analysis of the result of the 1984 local election in the city provides the background for subsequent developments in the local party system. Secondly, in a discussion of the course of the debate between the SPD and Green Party council groups in Mainz, reasons will be given for the inability of the parties to reach agreement over the adoption of a common strategy for the period under analysis. It will be suggested that the New Local Politics approach favoured by the Greens could not be reconciled with the more established local political practices of the inner-party majority of the SPD.

The 1984 Local Election in Mainz

The local election of June 1984 represented a significant turning-point in Mainz's local politics. With the Greens gaining 9.2 per cent of the vote, it was the only time since the first local elections in Rhineland Palatinate of 1952 that a fourth party was able to gain representation on the Mainz city council (Table 8.1). Previously, only the NPD had posed a challenge to the established parties in Mainz, failing to clear the 5 per cent hurdle in 1969, when they secured 4.6 per cent of the vote.

In many ways, Mainz was not an ideal source of support for the Greens in terms of the existence of an alternative milieu (Veen 1989). The makings of an alternative sector, in the form of alternative cafés, bookshops and workshops, are only evident in some central parts of the city (Neustadt-Süd) and in a few suburbs (for example Gonsenheim). In this respect, Mainz was by no means comparable to the larger cities of the Federal Republic, with their highly developed alternative forms of culture (for example Berlin, Munich, Frankfurt, Hamburg). Nor could the Mainz Greens draw upon the presence of a university-based alternative culture, such as exists in the towns of Freiburg, Münster and Tübingen. Nevertheless, on the basis of their previous electoral performance in Mainz, it was widely anticipated that the Greens would gain council representation in 1984 (Table 8.2). Only the fact that the party was entitled to send five councillors to the newly constituted chamber came as a surprise to local political commentators.

Table 8.1 Local Elections in Mainz, 1952–1989 (in %)

Year	SPD	CDU	FDP	Greens	Other
1952	43.2	32.8	17.3	....	6.7
1956	51.9	35.0	11.3	....	1.8
1960	45.8	37.8	13.7	....	2.7
1964	51.9	38.2	10.0	....	....
1969	49.2	38.0	8.3	....	4.6
1974	44.1	45.0	8.4	....	2.4
1979	48.1	42.5	8.0	....	1.4
(seats)	(29)	(26)	(4)	(0)	(0)
1984	43.7	40.0	6.1	9.2	0.4
(seats)	(27)	(24)	(3)	(5)	(0)
1989	40.5	33.5	7.5	11.9	6.1
(seats)	(26)	(21)	(5)	(7)	(0)

Source: Ausschuß Wahlforschung 1987:151; Stadtverwaltung Mainz

However, the electoral data presented in Table 8.2 suggest that the success of the Greens in the 1984 local election resulted more from the low electoral turnout than from a positive expression of support for the Greens' programme. Although a large number of Mainz voters were undoubtedly tempted to vote Green in order to articulate their opposition to the continuation of the Mainz Model, described in Chapter 7, the Green Party's level of support in the 1984 local election was not significantly greater than it had been in previous elections. When treated as a proportion of the entire electorate, for example, the Green vote of 6.4 per cent in this election was not much different from that recorded at earlier federal and regional elections.

Table 8.2 Green Electoral Participation Mainz, 1979–1991

Election	Votes	in %	as % of electorate
EW 1979	2,767	3.1	2.3
BW 1980	1,878	1.8	1.6
BW 1983	7,518	6.9	6.1
LW 1983	7,053	6.5	5.8
EW 1984	8,417	9.7	6.7
KW 1984	7,959	9.2	6.4
BW 1987	14,557	13.2	11.1
LW 1987	9,949	10.1	7.6
EW 1989	11,814	12.5	8.9
BW 1990	7,562	7.1	5.6
LW 1991	10,727	11.4	8.0

Source: Amt für Statistik und Stadtentwicklung Mainz
BW – Federal elections: EW – European elections
KW – Local elections; LW – Regional elections

Table 8.3 Mainz: Party Support by Age Groups, 1979–1984

Election year/age groups	SPD	CDU	FDP	Greens
1984				
18–24	44.4	28.1	5.1	22.3
25–34	42.2	27.7	4.3	24.5
35–44	44.2	38.7	7.1	9.3
45–59	45.6	41.0	9.0	3.9
60 and above	42.9	48.5	6.0	2.0
All ages	43.9	39.8	6.7	9.0
Change 1979–1984				
18–24	–4.7	–6.1	–5.3	22.3
25–34	–14.0	–4.7	–5.1	24.5
35–44	–2.0	–4.6	–3.0	9.3
45–59	–3.9	–1.3	0.7	3.9
60 and above	–3.7	2.3	–0.2	2.0
All ages	–5.1	–1.7	–1.6	9.0

Source: Mainz 1984

Table 8.4 Mainz: Party Support in City Boroughs, Local Election 1984

City Borough	SPD		CDU		FDP		Greens	
	1984	1979–84	1984	1979–84	1984	1979–84	1984	1979–84
Alstadt-Süd	40.4	-4.6	46.7	-1.3	3.6	-1.2	8.7	8.7
Alstadt-Nord	47.1	-4.7	37.0	-3.2	4.6	-2.0	10.5	10.5
Neustadt-Süd	47.8	-4.9	36.4	-2.9	4.4	-1.7	10.3	10.3
Neustadt-Nord	59.8	-1.6	28.6	-3.5	2.5	-2.1	8.4	8.4
Oberstadt-Süd	41.4	-3.2	42.3	-1.9	7.7	-2.2	8.3	8.3
Oberstadt-West	46.7	-2.2	38.0	-3.9	5.3	-2.2	9.5	9.5
Wallstraße	43.2	-4.0	41.1	-1.5	5.2	-3.6	10.2	10.2
Mombach	47.5	-2.7	39.6	-1.9	4.4	-2.5	8.0	8.0
Gosenheim	38.6	-4.0	44.2	-3.2	6.3	-2.5	10.6	10.6
Finthen	40.3	-5.0	42.0	-1.5	9.2	-0.7	8.2	8.2
Bretzenheim	42.4	-4.1	40.3	-3.0	6.8	-1.9	9.9	9.9
Marienborn	47.5	-1.6	38.4	-4.7	4.2	-2.1	9.7	9.7
Lerchenberg	41.2	-5.5	35.9	-2.7	12.0	-1.5	10.7	10.7
Drais	31.0	-3.5	43.8	-8.6	15.5	2.6	9.5	9.5
Hechtsheim	37.6	-5.0	47.5	-1.5	5.7	-1.7	9.0	9.0
Ebersheim	33.2	-2.4	53.9	-4.3	5.3	-0.5	7.4	7.4
Weisenau	52.2	-4.4	35.3	-1.1	5.1	-1.0	7.2	7.2
Laubenheim	41.3	-7.1	41.3	5.0	8.6	-5.6	8.7	8.7
Mainz	43.7	-4.4	40.4	-2.1	6.1	-1.9	9.2	9.2

Source: Amt für Statistik und Stadtentwicklung Mainz

The structure of Green Party support in the 1984 local election in Mainz corresponds fully with that outlined in Chapter 4 with regard to other German towns and cities. The highest levels of Green support were recorded amongst the youngest age-cohorts (Table 8.3). The heavy losses of the SPD in the 25–35 age-group (-14 per cent) suggest that this party was most acutely affected by the Green candidature. However, a comparison of the representative electoral statistics for the 1984 and 1979 local elections indicates that the Greens gained the support of former voters of each of the established parties in Mainz (Mainz 1984b). This finding is supported by a more localised analysis of the results of the 1984 local election in Mainz. In only two Mainz boroughs could any of the three established political parties increase their 1979 proportion of the vote, whilst the Greens gained votes throughout the city (Table 8.4). The SPD lost support in every one of Mainz's eighteen boroughs, and the CDU and FDP increased their share of the vote in just one borough each.

Table 8.4 shows no clear correlation between Green gains and the losses of any one of the established political parties. The Green Party vote was well below average in the SPD strongholds of Neustadt-Nord, Weisenau and Mombach and in the CDU stronghold of Ebersheim. With regard to FDP support, the Greens did well in the Lerchenberg borough, in which the FDP recorded its highest proportion of the vote, but also in Altstadt-Nord, in which FDP support was below average. The major factors which appear to have influenced the level of Green support in the various boroughs stem from the boroughs' unique social structures (see Köth and Kolmer 1983:19; Erfurth-Hirtz 1985). The Greens performed best in Mainz's middle-class suburbs (Lerchenberg, Gonsenheim) and in more central districts characterised by the presence of cheaper forms of housing (Neustadt-Süd, Altstadt-Nord). However, in the working-class suburbs of Mombach and Weisenau the Green vote was below average. This also ties in with social ecological analyses of local voting behaviour (see Chapter 4).

For an understanding of the development of the local party system in the period following the 1984 election, it is essential to stress the implications of the new political constellation brought about by the vote. As the largest party on the Mainz city council, the SPD had previously depended upon the support of the

Christian Democrats to guarantee their prime position. To rely on the support of the small FDP council group was regarded by the right-wing majority in the SPD as introducing an unnecessary element of uncertainty into council proceedings. This derived from the traditionally weak cohesiveness of the SPD council group. Since the first members of the SPD youth wing (*Jusos*) gained council representation in 1974 there had been an element of inner-party opposition to the continuation of the Mainz Model. However, as long as there was no suitable alternative coalition partner, the *Jusos* were unable to break the long-established link with the CDU. In 1984 a new choice was opened up to the SPD by the election of the Greens. Together the SPD and the Greens could technically have exercised control over the development of local policy in Mainz for the duration of the 1984–9 legislative period. For the SPD left wing this possibility presented a seemingly ideal opportunity of separating the two major parties on the city council once and for all.

The fact that the SPD and the Green Party ultimately failed to reach agreement in Mainz over the adoption of a common strategy for the period under review requires closer attention. In the following section a number of possible reasons for the failure of a potential red–green alliance in Mainz will be cited. In particular, it will be argued that the Old Politics predispositions of the majority of SPD councillors in Mainz could not be reconciled with the New Politics approach of the city's Green council group. However, it will also be suggested that the manner in which the Greens sought to participate in local political affairs between 1984 and 1987 reduced the effectiveness of their work in the council chamber.

The Greens and the SPD in Mainz

A contrast was drawn in Chapter 3 between the ideal-typical New Local Politics approach of the Greens and the Old Local Politics approach which has characterised German politics at local level in the past. Three main sources of potential conflict arising from a realignment along a New–Old Local Politics dimension were identified. These exist in the competing styles of the Greens and the established political parties at local level, in differing interpretations of the scope of Article 28.2 of the Basic Law and in contrasting views held of democratic decision-making structures. A further conflict in terms of competing agendas will be discussed in Chapters 9 and 10 below. In charting the course of the relationship between the Greens and the SPD in Mainz in the three years following the Greens' election to the city council in 1984, the contrasting styles of the New and Old Local Politics approaches are to be brought to the fore. Two major questions pertaining to Green local politics will be broached. Firstly, attention will be drawn to the extent to which Green local politics gives rise to conflict as a result of its New Politics orientation. Secondly, light is to be cast upon the degree to which the parliamentary styles adopted by the Greens run counter to established, collegial forms of local political behaviour and result in a politicisation of all aspects of local council activity.

As previously discussed, a number of potential difficulties exist with regard to the operationalisation of the New Politics model at local level. In particular, a fault with existing research on the New Politics is its tendency to treat political parties as homogeneous bodies, representing either a New Politics or an Old Politics dimension. In this sense it would be wrong simply to categorise the Greens as a New Politics party, given their heterogeneous nature and strength of the internal divisions between competing factions. Instead, there is a need to locate the various Green factions on the New–Old Politics dimension. On the one hand, the fundamentalist wing represents the extreme example of a New Politics grouping, rejecting any form of cooperation with established political forces and laying emphasis upon the adoption of radical democratic organisational structures. On the other, the realist faction should be perceived in terms of its more moderate New Politics approach, favouring alliances with other political parties and encouraging the adoption of representative democratic structures.

When examining the relationship between the Greens and the SPD in Mainz, the role played by factions in both parties is crucial. Attention has already been drawn to divisions within the Mainz SPD. Significantly, the Mainz Greens were also divided, essentially between its realist and fundamentalist (mainly *Öko-Sozialisten*) wings. It can be anticipated that such divisions would influence to a greater or lesser extent the course of the red–green debate in the city's local politics. In Mainz, the most stark political contrast could be expected to exist between the New Politics-oriented fundamentalist wing of the Greens and the Old Politics-oriented right wing of the SPD. Conversely, the most likely sources of support for the creation of a red–green alliance in Mainz would exist in the more moderate realist faction of the Greens and the New Politics-oriented left wing of the SPD. The fact that the latter groups were in the minority in their respective parties between 1984 and 1987 did not bode well for the establishment of an alliance between the Greens and the SPD on the Mainz city council.

This provides the background to a discussion of political events in Mainz between June 1984 and July 1987. Three distinct phases in the relationship between the Greens and the SPD can be discerned. In Phase One, the opening stages of the relationship will be addressed. Phase Two encompasses the key turning-point in the red–green debate in Mainz, the passing of the city budget in the winter of 1985/6. The inability of the two parties to reach agreement on this major policy area led to the re-establishment of the Mainz Model and the exclusion of the Greens from positions of authority for the remainder of the legislative period. Finally, Phase Three was characterised by the effects of the collapse of a potential alliance between the Greens and the SPD.

Phase One: The Developing Relationship

During the first year of Green council representation in Mainz, the city's various political forces sought to define their positions with regard to the major local political issues. Above all, this entailed a clarification of the relationship between the Greens and the SPD, since the respective strategies of the CDU and FDP council groups required little modification in the newly convened council. Having lost both electoral support and council seats, the aim of both the CDU and FDP was primarily to ensure the stability of the *Mainzer Modell* and thereby secure the continuation of their influence upon the development of Mainz's local politics.

The problems faced by the SPD and Greens were of a different nature to those of the Christian and Free Democrats. A stable alternative to the established parties' Grand Coalition could only be found in the creation of a red–green alliance in Mainz. However, for such an alliance to come about, it would be necessary to overcome significant internal opposition in both the Green Party and the SPD to the adoption of a joint strategy. In this respect, it should be recognised that the main strategic function of any local political alliance must be to reach consensus on two areas of overriding significance: the selection of personnel to fill council executive positions and the passing of the city budget (Naß-macher 1989). For any alliance between the Greens and the SPD in Mainz to be successful, these two issues would have to be tackled to the parties' mutual satisfaction.

Even in the early months of the new legislative period, the extent to which the Greens and the SPD were at cross purposes with regard to the formulation of a joint strategy on both policy and personnel matters was evident. Whilst the Greens were most keen to reach agreement on policy issues, the SPD was primarily interested in establishing a consensus on personnel matters. This fundamental divergence in the aims of the two parties dictated the development of the subsequent relationship between the Greens and the SPD. On the one hand, the Greens were only willing to discuss personnel issues within the framework of a common programme, totally rejecting any participation of their own in the council executive. On the other, despite the SPD's willingness to discuss policy matters on a one-off basis, it would only do so if such discussion did not impinge upon decisions regarding the appointment of council executive personnel. Indeed, a fateful resolution passed by an SPD party general meeting held in Mainz in October 1984 expressly restricted the room for manoeuvre of the party's council group. At this meeting it was resolved that the priorities for the party's council group in the new legislative period would be to ensure the succession of an SPD mayor upon the retirement of Mayor Jockel Fuchs, to guarantee the maintenance of an SPD majority in the council executive, to stick to agreements made with parties before the 1984 local election and to seek to implement a maximum number of SPD policies without entering into talks with any other party over a common programme. The course of events during the first nine months of the new council period demonstrated the effect of such contrasting strategies upon the development of Mainz's local politics in the first phase of this analysis. Whilst the SPD and Greens managed to reach agreement on limited aspects of policy on an *ad hoc* basis, it proved impossible to agree upon a common strategy in more significant areas.

The first signs of attempted agreement between the Greens and the SPD came at the neighbourhood council level. In the most populous Mainz borough (Gonsenheim), for example, the SPD and Greens jointly agreed on the election of an SPD *Ortsvorsteher* (chairman of the neighbourhood council). The local election of 1984 gave the Greens the balance of power in this borough, allowing agreement to be reached without much controversy emerging on either side following a series of public meetings. In hindsight, the course of this loose alliance should have alerted the Greens to the SPD's local strategy. Having secured the election of their representative to local office, the SPD in Gonsenheim allowed the alliance with the Greens to fade into disuse. As Green councillor Günter Beck wrote about the arrangement with the Gonsenheim SPD in an (undated) report: '... in the last two years we've often had to struggle with the SPD and constantly insist upon their keeping to the agreement'. The experience of this alliance served to reinforce the attitude of Green fundamentalists towards the SPD, given an absence of positive achievements. However, the modest budget of the neighbourhood council and its limited competences ensured that the first red–green alliance in Mainz aroused little attention beyond the boundaries of the relevant borough.

In the city council, agreement was reached in principle between the SPD and Greens on various important policy measures. The declaration of Mainz as a nuclear-free zone resulted from a joint initiative of the parties. Both parties were also able to back the introduction of a new transport policy for the city, which laid more emphasis upon public rather than upon private means of transport; and backing was also given to the establishment of a partnership link with the Nicaraguan town of Diriamba. Yet the first real test of a potential red–green alliance in Mainz as a whole came in a different policy area, when the need arose to pass a supplementary budget (*Nachtragshaushalt*) in the autumn of 1984. A series of meetings took place in which the

147

Greens and SPD discussed making changes to the existing budget. After an initial meeting, the SPD indicated their intent to make changes to the budget in key policy areas, thus laying the foundation for a joint agreement on the 1986/7 dual budget: 'There can and should be no question of changing the entire structure of the existing budget, but rather – against the background of an as yet unclarified financial scope – to facilitate the making of necessary changes or to lay the foundations for the 1986/87 dual budget.'[1] However, a number of barriers to a potential agreement between the Greens and the SPD existed. Above all, fundamentalists were in full control of the Green Party organisation in Mainz. Extracts from a discussion paper prepared for a meeting of the Mainz Green Party by councillor Alf Haenlein serve to illustrate the gulf which existed between the approaches of the two parties:

> The suggestion to submit a supplementary budget ... could have come from any of the parties in the council. The only thing which matters is the policy content. ... The SPD policy of 'changing majorities' should not be tolerated by us. Collaboration on certain points should only come into question if, for the entire electoral period, there really are no policy measures which are forced through by the SPD with the help of the bourgeois parties and which contradict Green local politics.[2]

In general, the fundamentalist critique sought to emphasise the similarities between the established parties rather than to differentiate between the SPD on the one hand and the CDU and FDP on the other. According to Haenlein, any agreement between the Greens and the Social Democrats on a joint strategy could only be reached if the SPD withdrew from the Mainz Model once and for all: 'We have to make it clear to the SPD that there can be no continuation of the old policies with the Greens. We have to make it clear that we will not allow ourselves to be treated as an "Eco-FDP".'[3]

---

[1] Letter to Green council group from SPD council group leader Eckhard Pick, dated 5 September 1984.

[2] Extracted from discussion paper entitled *Mainzer Modell, Umweltdezernat, SPD-Gespräch und Nachtragshaushalt*, prepared by councillor Alf Haenlein for Mainz Green Party meeting on 22 September 1984.

[3] Extracted from follow-up paper to that cited in previous note, prepared by councillor Alf Haenlein for Mainz Green Party meeting on 4 October 1984.

As a result of the internal discussion over the supplementary budget, the Green Party resolved at a party meeting on 4 October 1984 to enter into talks with the SPD only on condition that the Social Democrats declined to elect CDU or FDP members to the council executive. Given the unlikelihood of such a concession's being wrung from the SPD, the Greens also decided to put forward their own budget. However, by the time this had been achieved, the SPD had sought and secured backing for their own supplementary budget in the council meeting of 12 December 1984, and the Greens lost a key opportunity to influence subsequent local political developments in Mainz.

During this first phase of Green involvement in Mainz's local politics discussions with the SPD on policy matters were possible. However, given the conflicting strategies outlined above, it was not surprising that the most serious conflicts between the two parties emerged with regard to personnel matters in respect of the appointment of new members to the council executive committee (*Stadtvorstand*), the composition of which is stipulated in the city's governing statutes. In addition to the city mayor, this committee comprises five full-time executive members and two honorary members (see Hess and Hundertmark 1987). As has been previously noted, the foundation of the Mainz Model existed in the distribution of these executive positions according to the relative strengths of the parties represented in the council chamber. The Greens' aim of bringing about the end of the Mainz Model could only be achieved by securing the withdrawal of the SPD from the established consensus of over thirty years' standing. In this major respect, the SPD majority proved unwilling to abandon its adherence to the tradition of a consensus-oriented local politics. Instead, the Social Democrats set store by keeping to the agreements made with the other established parties on personnel matters before the 1984 local election. The debate over the election of a CDU representative, Josef Hofmann, to the position of honorary executive member in February 1985 was indicative of the gulf which existed between the Green and SPD strategies. The course of the discussion is presented here as a means of symbolising the contrasting approaches and styles of the Greens and the established parties in Mainz.

The Christian Democrats had made it clear to the SPD that support for their candidate for the executive post was vital for the continuation of CDU cooperation in the executive committee. Despite the opposition of ten left-wing SPD councillors, the inner-party majority was unwilling to resist the CDU's demands. The fact that the SPD felt obliged to concede to the CDU request on this occasion presented the most obvious indication that the SPD was unwilling to relinquish its adherence to the Mainz Model. A certain poignancy was added to the heated discussion in the council session of 26 February 1985 by the fact that the council had voted unanimously to keep the position vacant shortly after the 1984 local election. Extracts from the minutes of the relevant council meeting illustrate the fundamental differences which characterised the approaches of the Greens and the representatives of the other political parties in Mainz. In justifying their support for the CDU candidate, SPD council group leader Eckhard Pick cited the three main reasons for the party's strategy. Firstly, the CDU's decision to support the SPD nominee for the position of mayor upon the retirement from office of Mayor Fuchs was regarded as guaranteeing: 'for us a maximum amount of freedom to reach a decision. The SPD can choose its candidate in peace and composure without external pressures.' Secondly, Pick pointed out that no fixed agreements had been made with regard to policy matters: 'As before, the SPD can continue to follow its own, independent policy line on the basis of its manifesto.' Finally, the question of possible alternatives was addressed. Without specifically mentioning the Greens, Pick suggested that the failure of the SPD to support the CDU candidate would lead to a political crisis in Mainz: 'Bearing in mind the statements of the CDU, any other decision would have led to a serious political crisis in Mainz with risks which cannot be overlooked' (Council minutes, 26 February 1985).

The election of the CDU candidate presented an ideal opportunity for the Greens to express their opposition to the established practices of Mainz's local politics. A contribution criticising both the CDU and SPD was made by Councillor Haenlein. First the CDU was addressed: 'Not once have you managed to pluck up the courage to be an opposition. You have always wormed your way into power through the Mainz Model, this infamous all-party coalition. ... Executive positions are allocated like the sinecures of the Middle Ages ...'. Haenlein followed this critique of the role of the CDU with a direct criticism of the strategy of the SPD and the speech of SPD group leader Pick:

... in reality the SPD can be blackmailed. ... What you are doing in the all-party coalition is continuing to falsify the electorate's wishes. For decades you have been voting yourselves and each other back into office, without taking the person into account and without any public discussions having taken place. ... It's a good job that the Greens are here now. Now the atmosphere has changed. We have talked a lot about how we should act in the future, and it will largely depend upon the course of today's events. We have a very ambivalent attitude towards the work in this council; we stand outside the ruling club and don't wish to be in the ruling club (Council minutes, 26 February 1985).

In the ensuing debate Councillor Haenlein clashed on a number of occasions with Mayor Fuchs over the Greens' assessment of Mainz's recent political history, leading to a closing of the SPD ranks around their mayor and the delivery of the following personal statement by Councillor Pick on behalf of the SPD council group:

I would like to stress that I find the way in which the mayor as a person has been disparaged in the Greens' contributions intolerable. I think it is unacceptable that a personality who for more than twenty years has influenced and determined this city's politics and the policies for its citizens is belittled in this manner. I believe that it does not correspond to the established style of this chamber that one treats one's political opponents in this way. ... A new style now appears to have entered into this chamber, which apparently derives from a particular tendency within the Greens, namely that of believing that they have a monopoly on the sole truth (Council minutes, 26 February 1985).

For the fundamentalist majority within the Greens, the discussion about the election of Dr Hofmann to the council executive served to confirm their suspicions (and hopes) that the SPD was unwilling to break with tradition. In effect, they succeeded in their aim of manoeuvring the party into the political sidelines, as regards key decisions over personnel matters. The only points on which agreement could now be sought with the SPD were linked to policy issues. Similarly, the forces within the SPD most strongly opposed to any form of alliance with the Greens were also strengthened by the events of February 1985. A joint statement by Mayor Fuchs, SPD council group leader Pick and local party chairman Anton Diehl reaffirmed the party majorify's belief that no agreement could be reached with the Greens: 'Whoever dismisses the successes of local politics in Mainz during the past decades and in particular the achievements of SPD mayors and SPD council groups in a subjective and defamatory manner, as the Greens did in the council meeting, puts him- or herself into the political sidelines.'[4]

By illustrating the course of this particular debate in some detail, it is possible to demonstrate the gap which had to be overcome, were the Greens and the SPD to reach agreement over the dual budget for 1986/7 in the autumn of 1985. In this respect, the ten SPD councillors who abstained from the vote over the election of a new executive member occupied a key role. For a consensus to be established, the balance of power within the respective party organisations would have to change in favour of the more moderate forces. Indeed, a number of important political events beyond the boundaries of Mainz served to slightly alter the balance in favour of an agreement between the SPD and the Greens. In March 1985, for example, the local elections in the neighbouring state of Hesse had led to the creation of a number of red–green alliances in its local communities (Bullmann 1987; Scharf 1989). Of particular relevance for Mainz was the election result in Wiesbaden. In the Hessian state capital, CDU Mayor Jentsch was voted out of office by a red–green majority and replaced with SPD nominee Achim Exner. Whilst the Mainz Greens sought to avoid participation in the council executive, the Wiesbaden Greens assumed executive responsibility for the development of the city's cultural policy. The existence of a series of local red–green alliances in Hesse represented a significant factor behind the establishment of Germany's first ever red–green coalition at regional level (see Scharf 1989). The gradual shift within the Green Party at all political levels towards a more realistic position and thereby towards the adoption of the red–green strategy was further encouraged in early 1985 by the result of two regional elections. The poor showing of the ecologists in the Saarland and North Rhine Westphalia was directly attributed to the fundamentalist stances adopted by the Green Party organisations in the two states (Kimmel 1985; Feist and Krieger 1985).

---

[4] Extracted from a joint statement on the executive election and the situation of the Mainz SPD, March 1985.

However, despite the fact that the general political context tended to favour the establishment of an alliance between the Greens and the SPD in Mainz, the heated discussions about the election of the new executive member served to demonstrate the gulf to be overcome were the 1985 budget talks to succeed.

Phase Two: The 1986/7 Budget Debate

This section perhaps more than any other addresses the extent to which the New Local Politics of the Mainz Greens conflicted with the traditional local political approach of the majority of the city's SPD council group. The analysis illustrates the conflicting styles and approaches adopted by the parties during the debate over the 1986/7 dual budget (*Doppelhaushalt*). The outcome of this debate played a significant role in the subsequent development of the Mainz party system, influencing all future personnel and policy matters in the local council.

The official inner-party debate over the 1986/7 budget began for the Greens in March 1985, a full nine months before the council meeting at which it was to be passed. Such was the importance accorded to the discussion, that this represented one of the few occasions during the period under analysis on which the Greens' council working group (*Fraktionsgruppe*) regularly carried local political matters into the meetings of the local party organisation. In a series of meetings of both the *Fraktionsgruppe* and the party membership, the Greens sought to clarify the strategy to be adopted in the talks envisaged with the SPD. Despite the repeated misgivings of party realists, the Greens opted to enter into discussion with the Social Democrats over a list of minimum demands, which would have to be accommodated were Green support for the budget to be forthcoming.[5]

It might appear surprising to onlookers that such a strategy could be adopted by the Mainz Greens, given its unmistakable similarity with that practised so unsuccessfully by the *Grün-Alternative-Liste* (GAL) in Hamburg in their talks with the SPD in the summer of 1982 (see Beyer 1983:36f.; Grupp 1986). In

---

[5] The minutes of a meeting of the Green *Fraktionsgruppe* on 29 July 1985, for example, identify conflicting views within the Greens about the concept of a list of minimum demands.

Hamburg the Greens' utopian demands could not be reconciled with the SPD's more moderate stance, ultimately leading to the holding of new regional elections and a sharp decline in the Green vote (Müller-Rommel 1983b). An explanation of the tactics adopted by the Mainz Greens can be found in the prominent position held within the local party organisation by a small group of *Öko-Sozialisten*, whose regional stronghold was to be found in Hamburg (see Ebermann and Trampert 1985). The tactics favoured by this inner-party faction are not significantly different to those of the more radical fundamentalists (see Murphy and Roth 1987).

With regard to the budget discussion in Mainz, a wide range of possible minimum demands were initially raised by local Green Party members and councillors. Under discussion were such topics as the refusal to grant additional land for (US) military purposes, a rejection of city involvement in new media technologies (cable and satellite television), a de-privatisation of certain local services, an increase in local business taxation, a ban on the construction of additional car parks in the city centre, a freezing of electricity prices for domestic users, a guaranteeing of the future of cultural facilities and a general increase in the proportion of the city budget set aside for environmental and social purposes. However, not only budgetary matters were of interest to the Greens. A unanimously agreed resolution at the local party meeting of 2 May 1985 outlined the Greens' aim to link budget discussions to a broader political context:

> The party general meeting notes that agreement to a city's budgetary statutes ... always represents a form of long-term cooperation with other city council groups. However, this situation demands the incorporation of the budgetary statutes into a political framework, which in other important social and ecological questions must allow the attainment of a minimal consensus; i.e. a precondition of the Greens' approval of the dual budget 86/87 is that resolutions are made on other political issues which we can support.

In the ensuing weeks, the Greens devoted their energies to resolving internal differences of opinion over the approach to be adopted and to clarifying the demands to be regarded as the minimum platform. In a meeting of the *Fraktionsgruppe* on 26 August 1985 sharp differences of opinion were evident over the manner in which the Greens should pursue their budgetary demands. Such differences were then masked over in a press statement, issued on 30 August 1985, in which the *Fraktions-gruppe* finally published a list of minimum demands, covering the five key areas of social policy, energy and the environment, women, peace issues and cultural policy. In order to avoid increasing the city's debt burden, all necessary expenditure increases arising from the Greens' proposals were to be met by a substantial rise in the rate of the local business tax.

The catalogue of demands provided a basis on which the Greens then sought talks with the SPD council group.[6] Following the failure of initial talks in October, the first real discussions between the relevant parties occurred in November 1985, at the Greens' invitation. In a letter to the SPD council group, the Greens outlined the subject areas to be discussed and the manner in which the talks were to be conducted. Working groups, meeting in public, were to be formed on the respective subject areas and to be given the task of resolving any differences of opinion: 'We assume that minutes of the talks in the respective working groups will be written, which should be checked and signed by representatives of the council groups. The results of the working groups should then be discussed and agreed upon in an open meeting of both council groups.'[7]

That any discussions occurred at all between the Greens and the SPD in Mainz represented a major victory for the left wing of the city's SPD. They had succeeded in persuading party right-wingers, including key members of the council executive, that the Greens should at least be regarded as a possible alternative to the party's continued reliance upon the CDU and FDP. Even before discussions began, it was evident that the forces opposed to a possible red–green budget were in a majority in both party organisations, and that any failure to reach agreement would not be regarded unfavourably by Green fundamentalists or SPD right-wingers. Nevertheless, meetings were held between the Greens and the SPD, although agreement could not be reached on the Greens' key demands. From an SPD point of view, the previously cited party resolution of October 1984, in which the creation of an alliance with another party and

---

[6] Letter from Green *Fraktion* to SPD council group, dated 19 September 1985.
[7] Letter from Green *Fraktion* to SPD council group, dated 6 November 1985.

agreement upon policy matters were rejected, offered ample justification for their refusal to follow the Greens' approach to the discussions. Moreover, the fact that there was still no consensus within the Green *Fraktionsgruppe* over the manner in which their aims were to be achieved, made internal discussions increasingly fraught. The Greens repeatedly changed their negotiating stance. At a meeting of the group on 14 October 1985, for example, two broad strategies were identified: '... one side wants to negotiate with the SPD for as long as possible, the other side only wants to negotiate if the SPD signals its willingness to consider seriously our principal demands.'[8]

With time for further deliberation running out, both sides became increasingly frustrated with the course of their discussions. The prevailing mood was not helped by persistent rumours that the SPD and CDU had already agreed a common budget in secret. In a letter of 5 September 1985 from Gerold Brand to Green Party colleagues, the implications of such a secret arrangement between the two largest council groups were outlined: 'If this is the case, we must recognise that for the next two years at least there will be little opportunity of changing things by parliamentary means.' Feeling that the SPD had not moved far enough to accommodate their minimum demands, the Greens' stance gradually shifted to a more radical, fundamentalist position. This was represented in their decision to press for a one-month postponement of the council meetings in which the budget was to be passed. The aim of the Greens was to allow additional time for further deliberation, and in a final, key meeting between the Greens and the SPD prior to the introduction of the budget on 4 December 1985, the Green delegation acted upon the following resolution of the *Fraktionsgruppe*:

> We demand that the council meetings regarding the dual budget be postponed until January.
>
> If the SPD suggests that the council meetings be postponed for one week, we will accept this compromise.
>
> If the SPD is neither prepared to postpone until January nor suggests postponing for one week, we will listen to the SPD's offers without

[8] From minutes of meeting of Green *Fraktionsgruppe*, held on 14 October 1985.

comment and then leave. Under no circumstances are negotiations to occur prior to the council meeting.[9]

Whilst agreement was reached in principle on a number of the Greens' minimum demands, the SPD was unwilling to allow additional time for discussion on the formal grounds that this would cause difficulties for the city's administration and that its councillors might not be available for later council sessions:

> The administration must be put in a position in which they can grant contracts as quickly as possible to craftsmen and the middle class. They can only do this after the publication and ensuing legal validation of the budget.

> Many members of our council group have set their minds on the dates of the tenth and eleventh of December 1985. The full presence of the council group could not be guaranteed with a postponement.[10]

Instead of addressing outstanding policy differences, the debate between the Greens and the SPD therefore degenerated into a discussion about the timing of the passing of the budget. The underlying conflicting approaches of the two parties could no longer be reconciled. On the one hand, the Greens insisted that all policy difficulties would have to be ironed out before they could give their consent to a joint budget. On the other, the SPD felt that they had conceded enough to the Greens and set great store by the fact that the budget agreed so far would establish a framework within which policy changes along the Greens' lines would be possible. Such conflicting approaches could not be reconciled in time for the vital council session of 10 December 1985. Nevertheless, the SPD still operated under the illusion that, even if the Greens did not vote in favour of the budget, they would not vote against it, since a number of the Greens' demands were met in it. By abstaining, the Greens would have allowed the budget to be passed with the casting vote of Mayor Fuchs.[11] This represented a serious error of judgement on the

---

[9] Resolution passed by Green *Fraktionsgruppe* on 2 December 1985.

[10] Letter from SPD council group leader Eckhard Pick to Green *Fraktion* dated 5 December 1985.

[11] Some Green councillors argued unsuccessfully for an abstention in the budget debate during a meeting of the party's *Fraktionsgruppe* on 9 December 1985. With twenty-seven SPD councillors facing twenty-four CDU and three FDP councillors, the mayor's casting vote would then have been decisive.

part of the Mainz SPD, particularly when one considers that the Greens had passed the following resolution at their party meeting only the week before: 'The Greens can only vote in favour of the dual budget if the decision is postponed. If a postponement of the dual budget is still possible in December, an extraordinary general meeting of the party after the completion of negotiations with the SPD will determine the way in which the Greens are to vote in the council.'[12] As a result, it was evident that the only logical course of action for the Greens in the budget debate on 10 December 1985 was to reject the SPD's proposed budget. However, the fact that the Greens did not abstain in the budgetary debate still came as a shock to a number of political commentators in Mainz.

The ensuing change in mood of the SPD with regard to the Greens can be directly attributed to the two parties' inability to reach agreement over the budget. For the SPD's left wing in particular, the budget debate represented a serious set-back. In a letter to the Greens, SPD council group leader Pick expressed his disappointment with the Greens' behaviour, suggesting that the gulf between the two parties was not actually as great as was perceived by the Greens: 'A result was reached in our deliberations ... which, in our view, pointed to the beginning of new paths and priorities.'[13] From December 1985, the right-wing majority in the SPD was able to reassert its control over future discussions with the Greens, and even the most ardent supporters of a red–green strategy were forced to recognise the weakness of their case. Even realists within the Green *Fraktionsgruppe*, who appreciated the relevance of the SPD's decision to enter into talks with the Greens in the first place, argued in vain for a greater degree of flexibility in any future discussions with the SPD.[14]

Bearing in mind the loss of trust which resulted from the collapse of budget negotiations, it appeared increasingly likely that

[12] Resolution passed by Mainz Green Party on 6 December 1985. In a letter to the SPD council group of the same date, the Greens emphasised that they would vote against any budget which did not meet their demands.

[13] Letter from SPD council group leader Eckhard Pick to Green *Fraktion*, dated 18 December 1985.

[14] The minutes of a meeting of the Green *Fraktionsgruppe* on 16 December 1985 illustrate a growing divide between realists and fundamentalists within the group.

all future attempts to reach agreement over a new budget in the New Year would be doomed to fail. The SPD's insistence that the budget presented on 10 December 1985 represented the maximum to which they were prepared to agree characterised all further discussions with the Greens. Meetings held in January 1986 ended without agreement, whilst sessions of expert working groups on social and environmental themes failed to bridge the growing divide. Finally, a meeting of the Mainz Green Party rejected by a slender majority the existing state of agreements between the SPD and Greens and insisted that further significant concessions with regard to the party's initial minimum demands be sought from the SPD. As a direct result of this party meeting, the Social Democrats gave up all hope of reaching an agreement with the Greens. In a letter, dated 14 January 1986, SPD council group leader Pick formally informed the Greens that they were not willing to make any additional changes to the initially submitted budget: 'I would like to inform you that the SPD council group has taken note of the talks with you and has lately reaffirmed its view that no changes to the budget and employment plans introduced on 10 December 1985 can be accepted.' This opened the way for the passing of a budget with the CDU. The depth of disillusionment with the Greens was expressed by the fact that only four of the twenty-seven SPD councillors continued to support the holding of further talks with the Greens (*Tageszeitung* 17.01.86).

In the debate over the 1986/7 budget, the conflicting approaches of the Greens and the SPD with regard to local political activity are to be clearly seen. Whilst agreement was possible on limited policy areas, irreconcilable differences in style ultimately led to the collapse of negotiations. One SPD councillor summed up the contrasting approaches in an interview conducted some months later: 'The particular difficulty of negotiating with the Greens is that one can never know the composition of the Green's next party general meeting or which decisions it will make. On the other hand, the CDU can always rely on the fact that the SPD can be pressurized into reaching agreements which contradict their own programmes and decisions.'[15] The conflict

[15] Interview with SPD councillor Gabriela Wenke in *AMiGa, Rundbrief der SPD Ortsvereine Mainz Altstadt, Mitte, Gartenfeld*, No. 1, 1988.

between the two factions most divided along the New–Old Politics continuum, the Green fundamentalists and the SPD right wing, ultimately led to the collapse of the talks. However, for the Greens, the result of the failure to agree upon the 1986/7 budget was much worse than for the SPD, serving to restrict their future involvement in the key decisions affecting Mainz's local politics for the remainder of the period under review. This will be addressed in the following section.

Phase Three: The Mainz Greens in Isolation

As has previously been discussed, the most important decision to be made by any local council in the Rhineland Palatinate concerns the appointment of the mayor (Naßmacher 1989). In the region's large cities the mayor holds a position of great authority, being elected for a period of ten years. After its deliberations over the 1986/7 budget, the attention of the Mainz city council was immediately diverted towards the impending need to choose a new mayor to replace Jockel Fuchs, whose maximum two-term period of office was coming to an end.

One of the major side-effects of the Greens' failure to agree a common platform with the SPD was their subsequent exclusion from any negotiations with regard to the choice of a candidate for mayor. An invitation from the SPD to participate in discussions on the subject was clearly a tactical manœuvre, which elicited the following response from the Greens:

> We were surprised by your offer of talks on the mayoral election. We are unable to imagine what in particular about this subject could be discussed between us, since we assume that all decisions regarding the matter· have been made and that the required majorities have already been secured several times over by your council group. In our view there is, therefore, little sense in having discussions about the formality of the mayor's election.[16]

The Greens' stance changed only partially in the months to come, when it became evident that the SPD was to be forced to make significant concessions to the CDU in return for the Christ-

[16] Letter from Green councillor Hans-Jörg von Berlepsch to SPD council group leader Eckhard Pick, dated 9 July 1986.

ian Democrats' agreement on SPD mayoral candidate Herman-Hartmut Weyel. In a meeting of the Mainz Green Party on 2 October 1986, two weeks before the designated election of the mayor, a resolution was passed which sought to enter into new negotiations with the SPD over policy matters. The resolution included a shift in the Greens' stance with regard to the occupation of executive positions: 'Should negotiations prove successful, the Greens declare their willingness to assume personnel responsibilities in the future.'[17] However, this shift in attitude was not significant, given the limited prospects of success for the Greens' strategy. Indeed, a curt response from the SPD to this particular Green offer demonstrated the extent to which the party had become excluded from the decision-making process in the city.

Nevertheless, a comparison of the course of the SPD–CDU negotiations over the election of the mayor and those of the SPD and Greens over the budget serves to illustrate once more the differences between the Old and New Local Politics approaches. Whilst the Greens were unable to gain significant concessions from the SPD with regard to their policy priorities, the CDU was much more successful. SPD hopes that their candidate would be supported unconditionally by the Mainz Christian Democrats, as agreed in the course of the debate over the election of Josef Hofmann to the executive in February 1985, were dashed. The CDU's strategy was made clear in a six-page letter from council group leader Heinz-Georg Diehl to the SPD *Fraktion* on 1 October 1986: 'Neither for the SPD nor for the CDU can it only be a matter of the filling of leading positions in the city administration. There must also be a willingness to share responsibilities over decisive questions for Mainz.' In this letter the CDU's own list of minimum demands was outlined. Not only was a significant shift in the SPD's stance with regard to important policy measures required, the CDU also sought to secure greater influence for itself upon personnel matters: 'In the context of next year's redistribution of administrative tasks, the CDU-run administrative divisions will be given two further areas of responsibility. In line with current practice, the SPD and CDU

---

[17] Resolution of Mainz Green Party, expressed in letter from Green *Fraktion* to SPD group leader Eckhard Pick, dated 6 October 1986.

will ensure the right to propose and provide mutual support with regard to the occupation of chairmanships of those companies closely linked to the city.'[18]

In the absence of practicable alternatives, the Mainz SPD ultimately felt obliged to agree in full to the CDU's demands. A statement by local party chairman Anton Diehl which sought to justify the SPD's decision to give in to the CDU stressed the lack of alternatives for the SPD: 'The council group saw no other realistic possibility of reaching agreement, not least because of the experience with the Greens during discussions over the dual budget of 1986/7.'[19] The fact that major concessions in both policy and personnel matters could be granted to the CDU, but not to the Greens is significant in terms of the debate over the conflicting approaches to local politics of the Greens and the established parties. It proved more straightforward for the right-wing SPD majority to reach agreement with the CDU in a manner to which they were accustomed, than to comply with the limited, albeit less conventional, demands of the Greens. The fact that a serious conflict developed within the Mainz SPD over the agreement with the CDU and resulted in the withdrawal of several party members from council-related duties was taken in the party's stride.[20] The main aim of the SPD had been achieved, namely the election of its candidate to the office of mayor. For the Greens, conciliation was sought in attempts to seek political gain from their declared oppositional stance. In a press release to mark the election of Weyel to mayor, the future role of the Greens was clarified:

> From now on the Green council group will, in ever clearer circumstances, provide the only alternative to the Mainz Model of the hobnobbing SPD/CDU. This means that:
> — the Greens will increasingly assume the role of legal representative for social and ecological interests.
> — the Greens will continually force the SPD to come clean on their policies in the city council.

[18] Both quotes extracted from letter sent by CDU group leader Heinz-Georg Diehl to SPD council group, dated 1 October 1986.

[19] Letter from Anton Diehl, chairman of SPD *Unterbezirk* Mainz, to party members, dated 22 October 1986.

[20] SPD councillor Claus Scharf resigned his positions on a number of council committees as a result of the concessions made to the CDU in a letter to Mayor Jockel Fuchs, dated 15 October 1986.

— the Greens will publicise the deceits of the SPD's electoral promises, especially in its transport, building and budgetary policies.[21]

In practice, as a result of the budget fiasco of the winter of 1985/6, the Greens had succeeded in manoeuvring themselves out of any position of influence with regard to subsequent decisions affecting Mainz.

The collapse of budget negotiations with the SPD also had a long-term impact upon the Greens' links with the city's extra-parliamentary initiatives. Although Mainz does not have a substantial alternative sector, the Greens set great store in the maintenance of links with the few organisations which were active in this area. Indeed, the idealised view of party fundamentalists still dictates that the Greens are the parliamentary arm of a movement which is essentially based outside the parliaments. However, as was the case in a number of other cities addressed in Chapter 5, the impetus for cooperation between the Mainz Greens and local initiative groups came most often from the Greens themselves. The failure to agree a budget with the SPD in the winter of 1985/6 marked the last opportunity for a number of projects to receive the necessary funding to implement their goals. This applied in particular to those measures agreed in principle with the SPD during negotiations over the budget, such as the funding of a town partnership between Mainz and Diriamba (Nicaragua) and of an experimental night-taxi service for women. As a result, the Greens' influence over the initiative groups declined and the council group was obliged to go to even greater lengths to maintain any sort of links at all. Consequently, the Mainz Greens were not only isolated in terms of their influence upon council politics by the end of the period under analysis, they were also increasingly isolated with regard to the extra-parliamentary groups from which they sought support.

Summary: Why the Red–Green Strategy Failed in Mainz

This chapter began with a discussion of the differences between the New Local Politics of the Greens and the Old Local Politics of

---

[21] Extracted from a Green council group press statement, entitled 'Weyel – now SPD or CDU city mayor?', dated 15 October 1986.

the established parties. Two suggestions were made. Firstly, it was held that local politics in Germany would become more conflictual as a result of the Greens' unique New Local Politics approach. Secondly, the argument was made that the parliamentary styles adopted by the Greens would run counter to traditional forms of local political behaviour, leading to a politicisation of all aspects of council activity. Both elements can be supported by an analysis of political events in Mainz between 1984 and 1987. With reference to the first suggestion, the course of the 1986/7 budget negotiations demonstrated that the Greens and the SPD were operating at cross purposes. The Greens' overriding interest was in the implementation of their policy proposals, whilst the SPD laid greatest emphasis upon the placement of party representatives in key executive positions. The existence of competing factions within both political parties did not help matters and served to heighten the divide along the New–Old Local Politics continuum. Such events in Mainz serve to symbolise the developing conflict between the New Local Politics approach of the Greens and the traditional, Old Local Politics stance of the SPD. The contrasting approaches of the Greens and the SPD could not be reconciled in this particular city and ultimately led to the collapse of a possible agreement between the parties.

Evidence was also provided to support the second suggestion that local politics in Germany has become more political since the emergence of the Greens at local level. The discussion of the election of new members to the council executive was indicative of the extent to which areas traditionally regarded as being uncontroversial became highly political following the election of the Greens to the Mainz city council. The Greens represented the most vocal source of opposition to the consensual practices which had characterised Mainz's local politics for the preceding thirty years. Whether this role actually benefited the Greens in terms of achieving their policy aims must be called into question, given that their activities were characterised by a growing isolation in the wake of the budget negotiations, both in parliamentary and extra-parliamentary terms.

9

A New Politics Agenda?: Analysis of Local Council Initiatives in Mainz

A discussion of the political developments in Mainz between 1984 and 1987 points towards the existence of a New Politics dimension in the local party system. In this chapter the discussion will be taken one stage further. Having demonstrated that the style of local politics has fundamentally changed in the period following the election of the Greens to the Mainz city council, it is now necessary to examine the content of local political debate during the same period. In this respect, two questions are to be addressed. Firstly, it has been suggested, on the basis of an analysis of the activities of Green council groups throughout the country, that the Greens have been responsible for a change in the agenda of Germany's local politics. Whether or not such a development represents the establishment of a New Politics dimension at local level needs to be investigated. It has been demonstrated that the issues of the New Politics, which include questions linked to ecology, women's rights, participation in decision-making processes, consumer affairs and the North–South divide, already influence debate at higher system levels (Baker *et al.* 1981; Schmitt, Niedermeyer and Menke 1981; Gibowski and Kaase 1986). However, there is no clear proof that such topics are systematically being discussed at the local level of the German party system. The first issue to be assessed, therefore, is whether the Greens have introduced a New Politics dimension into the local politics of Mainz.

Secondly, it has been contended that the traditionally consensual nature of Germany's local politics is in a state of decline. Gabriel (1979b and 1984) has suggested that the local level was undergoing a process of parliamentarisation during the late 1960s and 1970s, whilst other commentators have noted that councillors in some service-sector centres in which the process of socio-economic modernisation has been most rapid were increasingly voting along party lines (Hesse 1982). In these cases the evidence suggested that fewer decisions, including the all-important passing of the annual budget, were being made in unison (see Gabriel 1984). Consequently, the second question to be addressed in this chapter is whether the Greens' New Politics orientation has contributed both to the politicisation process and to the demise of consensus politics. The precise nature of the conflict in local party systems is also a matter of importance. It is necessary to discover whether any emerging conflict cuts across established party lines along an Old–New Local Politics divide.

This chapter is divided into four main sections. The first section discusses the methodology of the analysis to be undertaken. The second section assesses levels of council activity in Mainz during the period under review and the extent to which the Greens were responsible for any changes in activity levels. This provides the basis for an analysis in the third section of the subject areas of debate in the Mainz city council between July 1984 and June 1987. Finally, the fourth section examines the conflict dimensions evident in the city's local party system. This discussion will identify the subject areas which give rise to discord and the council groups responsible for introducing conflictual issues at local level.

Methodology

The changing agenda of Mainz's local politics and any resulting decline in the level of consensus is to be addressed in this study by means of an analysis of the motions introduced by the four parties represented on the city council during a three-year period. The data encompass all 325 motions initiated between July 1984 and June 1987 by the SPD, CDU, FDP and Green council groups in thirty-five sessions of the Mainz city council. Such an analysis of council initiatives presents an ideal means of addressing the content of council debate. Especially for those council groups not involved in the council's administration, like the Greens in Mainz, motions provide a way of influencing the policy-making process. In order to judge the full impact of the Greens upon the local political agenda in Mainz, it also proved necessary to examine the motions introduced in a period preceding the party's election to the city council. In this respect, the parliamentary initiatives of the SPD, CDU and FDP were analysed for the twelve-month period of June 1983 to May 1984. During this control period forty-seven motions were introduced by the established parties' council groups in six council meetings.

The data on which the statistical analysis is based were collated by the council administration in Mainz and present information on the four key variables required for a discussion of the questions under review.[1] Firstly, a keyword is assigned to each motion, under its general heading. This assists in an identification of the subject area of the relevant initiative. Secondly, the council group responsible for introducing the motion is stated. Thirdly, the date of the council meeting in which the motion was debated is given. Finally, the council resolution affecting the motion is provided. Further supporting data were extracted from the texts of the relevant initiatives and from the minutes of the council sessions in which the motions were discussed.

By utilising the information provided by the Mainz city authorities, the data were coded according to the four key variables and then statistically manipulated using the SPSS/PC system. The cross-tabulation of these and newly created variables was utilised in testing the questions pertaining to the influence of the Greens upon Mainz's local politics. In this respect, particular attention was paid to the subject areas of the motions introduced during the two periods under review, the council groups responsible for initiating motions in each of the subject areas and the degree of conflict which arose in both periods. For the period in which the Greens were represented on the city council, it was of interest to identify whether the subject areas of the motions varied across the three years of the analysis and the extent to which a connection existed between the subject area of a particular motion and the type of decision made. With regard to the parliamentary activities of the council group of the Mainz Greens it was also necessary to establish whether any firm link could be made between developments in the local party system from 1984 to 1987 and the number of motions

---

[1] Since 1979 all initiatives submitted by the Mainz council groups have been stored in a central database. The author extends his gratitude to the Mainz city authorities and to Barbara Schneider, business manager of the Green council group, for making these data available.

introduced, the subject area of the motions and the outcome of the debate on their initiatives.

Changing Levels of Council Activity in Mainz

It has already been shown that the Greens adopt parliamentary styles of politics at local level. Indeed, this is a principal feature of their New Local Politics style. In this section a further aspect of their parliamentary approach is to be addressed, pertaining to the Greens' powers of initiation at local level. At the national and regional levels, the Greens have a reputation of being hard-working, in terms of the sheer volume of initiatives they introduce (Ismayr 1985; Poguntke 1987c). Whether such initiatives are successful appears to be of secondary importance to a party seeking to influence public opinion rather than to work actively within the system to produce reforms. It is necessary to judge whether this also applies at local level. In analysing variations in the levels of parliamentary activity of the council groups represented on the Mainz city council, conclusions are to be drawn in two areas. Firstly, it will be established whether the period following the Greens' election to the city council was marked by higher rates of activity than the control period which preceded their election. Secondly, the extent to which the Greens were responsible for any variations in activity will be demonstrated.

At surface level, a comparison of activity rates illustrates a marked difference between the periods prior to and subsequent to the election of the Greens to Mainz city council in June 1984. Whilst on average 7.83 motions per council session were introduced by the council groups during the twelve months which preceded the election of the Greens, the corresponding figure for the period following their election was 9.29 motions per session. However, when consideration is taken of the fact that four council groups were represented in the second period and only three in the first, the increase becomes less significant. On average, 2.61 motions per council session were introduced by each council group between June 1983 and May 1984. In the first three years of Green council activity in Mainz the four council groups initiated on average just 2.32 motions per session, representing a slight overall fall in the level of activity of the Mainz council groups between 1984 and 1987.

Any increase in activity, measured in terms of the number of motions introduced per council session, can largely be attributed to the election of a new party to the council. In this respect, the group's political orientation appears to be less important. However, it would be misleading to dismiss altogether the effects of the presence of a new party on the city council. One major result of the Greens' election to the city council was an increase in the average number of motions discussed in individual council sessions, which led to a significant increase in the duration of individual council meetings, since more motions were to be discussed by a larger number of parties.

Figure 9.1 Mainz: Motions per Council Session, 1983–1987

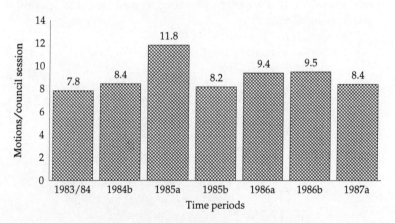

Time periods: suffix 'a' = January-June; suffix 'b' = July-December

In terms of the thirty-five meetings held in Mainz between July 1984 and June 1987, large variations in the level of council activity were recorded. The distribution of motions varied between a peak of twenty-one motions registered in the session held on 29 May 1985 and a low of two motions recorded in the sessions of 29 August 1984 and 29 July 1985 (both convened as special holiday sessions during council summer recess). However, there was no consistent trend with regard to the level of council activity. Nor could significant trends be identified when the sessions were regrouped into seven equal half-year periods (Figure 9.1). Whilst each of the time-periods following the Greens' entry to the Mainz city council was marked by a rate of activity higher than that of the control period, this derived mainly from the presence of four council groups, as opposed to the three represented in the period before. With the exception of the first half of 1985 (Period 1985a), in which on average 11.83 motions were initiated each session, the average number of motions introduced by the Mainz council groups between 1984 and 1987 fluctuated within a narrow range of between 8.4 and 9.5 motions per session. When account is taken of the number of council groups represented, only the time-period 1985a actually registered levels of activity above that of the period preceding the Greens' election to the city council. Between January and June 1985 an average of 2.96 motions per council group per council session were introduced, the corresponding figure for the period 1983/84 being 2.61.

Figure 9.2 Mainz: Motions by Initiating Group, 1984–1987

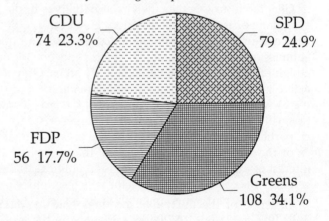

CDU
74 23.3%

SPD
79 24.9%

FDP
56 17.7%

Greens
108 34.1%

NB excludes 8 joint motions

When viewed globally, therefore, the slight increase in the average number of motions placed upon the agenda of the Mainz city council was mainly due to the election of a new council group. However, it is also interesting to examine the contribution of the individual political parties to the levels of council activity in Mainz. During the three-year period under review, the Green council group accounted for over one-third of all motions submitted to the Mainz city council (Figure 9.2). Such a rate of activity is clearly out of all proportion to the size of the Green council group. If the eight motions introduced by more than one council group are excluded from the analysis, the Greens were responsible for 108 (34.1 per cent) of the 317 motions introduced by the four council groups. In many ways this fact provides ample evidence of the extent to which the Greens have become almost fully integrated into the parliamentary process in Mainz. The sheer volume of parliamentary motions initiated by the Green council group suggests that the group's priorities lie in the parliamentary system and not in their extra-parliamentary activities. Party fundamentalists who prefer to regard councils as a forum for conveying their radical views might of course legitimately argue that the number of motions is not an adequate measure of the extent of Green integration into the parliamentary system. Indeed, greater attention will be paid in Chapter 10 to whether the Green initiatives in question were pragmatic or symbolic in intention. However, the proportion of time consumed in preparing detailed motions and questions for submission to council inevitably limits the scope for maintaining a high profile outside the parliamentary arena. Only if there is an active grassroots supporting the parliamentary work is it possible to withstand some of the pressures towards institutionalisation. As was discussed in Chapter 5, however, Green local council participation is characterised by the organisational weaknesses of the Greens' grassroots and by the overwhelming lack of interest of the party's adherents in local political affairs. This was certainly the case in Mainz: a factor which seriously undermined the ability of party fundamentalists to act as a mouthpiece for movement activists. Moreover, the Green council group in Mainz was partially responsible for disengaging from those grassroots that did show an interest in council politics. Councillors were often reluctant to justify their council activities in front of party members, as exemplified at a party meeting in January 1987. With the *Fraktionsgruppe* having begun to analyse the past two years' work, party members were keen that the results of the council group's discussions should be distributed widely to all

171

members and other interested people. The view of the parliamentary group was that this would be too much work: 'Interested people could apply to the council office and would then receive the results/minutes of meetings of the council group in the post'.[2]

When account is taken of the relative strengths of the Mainz council groups, the level of Green activity becomes even more apparent. Whilst each CDU and SPD councillor was responsible for an average of about three motions over the period of the analysis, the respective figure for the five Green councillors was 21.6 initiatives each. Nevertheless, when the level of activity of the FDP council group is brought into the discussion, it becomes evident that the level of activity differentiates less between the Green councillors and those of the established political parties, than between the large and small council groups. In order to establish a clear political profile, the Greens and the FDP are obliged to maintain a comparatively high rate of initiation. By contrast, SPD and CDU councillors are able to adopt a comparatively low level of activity.

In this context it is interesting to compare the level of council activity in the periods immediately preceding and following the Greens' election to the Mainz council. Here consideration is taken both of the number of council meetings held during the two periods and of the respective strengths of the individual council groups. Overall, there was only a slight change in the average level of activity for the two periods concerned, when measured in terms of the number of initiatives introduced by individual councillors per council session. The rate rose from a figure of 0.13 in the first period to 0.15 in the second. This increase can primarily be attributed to the presence of the Greens in the city council and to an increased level of activity on the part of the small FDP council group. Each of the major parties witnessed a fall in the average level of activity of their representatives. The decline was most noticeable in the case of the SPD, with a fall from a level of 0.13 motions per councillor before July 1984 to just 0.08 in the period which followed.

Again, any conclusions to be drawn from such a comparison should be treated with caution. The fact that the control period

---

[2] Minutes of Green Party meeting, 13 January 1987.

fell at the end of the legislative period 1979–84 could have served to affect the performance of the established parties' council groups in Mainz. By raising their levels of activity in the run-up to the 1984 local election, the SPD, CDU and FDP might well have sought to influence the course of the election. However, on the basis of the information presented, it is evident that the Greens have succeeded in adopting the role of being the principal initiating force in Mainz's local politics. On their own, they were more than able to compensate for the declining levels of activity of the larger council groups. This appears to have affected the SPD in particular. In this respect, the extent to which the Greens were consistently active at a higher level than the remaining council groups for the entire period under analysis must also be addressed.

Figure 9.3 Mainz: Important Political Events, 1984–1987

Time period	Events
Period 1	SPD-Green talks re supplementary budget; Red-Green alliance in Gonsenheim suburb (July-October 1984, 4 council sessions)
Period 2	Election of CDU members to council executive with SPD support (November 1984-May 1985, 8 council sessions)
Period 3	SPD-Green talks re budget 1986/87 (June-December 1985, 7 council sessions)
Period 4	Failure of SPD-Green budget talks; Election of new city mayor (January-October 1986, 9 council sessions)
Period 5	End of Mayor Fuchs era; Transitional period (November 1986-June 1987, 6 council sessions)

Notable fluctuations in the rates of initiation of the four council groups were recorded over the thirty-five council sessions held between July 1984 and June 1987. The Greens failed to introduce motions on just two occasions (8 May 1985 and 16 October 1985), but compensated for this lapse by initiating no fewer than nine motions in the session held on 29 May 1985. Of the four council groups, the level of Green activity varied most considerably between 1984 and 1987. The other council groups maintained more consistent levels of initiation, albeit at a generally lower rate than that of the Greens. The SPD introduced a maximum number of five motions on two occasions and initiated no motions at all on a further five. The CDU was the most consistent of the four council groups, recording a maximum figure of four motions per council session on five occasions and failing to introduce any motions at all on a further six. The FDP introduced three or more motions only eight times, with a peak of five motions recorded for the session of 29 May 1985. FDP motions were absent from the agenda of council meetings on eight occasions.

Such absolute variations in the level of activity of the individual council groups in Mainz allow few conclusions to be drawn about developments over the course of the analysis. For this reason it is useful to group council sessions together in time-periods in order to ascertain whether or not trends in the rate of activity could be identified. Figure 9.3 describes key developments in the Mainz party system between 1984 and 1987 for a series of five time-periods. Period One, running from July to October 1984, represented a period in which the Mainz parties sought to clarify their relationship with one another. In certain respects, a *rapprochement* between the Greens and the SPD was evident, with regard to the discussions about the supplementary budget for 1985 and the debate over the alliance in the neighbourhood council in the Gonsenheim suburb. However, Period Two marked a worsening of the relationship between the Greens and the SPD, in the wake of the election of new CDU members to the council executive committee in November 1984 and February 1985. In Period Three, the Greens and the SPD were engaged in discussions about the joint passing of the city budget for 1986/7. The failure to reach an agreement brought this period to an end. The fourth period was characterised by the debate of the election of a new city mayor in Mainz, a debate from which the Greens were excluded as a result of events surrounding the passing of the 1986/7 budget. Finally, Period Five marked the end of the twenty-year era of Mayor Fuchs in Mainz and the transition towards a new era under Mayor Weyel.

Figure 9.4 Mainz: Motions per Council Session by Size of Initiating Group

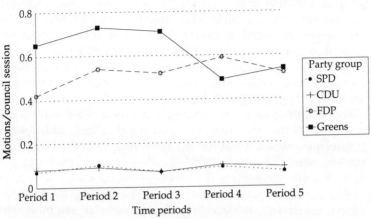

The information presented in Figure 9.4 serves to demonstrate the extent to which the major political events in Mainz influenced the levels of activity of the city's council groups between 1984 and 1987. The data are particularly illuminating from the point of view of the Greens. During the first three time-periods, the Greens' activity level reflected the prospect that their initiatives could gain some measure of success. Even if the motions were unsuccessful, the belief prevailed within the Green *Fraktionsgruppe* that certain political benefits could be secured from their implementation. The key factor underlying the high levels of activity registered between July 1984 and December 1985, was the potential alliance with the SPD. This engendered an optimistic mood within the Greens, rendering council activity worthwhile. However, when the budgetary talks between the Greens and SPD collapsed in December 1985, at the end of Period Three, the Greens' interest in local politics declined quite markedly. During Period Four, which directly followed upon the failure of the red–green budget negotiations, the level of activity of the individual Green councillors actually fell behind that of their FDP counterparts. In this period the Greens recorded an average figure of 0.49 motions per councillor per session, whilst the FDP reached a level of 0.59. Even in the final period of the analysis the Greens were unable to regain their earlier rate of activity. It is apparent from this analysis that the Mainz Greens became increasingly demoralised, unable to exert any influence over the all-important selection process for the new city mayor. This lack of strategic involvement was a direct result of the collapse of the budgetary talks in 1985.

Such an explanation of the varying levels of Green activity in Mainz naturally runs the risk of oversimplifying the complex factors underlying recorded changes in rates of initiation. The role played by the increasingly factionalised internal decision-making processes of the Greens should also be considered. Nevertheless, given the overriding significance of the dual budget of 1986/7 in Mainz's local politics in the period of analysis, it is apparent that the collapse of any prospect of an alliance with the SPD left the Greens in a political vacuum.

Regarding the levels of activity of the other council groups, it is noticeable that variations were less marked, although political events still influenced their performance in some notable ways. Both the SPD and CDU registered their lowest levels of initiation in the period in which the debate over a possible red–green alliance was most heated. Evidently both parties were waiting to see what materialised from the talks. The failure of the red–green talks and the decision of the SPD to agree a new budget with the CDU marked a return to the Mainz Model. With the budget out of the way, the established parties' council groups could once again concentrate upon their policy-making activities. The period following the passing of the city budget (Period Four) corresponded to that in which the highest levels of activity were recorded for the CDU (2.33 motions per session) and FDP (1.78 motions per session) council groups and the second highest for that of the SPD (2.56 motions per session).

Summary

An analysis of the changing levels of council activity in Mainz points to only a slight overall change in the rate of activity of the individual council groups in the periods immediately preceding and following the initial election of the Greens. This fact belies the Greens' enormous appetite for initiating motions. Over one-third of all motions introduced between July 1984 and June 1987 came from the five members of the Green council group. In the context of the debate over changing styles and practices in German local politics, it is significant that the Mainz Greens assumed the dominant role in seeking to influence the policy-making process by means of their motions. Nevertheless, it must be recognised that the power of initiation is largely a feature to be associated with the necessity for small council groups to maintain a political profile. The most likely explanation for variations in the rates of initiating activity lies in the events surrounding the passing of the city budget in the winter of 1985/6. with the Greens considerably reducing their level of activity in the period which followed the collapse of budgetary talks with the SPD.

The Changing Agenda of Local Politics in Mainz

The analysis of the changing agenda of Mainz's local council politics under the possible impact of New Politics topics necessitated the development of a means by which the subject areas of the issues under discussion in council sessions could be categorised. In the absence of comparable studies on which a classification of the subject areas of the motions of the Mainz council groups could be based, it was necessary to create one specifically for this study. The classification adopted in the ensuing analysis was developed pragmatically on the basis of a distillation of the key areas of debate during the period under review.

For the periods preceding and following the election of the Greens to the city council in 1984, thirteen broad subject-area categories were developed. These encompassed the great majority (93 per cent) of the 372 motions submitted between July 1983 and June 1987. In some cases there was no clear indication from the

177

motion's title or from the keyword assigned to it by the council administration of the subject-area to which it belonged. In these instances clarification was sought both by recourse to the text of the relevant motion and by an examination of the minutes of the council meeting in which the initiative was debated. The combination of these two approaches enabled the categorisation of borderline motions into the subject-area groups developed. Regardless of the creation of sufficiently broad categories, the content of certain motions defied precise categorisation. Where motions could not be adequately categorised, a final fourteenth heading of 'other' was adopted. The category 'other' subject-areas comprised some twenty-six motions (7 per cent of the entire sample).

The thirteen subject-area headings forming the basis of the analysis are: environment, transport, social, planning, culture, administration, military, economics, partnerships, law and order, democracy, education and youth. Figure 9.5 gives details of the topics included under each heading. The type of issues included within the subject-area categories are mainly self-evident. However, there are a number areas of the classification which require some justification. Some areas of local responsibility which traditionally belong to the repertoire of local politics were not represented by motions initiated during the period of the analysis and could therefore not be included. This applied for example to the case of health-related issues in the Mainz study. Other matters within local authorities' competences, such as the administration and maintenance of council buildings and facilities, were accommodated within the thirteen subject areas established, depending upon the content of the relevant motion. Thus a motion seeking to abandon admission charges to a local-authority-financed museum was placed in the culture category. The fact that women's affairs have been located in the 'social' category could also be open to criticism. However, this specific sphere of local political debate was not sufficiently well represented in the period of the analysis to warrant a category of its own. This also applied to motions with a sporting subject area, which were assigned to the 'culture' heading.

Even before the categorisation of the Mainz council groups' parliamentary motions could be undertaken, it became evident that significant problems existed with the global application of a

Figure 9.5 Classification of Motions' Subject Areas

Subject Area	Related Issues
Environment	Ecology, environmental planning and protection, energy, waste management, recycling, emissions, public information on ecology, natural habitats
Transport	Public and private transport services, parking, road maintenance, traffic flow, cycle paths, road lighting, speed limits, traffic calming measures
Social	Minority groups, immigration, women's issues, social security, unemployment
Planning	Town planning, construction, restoration, public and private sector accommodation, land use
Culture	Established and alternative forms of culture, festivals, conferences, museums and galleries, monuments, civic honours, street names, media affairs, sporting activities
Administration	Council affairs, personnel matters
Military	US forces, military bases, nuclear-free zone
Economics	Budgetary matters, local economy, privatisation
Partnerships	Domestic and foreign twinning arrangements
Law and order	Policing, demonstrations, public order
Democracy	Citizen participation, neighbourhood councils
Education	Schools
Youth	Youth and child welfare, youth clubs
Other	All remaining subject areas

'New Politics' label to certain subject-area headings. This demonstrates the extent to which debate about New Politics issues has perhaps been conducted in too simplistic a manner. It proved impossible to assign entire subject-area headings to the New

Politics agenda as such. Environmental issues, for example, which are commonly perceived as belonging to the New Politics agenda, incorporate topics which have been the subject of local political debate for many years in Germany. The same would apply to the questions of military activities and town partnerships, which have been on the local political agenda in the Federal Republic since the 1950s at least. In the absence of any clear means of establishing what constituted the agenda of the Old Local Politics no distinction could be drawn between environmental motions with a New Politics orientation and those that belonged to the established repertoire of local politics. Similarly, economics motions should not necessarily be assigned automatically to the category of 'Old Politics'. Such complex issues arising from the New Politics debate are best addressed in a more qualitative study of the parliamentary initiatives of the Mainz council groups (see Chapter 10 below).

In addition to the problems arising from a classification of motions into 'New' and 'Old' Politics types, the categorisation of the 372 individual motions introduced by the Mainz council groups between 1983 and 1987 itself presented a number of difficulties. Whilst the majority of motions could satisfactorily be assigned to one of the thirteen subject-area categories, some parliamentary initiatives transcended one or more of the headings. Such motions were introduced only in the period following the Greens' entry into the Mainz city council. This phenomenon is best illustrated with the assistance of an example. Following models adopted in other German cities, the SPD council group introduced a motion in 1985 calling for the adoption of a new integrated transport policy for Mainz (M94/85).[3] The key element of the policy lay in the initiation by the local transport authority of a new fare-pricing structure which would be accompanied by improvements in bus and tram services. The motive behind the initiative was primarily the protection of the environment. By reducing the cost of a monthly season ticket for the city's transport network and by improving the service on offer, it was hoped that more private-car users could be encouraged to

---

[3] In this and the subsequent chapter motions are referred to in terms of the number assigned to them by the Mainz city authorities. Thus M94/1985 represents the ninety-fourth motion submitted in 1985.

switch to public transport. Were the policy to be successful in the case of Mainz, the increase in the proportion of journeys made by public transport would serve to reduce the levels of air pollutants emitted from car exhausts and thereby contribute to a reduction in a prime cause of acid rain and global warming.

In the classification adopted here, motion M94/85 was placed in the 'transport' category, given that its focal point was the reform of the local transport system. However, as noted above, the motion had significant 'environmental' implications and could also conceivably have been placed in the 'social' category, since the reduction in public transport fares is of immediate benefit to those sections of the population unable to afford the luxury of a car and therefore most reliant upon the public transport network. In these social groups the new fare-pricing structure would automatically lead to an increase in the disposable income available, representing an improvement in living circumstances. In addition to the transport, environment and social categories it would have been possible to assign the SPD motion M94/85 to the planning or economic fields, given the long-term implications such a policy entails for the development of the local road infrastructure and for the finances of the city of Mainz.

Such difficulties of categorisation applied to only a small number of cases in this analysis. The possibility of assigning individual motions to more than one category and thereby allowing multiple values was rejected; there was judged to be no objective means of restricting the number of subject areas covered by a particular motion. In this respect, the majority of motions have 'economic' implications, since city funding is required for their implementation. To allow multiple values would have automatically reduced the clarity of the categories of analysis. Nevertheless, within the context of this study, some positive results can be derived from such categorisation difficulties. The fact that individual motions can belong to more than one category underlines the changing nature of German local politics. Parliamentary initiatives at this level increasingly incorporate elements from a range of subject areas, suggesting that local politicians are becoming more aware of the far-reaching effects of their decision-making processes. Furthermore, local issues are more frequently viewed in their supra-local contexts than has traditionally been the case. The Greens' concept of thinking globally and acting locally is also evident in the motions of the established political parties.

Whilst it is difficult to support the contention that such wide-ranging motions are in themselves indicative of the existence of a 'New Politics' dimension at the local level on the basis of the information available, this represents an area which certainly merits further investigation. The data available for this study can only point towards the possible emergence of a New Politics agenda at local level. To provide conclusive evidence that such a development has occurred would require a more detailed analysis, involving a comparison of the nature of the issues debated in local councils across a series of time-periods and incorporating a larger number of localities of differing social-structural types.

Despite the limitations inherent in the data available for this study, the ensuing analysis demonstrates that it is still possible to draw significant conclusions about the changing nature of local politics in Mainz between 1983 and 1987. It is also possible to judge the extent to which the Greens have contributed to the process of change.

The Local Political Agenda in Mainz 1983–1987

This section examines the suggestion that the Greens have contributed to a change in the agenda of local politics in Mainz. The basis for the analysis is provided by an examination of the subject areas of the motions introduced by the parties represented on the city's local council. A comparison of the extent to which the agenda of Mainz's local politics changed subsequent to the Greens' election to the city council is to be achieved by analysing the subject areas of the motions initiated by the council groups represented on the city council for the two periods June 1983 to May 1984 (Period One) and July 1984 to June 1987 (Period Two). In Period One the SPD, CDU and FDP were the only parties with seats on the council, whilst in Period Two these parties were joined by the Greens. Again, it should be stressed that this tells us little about the style and precise content of the motions within the respective subject-area categories.

Table 9.1 Mainz: Motions by Subject Areas, Periods 1 & 2 (in %)

Subject area	Period 1 1983/84	Rank	Period 2 1984/87	Rank	Change in %
Environment	21.3	1	26.2	1	4.9
Transport	10.6	4	17.2	2	6.6
Social	8.5	5	10.2	4	1.7
Planning	12.8	3	9.8	5	3.0
Culture	6.4	7	13.5	3	7.1
Administration	2.1	9	2.8	8	0.7
Military	2.1	9	1.5	12	–0.6
Economics	17.0	2	2.2	9	–14.8
Partnerships	0.0	13	3.4	7	3.4
Law and order	0.0	13	2.2	9	2.2
Democracy	2.1	9	0.9	14	–1.2
Education	2.1	9	2.2	9	0.1
Youth	6.4	7	1.2	13	–5.2
Other	8.5	5	6.8	6	–1.7
(n)	47		325		

At first glance, the data presented in Table 9.1 suggest that the agenda of local politics in Mainz only partially changed following the election of the Greens. In both periods under analysis, the five broad subject areas of environment, transport, social, planning and culture accounted for the great proportion of all motions (59.6 per cent in Period One, 76.1 per cent in Period Two). Issues of an environmental nature dominated the local political agenda in Mainz in each period. However, a significant increase in the introduction of such issues was evident during the second period (+4.9 per cent). Of particular relevance was the declining salience of motions with an economic subject-matter over the course of the analysis. Whilst this category accounted for 17 per cent of all motions introduced in Period One, following the election of the Greens to the city council in 1984 only 2.2 per cent of all motions were judged to belong to an economic subject area. The declining significance of the economic motions across the two time-periods can be illustrated by the category's change in rank with respect to the other subject areas. In Period One the economics heading was ranked second in importance to that of environment, whilst in Period Two it only ranked ninth. Other subject areas of increasing importance in Mainz during the second period were those of culture (+7.1 per cent) and of transport (+6.6 per cent). To a lesser extent, the social (+1.7 per cent), partnerships (+3.4 per cent) and law and order (+2.2 per cent) categories also registered an increase in importance. The categories planning (–3.0 per cent) and youth (–5.2 per cent) were of declining significance. Only a negligible change in the proportion of motions belonging to the remaining subject-area categories was recorded.

Table 9.2 Mainz: SPD, CDU and FDP Motions by Subject Areas, Periods 1 & 2 (in %)

Subject area	Period 1 1983/84	Rank	Period 2 1984/87	Rank	Change in %
Environment	21.3	1	23	1	1.7
Transport	10.6	4	21.1	2	10.5
Social	8.5	5	7.7	5	–0.8
Planning	12.8	3	10.5	4	–2.3
Culture	6.4	7	16.3	3	9.9
Administration	2.1	9	2.9	8	0.8
Military	2.1	9	1.0	13	–1.1
Economics	17	2	1.9	11	–15.1
Partnerships	0.0	13	2.9	8	2.9
Law and order	0.0	13	2.4	10	2.4
Democracy	2.1	9	1.4	12	–0.7
Education	2.1	9	3.3	7	1.2
Youth	6.4	7	1.0	13	–5.4
Other	8.5	5	4.8	6	–3.7
Total	100.0		100.2		
(n)	47		325		

On the basis of such an analysis alone it is not possible to assert that there has been a fundamental shift in the agenda of Mainz's local politics since the election of the Greens to the city council in June 1984. Nevertheless, by examining the motions of the council groups of the established parties in Mainz for the two periods under review, it is possible to assess whether or not the changes outlined above have occurred as a result of the Greens' presence in Mainz or whether the increasing salience of certain issues has happened regardless of the Greens' presence. Table 9.2 presents the same information as Table 9.1, with the exception that the Greens have now been excluded from the analysis.

A comparison of the agendas of the two periods concerned shows differences between the priority accorded to certain subject areas by the established parties' council groups. The increasing salience of environmental issues, for example, was much less marked in the case of the established parties during Period Two (+1.7 per cent) than it was when the Greens' motions were incorporated into the analysis (+4.9 per cent). Other subject areas witnessed a greater increase in the priority placed upon them by the SPD, CDU and FDP councillors. This applied particularly to the transport (+10.5 per cent) and cultural (+9.9 per cent) categories. The declining salience of motions with an economic subject area (−15.1 per cent) was slightly more dramatic than that measured with the inclusion of the Greens (−14.8 per cent). In certain areas, therefore, the established parties' councillors were discussing the same issues after the local election of June 1984 that were on the agenda before the Greens' entry to the city council. However, the greater relevance of environmental issues since July 1984 can largely be attributed to the presence of the Greens. Without the Greens only transport and cultural themes would have become significantly more important.

On the basis of the data available and in the absence of a precise means by which such a concept can be operationalised, there is therefore insufficient evidence to suggest that issues of the New Politics dominated the agenda of local politics in Mainz during the period under review. This is despite the fact that economics issues, regarded as belonging to the traditional agenda of Germany's local politics, have been of declining relevance since the Greens' presence on the local council. Similarly, evidence that environmental, military and partnerships issues have become more important does not necessarily point towards the emergence of a New Politics agenda. Even before the Greens' entry to the city council, the environment category accounted for the majority of all motions initiated by the SPD, CDU and FDP council groups. Nevertheless, were the Greens absent from the Mainz city council, it is clear that motions with an environmental subject area would not have ranked so highly.

Given the difficulties inherent in attempts to prove the existence of a New Local Politics agenda in Mainz, greater significance should perhaps be accorded to the extent to which each of the political parties has been able to represent certain issues at the local level. Is there evidence to suggest that the declining salience of economic issues and the relative increase in importance of environmental, cultural and transport issues derives directly from the Greens' involvement in Mainz's local politics?

Subject areas of Motions by Initiating Parties

In this section the subject areas of the motions of the individual council groups represented in Mainz will be examined. Although the motions of the first period preceding the election of the Greens to the Mainz council in 1984 will be used as a means of comparison for the motions of the established council groups, greater attention will be paid to the period in which the Greens were represented. By excluding the small number of motions initiated by more than one council group (eight motions in Period Two), 317 motions form the basis for the analysis to follow.

A comparison of the distribution of the motions of the SPD, CDU, FDP and Green council groups in Mainz across the fourteen subject-area headings allows certain conclusions to be drawn about their political priorities for a three-year period (Tables 9.3 and 9.4). Between 1984 and 1987 26.8 per cent of all motions placed upon the agenda of council sessions in Mainz had an environmental subject area. As indicated above, the Greens were largely responsible for the predominance of this category of issues. In this respect there is little evidence to suggest that the Greens have forsaken their roots within the ecology movement. Given the fact that over one-third (34.3 per cent) of the motions introduced by the Mainz Green council group between 1984 and 1987 belonged to the environmental category, representing 43.5 per cent of all initiatives under this heading, it is evident that the party continues to attach the utmost significance to this particular subject area. Only the FDP accorded a similar priority to green issues during the period under analysis. Of the SPD's seventy-nine motions, 22.8 per cent fell into the environment category, whilst the corresponding figure for the CDU was just 16.2 per cent. Environmental issues dominated the agendas of the Greens, FDP and SPD council groups, but only ranked third in importance for the Christian Democrats. Culture and transport issues were far more important to the CDU council group.

Table 9.3 Mainz: Subject Areas of Motions by Council Groups, 1984–1987 (in %)

Subject area	SPD	CDU	FDP	Greens	Total
Environment	22.8	16.2	32.1	34.3	26.8
Transport	17.7	21.6	25.0	10.2	17.4
Social	12.7	4.1	5.4	13.9	9.8
Planning	8.9	13.5	8.9	8.3	9.8
Culture	15.2	21.6	10.7	9.3	13.9
Administration	2.5	2.7	3.6	2.8	2.8
Military	2.5	0.0	0.0	2.8	1.6
Economics	2.5	0.0	3.6	2.8	2.2
Partnerships	2.5	5.4	0.0	3.7	3.2
Law and order	3.8	1.4	1.8	1.9	2.2
Democracy	3.8	0.0	0.0	0.0	0.9
Education	2.5	4.1	3.6	0.0	2.2
Youth	1.3	1.4	0.0	0.9	0.9
Other	1.3	8.1	5.4	9.3	6.3
Total	100.0	100.1	100.1	100.2	100.0
(n)	79	74	56	108	317

In the social category the Greens also initiated an above-average proportion of motions. Whilst motions with a social subject area accounted for 9.8 per cent of all motions initiated between 1984 and 1987, some 13.9 per cent of Green motions belonged to the category, accounting for 48.4 per cent of all social issues raised. Social themes ranked lower in the priorities of each of the other council groups. Only the SPD came close to sharing the Greens' preference for social issues (rank four), with both the FDP (rank five) and CDU (rank seven) assigning the category a very low priority. The Greens' contribution to the other main subject areas was less marked. This applied in particular to the

The German Greens: Challenging the Consensus

areas of transport issues and cultural matters. In these two categories the Greens introduced 20.0 per cent and 22.7 per cent of all motions respectively. Whereas transport issues constituted 17.4 per cent of all motions introduced during the three years of the analysis, only 10.2 per cent of the Green council group's motions fell within this subject area. The proportion of Green motions assigned to the culture category was 9.3 per cent, whilst that of all the council groups together was 13.9 per cent.

Table 9.4 Mainz: Subject Areas by Council Groups, 1984–1987 (in %)

Subject area	SPD	CDU	FDP	Greens	(n)
Environment	21.2	14.1	21.2	43.5	85
Transport	25.5	29.1	25.5	20.0	55
Social	32.3	9.7	9.7	48.4	31
Planning	22.6	32.3	16.1	29.0	31
Culture	27.3	36.4	13.6	22.7	44
Administration	22.2	22.2	22.2	33.3	9
Military	40.0	0.0	0.0	60.0	5
Economics	28.6	0.0	28.6	42.9	7
Partnerships	20.0	40.0	0.0	40.0	10
Law and order	42.9	14.3	14.3	28.6	7
Democracy	100.0	0.0	0.0	0.0	3
Education	28.6	42.9	28.6	0.0	7
Youth	33.3	33.3	0.0	33.3	3
Other	5.0	30.0	15.0	50.0	20
Total	24.9	23.3	17.7	34.1	100.0
(n)	79	74	56	108	317

In each of the subject areas outlined above, with the partial exception of the transport category, on which the FDP placed most priority, the Greens' position was furthest from that of the CDU. On this level at least it can be contended that the principal areas of differences in priority exist between the Greens and Christian Democrats. In the more minor subject areas of the classification there are considerable variations in the proportion of motions initiated by each of the council groups. Although this partly derives from the low numbers of motions involved in each case, some interesting observations arise. In the military category, for example, only the Greens and SPD submitted motions; the Greens being responsible for three of the five (60 per cent). In the area of partnerships the Greens and CDU were responsible for the same proportion of motions raised (40 per cent or four each). The SPD on the other hand was the only council group to raise issues belonging to the democracy subject area.

Summary

The analysis of the subject areas of the motions introduced by the Mainz council groups between July 1984 and June 1987 provides a means of identifying the policy-making priorities of each. On the basis of the information available it is not possible to prove conclusively the emergence of a new agenda in the local politics of Mainz following the election of the Greens to the city council in 1984. Nevertheless, certain trends suggest that there has been a certain movement towards issues generally identified with the New Politics (environmentalism, military and partnerships) and a decline in the significance of more traditional issues (economics). The priorities of the individual council groups varied quite considerably. Whereas the Greens favoured the areas of environmental and social policy, the CDU laid most emphasis upon transport and cultural issues. Both the SPD and FDP concentrated upon environmental and transport issues during the course of the analysis. An initial analysis of the differing subject-area priorities of the Mainz council groups suggests that the greatest potential for conflict within the local party system in Mainz existed between the Greens and CDU.

Conflict Dimensions in Mainz

In this section the second question raised at the beginning of the chapter is to be addressed. It has been suggested that the Greens have contributed to a decline in the degree of consensus affecting local party systems in the Federal Republic and that this decline has partially occurred as a result of the discussion of New Politics issues at local level. In the previous section,

189

difficulties were identified with regard to attempts to place individual motions into either New or Old Politics categories. As a result, this section will concentrate upon identifying the existence of conflict and an examination of the origins of such conflict. This task is to be undertaken by reference to the decisions made by the city's council groups with respect to the motions discussed in the previous sections.

Figure 9.6 Conflict Dimensions of Council Resolutions

CONSENSUAL	CONFLICTUAL
Unanimously accepted Unanimously accepted (amended)	Accepted by majority Accepted by majority (amended)
Unanimously referred Unanimously referred (amended)	Referred by majority Referred by majority (amended)
	Rejected
	Removed from agenda

Whilst a number of decisions can result from the discussion of a particular motion in a local council chamber, for the purposes of this analysis two basic types of decision were identified. On the one hand, motions which resulted in a unanimous resolution of the four council groups represented in Mainz were judged to be 'consensual'. On the other, motions which gave rise to an element of disagreement were regarded as being 'conflictual'. Each of these broad categories incorporates a series of additional council decisions witnessed during the period under discussion in Mainz. Figure 9.6 indicates the types of decision which fall into each of the basic categories. All decisions made in unison by the Mainz council groups were judged to belong to the 'consensual' category. This included motions unanimously accepted by the council, those unanimously accepted in amended form, those unanimously referred to council committee and those unanimously referred to committee in amended form. A second category of decision involved a degree of conflict. Motions subject to conflictual decisions were broken down in two stages. In a first stage, the nature of the conflict was determined. In the second stage, the motions were established as being conflictual. Motions which were accepted by a majority, accepted by a majority in amended form, referred by a majority, referred by a majority in amended form, rejected by the majority of council members or removed from the agenda of council sessions contain a conflictual element. Several motions in the Mainz study were subject to other types of decision. Some motions were withdrawn before the relevant council session by the initiating council group, and others were resolved without the necessity of a vote in the plenary session. A very small number of motions were subject to decisions which could not readily be placed in either of the categories developed. In such cases certain sections of the motion were approved unanimously by the council whilst others were subject to a majority decision. To facilitate the analysis, this group was also placed into the category of 'other' decision.

The categorisation of the types of decision into the two broad categories of 'consensual' and 'conflictual' inevitably involves a number of assumptions. For example, no judgement can be made about the motives of a particular council group or of individual councillors in supporting the referral of a motion to council committee (by far the most common council resolution). It is conceivable, for instance, that a council group could reject the policy implications involved in a particular issue, yet still vote for its referral for tactical reasons; be it as part of a reciprocal arrangement with the initiating council group, in order to assure its amendment in council committee to the group's own satisfaction, or even to introduce an element of delay. Nevertheless, there was sufficient evidence in Mainz to suggest that whenever council groups opposed a particular motion in principle, this opposition was reflected in their decision on the initiative. As a result, genuine sources of conflict were reflected in the majority decisions made.

Table 9.5 shows the frequencies of the basic types of decision made during Period Two of the analysis. By far the most common decision made by the council in Mainz was the unanimous referral of motions to the council's specialist committees, occurring in 62.5 per cent of cases. When other, smaller unanimous decision categories are added to this figure the total rises to 69.3 per cent. By combining the majority decision categories (see Figure 9.6), 13.2 per cent of the initiatives introduced between 1984 and 1987 were supported by more than half of the councillors. The remaining categories required no further adjustment.

Table 9.5 Mainz: Frequency of Decision Types, 1984–1987

Type of decision	Frequency	%
Unanimously accepted	10	3.1
Unanimously accepted (amended)	1	0.3
Unanimously referred	203	62.5
Unanimously referred (amended)	11	3.4
(All consensual)	*225*	*69.3*
Accepted by majority	5	1.5
Accepted by majority (amended)	7	2.2
Referred by majority	26	8.0
Referred by majority (amended)	5	1.5
Rejected	31	9.5
Removed from agenda	8	2.5
(All conflictual)	*82*	*25.2*
Other decisions	18	5.5
Total	325	100.0

Table 9.6 Mainz: Levels of Council Conflict, 1983/84 and 1984–1987 (in %)

Type of decision	1983/84		1984–87		1983–87	
	%	n	%	n	%	n
Consensual	89.4	42	73.3	225	75.4	267
Conflictual	10.6	5	26.7	82	24.6	87
(n)		47		307		354

NB excludes 'other' decisions

The categorisation of the decision types makes a comparison possible between the levels of conflict within the Mainz city council for the periods preceding and following the 1984 local election. Although one might expect the period prior to an election to be more conflictual than usual, with all council groups seeking to clarify their position on key issues for the benefit of the electorate, this was not the case in Mainz in the control period between June 1983 and May 1984. Almost 90 per cent of all motions submitted by the established parties' council groups resulted in unanimous resolutions (Table 9.6). This serves to underline the all-encompassing nature of the Mainz Model, with agreement on all important policy and personnel matters being reached in unison. In contrast to the relatively high levels of unanimity recorded in the period preceding the Greens' election to the city council, the second period of the analysis witnessed a marked increase in conflict. Between 1984 and 1987 the proportion of conflictual decisions made in the Mainz city council more than doubled to 26.7 per cent when compared with the figure of only 10.6 per cent during Period One.

Whilst the overwhelming majority of decisions continued to be made in unison by the four council groups, it is clear that the period following the election of the Greens was substantially more confrontational, lending support to the contention that the Greens were responsible for the declining levels of unanimity in Mainz. Although on average over 70 per cent of all motions resulted in a unanimous decision, this figure varied considerably over the three years of the analysis, with some periods being marked by a greater degree of conflict than others. No conflict at all was registered in five council sessions.[4] In a further nine cases there was a disproportionately low level of conflict, with over 80 per cent of motions being agreed in unison by the four council groups. However, in certain council meetings a high level of conflict arose. In the very first meeting following the Greens' election, for example, three of the four motions on the council agenda created conflict. In a further five council sessions 50 per cent or more of the motions created an element of conflict.[5]

Despite this wide variation, it was not possible to identify a consistent trend with regard to the level of conflict registered in the Mainz council chamber. Sessions in which conflict had been particularly marked were followed directly by relatively consensual

[4] Council sessions held on 29 August 1984, 19 March 1985, 29 July 1985, 15 October 1986 and 25 March 1987.
[5] Council sessions held on 7 November 1984, 21 May 1986, 10 December 1986, 20 May 1987 and 24 June 1987.

council meetings. Similarly, council sessions characterised by above average levels of unanimity preceded sessions in which a high proportion of motions had led to some form of conflict. A number of factors, acting either alone or concurrently, could lead to such variations in the degree of consensus between meetings of the Mainz city council. Of particular relevance in this study are possible linkages to the changing political context in which the sessions were located, the council group responsible for initiating the motions on the agenda and the subject areas of the motions. Evidence suggests, for example, that council meetings characterised by low levels of consensus tended to coincide with conflict arising in other aspects of the city council's activities. Thus the session on 7 November 1984, in which three-quarters of the motions introduced resulted in conflict, coincided with the election of two CDU members to the council executive. The opposition of the left wing of the Mainz SPD and the Greens to this event was translated into confrontation with regard to the motions under debate in the relevant council session. Similarly, in the council meeting held on 21 May 1986, the fact that five of the nine motions introduced (55.6 per cent) caused conflict can be linked to events surrounding the Chernobyl nuclear accident in the Soviet Union. The Greens sought to exploit this occasion to commit Mainz to a rejection of the Federal Republic's nuclear energy programme and secure the city's withdrawal from its limited reliance upon nuclear power. A further meeting on 10 December 1986 saw three out of the five motions initiated result in some form of conflict. This meeting can be placed within the context of events surrounding the course of a peace-movement demonstration in Mainz, broken up by the police in an unusual manner. The lowest level of consensus was recorded in the final council session to be included within the analysis, of 24 June 1987. In this council meeting, the CDU and SPD council groups were at odds over the appointment of further members to the council executive.

In this respect, it is possible to identify some party-political causes of conflict arising within sessions of the city council. Nevertheless, on other occasions in which one might have anticipated conflict, meetings passed quietly. In December 1985, for instance, a council meeting which followed immediately upon the collapse of the budgetary talks between the Greens and the SPD still resulted in over half the motions introduced being passed in unison (55.6 per cent). In the first meeting of 1986 this figure rose to 80 per cent. It is much easier to identify factors underlying above-average levels of conflict than those responsible for above-average levels of unanimity. With this in mind, it would appear that the causes of variations in the degree of consensus affecting individual council sessions are of a more complex nature. The evidence is that the variations were not simply related to the course of political events in Mainz.

An examination of the decisions made with respect to the motions of the individual council groups reinforces the extent to which the Greens were responsible for the increasing amount of conflict within the Mainz party system.

Types of Decision by Initiating Group

In the control period preceding the entry of the Greens to the Mainz city council high levels of agreement between the council groups were recorded, irrespective of the initiating council group (Table 9.7). In the case of the FDP each of the council group's eight motions of the period resulted in a unanimous decision being made. Both the CDU and SPD secured all-party support for over four-fifths of their parliamentary initiatives. Of the conflictual motions only the SPD had motions rejected outright by the council and this occurred just twice. During this period there was no clear link between the council group which introduced a particular motion to the council and the council's ultimate decision with respect to the motion.

The experience following the Greens' election in June 1984 contrasted directly with that of the control period (Table 9.8). Between July 1984 and June 1987 a very strong link was identified between the initiating council group and the outcome of their parliamentary initiatives. This link was most pronounced for the Greens. Whilst 73.3 per cent of all council motions initiated during the three-year period were accepted or referred to committee unanimously, this applied to only 56.1 per cent of Green motions. By contrast, 81.7 per cent of the established parties' motions gained all-party support. Whereas the Greens were responsible for initiating almost one-third of all motions (32.7 per cent), only a quarter of the consensual motions stemmed from the council group. Over half (53.8 per cent) of all conflictual motions introduced between July 1984 and June 1987 in Mainz were initiated by the Greens.

Table 9.7 Mainz: Council Decisions by Party Group, 1983/84 (in %)

Decision	SPD	CDU	FDP	All
Consensual	86.4	87.5	100.0	89.1
Conflictual	13.6	12.5	0.0	10.9
of which:				
Majority	4.5	12.5	0.0	6.6
Rejected	9.1	0.0	0.0	4.3
Removed	0.0	0.0	0.0	0.0
(n)	22	16	8	46

NB excludes 'other' decisions

Table 9.8 Mainz: Council Decisions by Party Group, 1984–87 (in %)

Decision	SPD	CDU	FDP	Greens	All
Consensual	85.7	78.9	79.6	56.1	73.3
Conflictual	14.3	21.1	20.4	43.9	26.7
of which:					
Majority	13.0	12.7	9.3	17.3	13.7
Rejected	1.3	8.4	11.1	18.4	10.3
Removed	0.0	0.0	0.0	8.2	2.7
(n)	77	71	54	98	300

NB excludes 'other' decisions and joint motions

The SPD and FDP contributed eleven motions each (13.8 per cent) towards a total of eighty conflictual motions, and the CDU accounted for fifteen (18.8 per cent). As a result, it is evident that the Greens were largely responsible for the unprecedented degree of conflict registered in the Mainz party system between 1984 and 1987. Each of the other council groups were far more successful than the Greens in terms of the support gained from other council groups for their measures. The SPD in particular continued to achieve a high level of support for its proposals. Over 85 per cent of SPD motions were passed unanimously; a figure similar to that registered for the party during the period preceding the election of the Greens to the city council (86.4 per cent). Both the CDU and FDP experienced a greater degree of opposition to their proposals following the Greens' election than had previously been the case, but still gained all-party support in the first instance for almost 80 per cent of their motions. It can be inferred that these lower levels of support for the CDU and FDP motions were themselves a result of the Greens' presence in the council chamber.

If the conflictual motions are subjected to a more precise analysis the antagonistic role of the Greens in the local politics of Mainz can be more clearly identified. Of the thirty-one motions rejected outright by the Mainz council between 1984 and 1987, 58.1 per cent were introduced by the Greens. This proportion is three times that pertaining to the initiatives of either the CDU or FDP council groups. The SPD only suffered outright defeat on one occasion during the same time-period. In a further category, in which motions were removed from the agenda of the council meeting, only the Greens were represented. In all, eight Green initiatives were voted off the agenda of council meetings (representing 8.2 per cent of the council group's motions).

Table 9.9 Mainz: Green Initiatives by Party Group Decisions, 1984–1987 (in %)

Decision	SPD	CDU	FDP
Accept	10.1	4.3	4.4
Refer	74.2	59.1	59.3
Reject	9.0	30.1	29.7
Remove	6.7	6.5	6.6
(n)	89	93	91

NB excludes 'other' decisions and missing cases

The evidence suggests that the Greens lie at the heart of increasing conflict in the local politics of Mainz. Such conflict was largely absent from the period prior to the Greens' election to the city council in June 1984. It is useful to identify whether the incidence of conflict in Mainz is restricted to the Greens, or whether it has spilled over to affect the other parties. Such an analysis can be undertaken on the basis of an assessment of the voting patterns of the established parties' council groups with regard to both the Greens' and their own initiatives. If the eighteen motions which resulted in a decision falling into the 'other' category and the eight motions introduced by more than one council group are ignored, 300 motions can be assessed. Ninety-eight of these motions were initiated by the Greens and 202 by the established parties. In Table 9.9 the decisions made by the established parties' council groups with respect to the Greens' motions are shown. The findings clearly indicate the origins of party-political conflict in Mainz. Whereas the CDU and FDP recorded high levels of opposition to the initiatives of the Green council group, the SPD was far more reserved. In 10.1 per cent of cases the Social Democrats supported the motive underlying a particular initiative and in an additional 74.2 per cent of cases they agreed to the further discussion of Green motions in committee. The preference for the treatment of such Green issues in committee could be regarded as a tactical manoeuvre by the SPD council group. In a number of cases the Greens sought to expose the SPD's lack of commitment to party policy by adapting SPD manifesto proposals and introducing them into council sessions in the form of a motion of their own. Where these issues were no longer a priority matter for the SPD council group or where there was perceived to be no means of funding their implementation, the referral of the motion to committee could be regarded as a means of saving face.

The decisions affecting the motions of the three established party groups in the Mainz city council were substantially different to those affecting the Greens' initiatives (Table 9.10). The 202 motions of the SPD, CDU and FDP were subjected to practically the same type of decision from all parties. Even the Green council group supported the referral of over 80 per cent of the established parties' motions to committee, with only 9.6 per cent being rejected by the council group. This analysis points clearly towards the existence of differing voting patterns according to the council group responsible for initiating particular motions. Green motions were subject to much higher levels of conflict than those of the established parties. The Greens' initiatives tended to raise more opposition from the CDU and FDP than from the SPD. However, this feature does not apply in reverse. On the contrary, the Greens tend to treat the motions of the established party groups in an identical fashion to that employed by these groups themselves.

Table 9.10 Mainz: SPD, CDU and FDP Initiatives by Party Group Decisions, 1984–1987 (in %)

Decision	SPD	CDU	FDP	Greens
Accept	7.5	8.0	7.1	6.6
Refer	85.5	86.0	87.4	83.6
Reject	7.0	6.0	5.6	9.6
(n)	200	200	198	197

NB excludes 'other' decisions and missing cases

Without the participation of the Greens, the evidence presented in this section suggests that the Mainz city council would have continued to be characterised by consensual decision-making processes and all-party agreement. Indeed, the Greens' preference for referring the established parties' motions to committee suggests that were the party denied the right to initiate motions, they would have done little to alter the degree of consensus with regard to council motions. The council group responsible for initiating motions in a particular council session exerts a major influence upon the level of conflict affecting the meeting. As a result, sessions marked by low levels of Green activity were more likely to be consensual than those in which the Greens were responsible for a high proportion of the initiatives on the agenda. Consequently, both the political context of the individual council sessions and the council group responsible for introducing motions in the relevant session represent key contributory factors underlying differing levels of conflict in Mainz between 1984 and 1987.

Subject Areas of Conflict in Mainz

This section concentrates upon the subject areas of those initiatives introduced in the Mainz city council between 1984 and 1987 which gave rise to conflict. Table 9.11 links the type of council decisions to the individual subject-area categories of the analysis. By their very nature, some issues proved more conflictual than others. The sub-ject-area categories which led to the lowest amount of conflict in Mainz were those of environment, transport, social, culture and democracy. Whilst 26.7 per cent of all motions introduced by the Mainz council groups gave rise to a conflictual decision, this applied to only 16.9 per cent of the motions with an environmental subject area. In the transport, social and culture categories the respective figures were 19.2 per cent, 19.4 per cent and 20.9 per cent. In contrast to such levels of unanimity, a number of categories attracted above-average levels of conflict. Under the larger subject-area headings only planning motions aroused a significant degree of controversy, with eleven of the thirty motions in question lead-ing to a majority decision (36.7 per cent). However, minor subject-area categories, such as partnerships, military, law and order and administration were all characterised by high levels of conflict. Four of the five motions in the military category, for example, resulted in disagreement of some form or other, whilst two-thirds of initiatives relating to town partnerships led to conflict.

Table 9.11 Mainz: Consensus Levels by Subject Areas, 1984–1987 (in %)

Subject area	Consensual		Conflictual	
	%	n	%	n
Environment	83.1	69	16.9	14
Transport	80.8	42	19.2	10
Social	80.6	25	19.4	6
Planning	63.3	19	36.7	11
Culture	79.1	34	20.9	9
Administration	50.0	4	50.0	4
Military	20.0	1	50.0	3
Economics	33.3	3	66.7	6
Partnerships	42.9	3	57.1	4
Law and order	100.0	3	0.0	0
Education	71.4	5	28.6	2
Youth	50.0	2	50.0	2
Other	63.2	12	36.8	7
Total	73.3	225	26.7	82

NB excludes 'other' decisions

Evidence also suggests that the party responsible for initiating a motion dictated the extent to which that motion caused conflict.

Also evident were notable variations in the levels of conflict affecting the motions of the Mainz council groups with respect to their subject areas. Table 9.12 details the proportion of conflictual motions within each subject area emanating from each council group in Mainz between 1984 and 1987. The most striking finding to be drawn from these data is that the Green council group was not only responsible for initiating more than half of all conflictual motions, but that this conflictual element characterised their initiatives irrespective of the subject area to which they belonged. Despite this fact, however, Green motions belonging to certain subject areas were more consensual than those in other categories. Within the fourteen subject-area categories variations in the levels of conflict affecting the motions of the four council groups were discernible. This was particularly evident in the four subject-area categories in which all motions initiated by the Green council group aroused dissent; the categories of military, partnerships, law and order and youth. Even in the environmental category, in which the Greens recorded their highest level of unanimity, with 75 per cent of the council group's motions gaining all-party support, the Greens were responsible for introducing 64.3 per cent of all conflictual motions. The environmental motions of the established parties' council groups tended to be of a far more consensual nature than those of the Greens. The SPD, for example, gained unanimous support for all but one of its eighteen environmental motions, whilst each of the CDU's motions in this category received unanimous backing. Only the FDP approached the Greens' level of conflict in this category, with four of their fourteen motions (77.8 per cent) leading to a majority decision of some type.

In the social category the Greens were again responsible for introducing the great majority of conflictual motions. Five out of six of such motions (83.3 per cent) were placed upon the council agenda by the Greens. Only the CDU was represented in the conflictual motions of this category in addition to the Greens, albeit with only a single initiative. Neither the SPD nor the FDP encountered opposition to their motions with a social subject area over the course of the analysis. Of all the subject areas included within the classification that of planning was responsible for causing most conflict irrespective of the council group responsible for introducing the relevant initiatives. Whilst the Greens' planning motions were most likely to give rise to conflict – only two of the council group's seven motions in this subject area were passed unanimously – the other council groups were responsible for a further two conflictual planning motions each. Taking account of the differing policy priorities of the established parties' council groups, this represented 40 per cent of FDP, 28.6 per cent of SPD and 20 per cent of CDU planning motions. Variations in the level of unanimity affecting the council groups' motions also arose in the culture category. Whereas only four of the Greens' nine motions with a cultural subject area resulted in a unanimous resolution, the FDP received all-party support for each of its six cultural motions. Both the SPD and CDU received unanimous backing for over 80 per cent of their initiatives in this category. Finally the subject area of partnerships is also worthy of attention. In this case a clear difference was also found in the decisions made affecting the Greens' initiatives and those of the established parties' council groups. Whereas each of the Greens' three partnerships motions resulted in a conflictual decision, the CDU had an equal proportion of motions in both categories and the SPD received all-party support for its single initiative.

Table 9.12 Mainz: Conflictual Motions by Subject Areas and Initiating Party, 1984–1987 (in %)

Subject area	SPD %	SPD n	CDU %	CDU n	FDP %	FDP n	GREENS %	GREENS n	All %	All n
Environment	7.1	1	0.0	0	28.6	4	64.3	9	17.5	14
Transport	22.2	2	11.1	1	33.3	3	33.3	3	11.3	9
Social	0.0	0	16.7	1	0.0	0	83.3	5	7.5	6
Planning	18.2	2	18.2	2	18.2	2	45.5	5	13.8	11
Culture	22.2	2	33.3	3	0.0	0	44.4	4	11.3	9
Administration	25.0	1	50.0	2	0.0	0	25.0	1	5.0	4
Military	25.0	1	0.0	0	0.0	0	75.0	3	5.0	4
Economics	0.0	0	0.0	0	33.3	1	66.7	2	3.8	3
Partnerships	0.0	0	40.0	2	0.0	0	60.0	3	6.3	5
Law and order	25.0	1	0.0	0	25.0	1	50.0	2	5.0	4
Education	0.0	0	100.0	2	0.0	0	0.0	0	2.5	2
Youth	50.0	1	0.0	0	0.0	0	50.0	1	2.5	2
Other	0.0	0	28.6	2	0.0	0	71.4	5	8.8	7
Total	13.8	11	18.8	15	13.8	11	53.8	43	100.0	80

NB excludes 'other' decisions and joint motions

A New Agenda? Analysis of Council Initiatives in Mainz

Table 9.13 Mainz: Green Motions by Subject Areas and Council
Decision, 1984–1987 (in %)

Subject area	Unanimous	Majority	Decision Rejected	Removed	(n)
Environment	75.0	13.9	11.1	0.0	36
Transport	72.7	18.2	0.0	9.1	11
Social	64.3	14.3	14.3	7.1	14
Planning	28.6	14.3	28.6	28.6	7
Culture	55.6	22.2	22.2	0.0	9
Administration	50.0	0.0	50.0	0.0	2
Military	0.0	66.7	0.0	33.3	3
Economics	33.3	0.0	66.7	0.0	3
Partnerships	0.0	33.3	33.3	33.3	3
Law and order	0.0	0.0	100.0	0.0	2
Youth	0.0	100.0	0.0	0.0	1
Other	28.6	14.3	28.6	28.6	7
Total	56.1	17.3	18.4	8.2	
(n)	55	17	18	8	98

NB excludes 'other' decisions

Such findings invite the conclusion that the Greens' motions were, in general, more provocative than those of the established parties' council groups, irrespective of the subject area to which they belonged. However, when the subject area of the motions was taken into consideration, the evidence suggests that the party's initiatives in selected subject areas were even more conflictual than those belonging to others. Given the existence of a strong link between the subject area of the Greens' motions and their ultimate outcome in council, it is worthwhile examining in closer detail the precise type of decision made to take account of differing levels of conflict. Table 9.13 provides more detailed information about the nature of the council decisions made in respect of the Green motions introduced during the three-year period of the Mainz analysis for which the relevant information is available.[6] The data corroborate the finding previously

[6] How individual parties had voted on Green issues could not always be inferred from the council minutes. Some motions were agreed in part only, with individual clauses being rejected.

established of the existence of a very strong link between the subject area of the Greens' motions and the degree of unanimity affecting them. The level of all-party support arising from the council group's environmental motions is of great relevance. Three-quarters of all motions belonging to this category were either unanimously accepted or referred to committee by the four council groups. A further five environmental motions (13.9 per cent) were the subject of a majority decision in their favour. This indicates that the Greens gained the support of at least one of the large council groups, most commonly of the SPD, for these initiatives. Only four Green motions with an environmental subject-matter were rejected outright in the first instance (11.1 per cent of the group's motions in this category).

The Mainz Greens were most successful in an area in which they possessed a degree of technical expertise. Motions based on the Greens' detailed knowledge of ecological matters tended not to be so readily dismissed by the council groups of the established political parties as motions in other subject-area categories. This reflects both the established parties' informational deficit on environmental issues and the Greens' internal decision-making processes with regard to environmental themes. The two Green council group working groups operating in this area, the environmental protection group and the ecology group, tended to fulfil their duties in a different way to other party working groups. Great stress was placed by the (realist-dominated) environmentalists upon the practicalities of introducing policies which would have some chance of implementation. Other working groups tended to work at a more abstract level.

In other subject areas the Greens' initiatives led to a disproportionately high level of conflict within the Mainz city council. This applied particularly to the subject areas of partnerships and military matters, in which all Green motions were subject to some degree of conflict and in which the Greens had motions removed from the agenda of council sessions, the most extreme form of conflict possible. In the two subject areas of law and order and youth the Greens also failed to gain all-party support for any of their motions, although the number of motions involved was perhaps too small to be able to draw significant conclusions. Other subject areas in which there was a disproportionately high level of conflict affecting Green motions were planning and economics. The category 'other' also was under-represented in the consensual category.

This analysis illustrates the differing attitudes of the established parties' council groups with respect to the content of the Greens' proposals. In general, motions introduced in established areas of local politics in which the Greens were judged to possess a degree of technical expertise, such as on environmental or transport matters, were more likely to be successful than motions belonging to 'new' areas which traditionally lay beyond the scope of German local politics. This particularly applies to military issues and to the increasing amount of debate on town twinning arrangements, but also to economic issues when placed in supra-local context. Planning issues were also increasingly emotive under the Greens, given the party's concerted opposition to specific local developments which it perceived to be a threat to the local environment.

Figure 9.7 Mainz: Classification of Subject Areas by Level of Conflict

Level of conflict	Subject areas
Very high	Military, Partnerships, Law and order, Youth
High	Planning, Economics, Other
Moderate	Culture, Administration
Low	Environment, Transport, Social

As a result, it is possible to establish a model which exploits the fact that varying types of subject area can give rise to differing types of decision. Four categories of subject-area type were established to take account of the varying levels of conflict arising from the Greens' initiatives in Mainz (Figure 9.7). Low levels of conflict arose in the environmental, transport and social categories. In the administration and culture subject areas moderate levels of conflict were recorded. In the remaining subject areas in which the Greens introduced motions either high or very high levels of conflict arose within the city council. The level of conflict deriving from this modified classification of the Greens' motions is displayed in Table 9.14. Of the motions belonging to the category which aroused least conflict some 72.1 per cent were passed unanimously. In direct contrast to this relatively high level of agreement, the subject areas grouped under the 'high' and 'very high' headings gave rise to greater dissent. In the case of the seventeen motions within the 'high' category, twelve led to conflict (70.6 per cent), whilst all nine motions belonging to the 'very high' category aroused conflict.

Table 9.14 Mainz: Green Motions by Subject Area Groups and Decisions, 1984–1987 (in %)

Decision type		Low	Moderate	High	Very High	All
Unanimous	%	72.1	54.5	29.4	0.0	56.1
	n	44	6	5	0	55
Majority	%	14.8	18.2	11.8	44.4	17.3
	n	9	2	2	4	17
Rejected	%	9.8	27.3	35.3	33.3	18.4
	n	6	3	6	3	18
Removed	%	3.3	0.0	23.5	22.2	8.2
	n	2	0	4	2	8
(n)		61	11	17	9	98

(Conflict level spans Low, Moderate, High, Very High.)

NB excludes 'other' decisions

In Mainz, therefore, it has been possible to illustrate a very strong link between the subject areas of Green motions and the council resolutions affecting them. It can be anticipated that similar findings would prevail in other communities across Germany. However, it would be useful to apply methods similar to those adopted here to studies of a range of additional German localities in order to assess whether the results have a more universal relevance. Unfortunately an absence to date of readily accessible comparable data means that it is not possible to undertake such a comparative analysis here.

Summary: The Changing Agenda of Local Politics in Mainz

At the start of this chapter two principal questions relating to Green local politics were outlined. On the basis of the information presented in this chapter it is now possible to draw some tentative conclusions about the changing agenda and style of local politics in Mainz, as reflected in the legislative initiatives of the parties represented on the city council.

Firstly, the changing levels of activity of the Mainz council groups were examined for the periods preceding and following the election of the Greens to the Mainz city council in June 1984. Although only marginally higher rates of activity were registered for the period in which the Greens were represented, this factor masked variations in the levels of activity of the individual council groups. The Green council group maintained a very high level of initiation for the period under review, introducing over one-third of all motions. However, when account was taken of the respective strengths of the council groups it emerged that not only the Green councillors, but also the members of the smaller FDP council group, were responsible for high rates of performance. The levels of activity of the larger council groups of the SPD and CDU were correspondingly lower.

The suggestion that the Greens have contributed towards a change in the agenda of local politics was tested for the case of Mainz on the basis of a classification of the motions of the council groups into a range of subject areas. At this early stage of the analysis difficulties could already be identified with attempts to locate topics on a New–Old Local Politics dimension. Nevertheless, certain variations in the agenda of local politics in Mainz following the entry of the Greens to the council chamber were identified. Environmental, transport and cultural issues were discussed more frequently, whilst the previously important economics category suffered a decline in significance. A number of changes also occurred with regard to the policy-making priorities of the individual council groups. The Greens laid most emphasis on environmental and social issues and were also responsible for the great proportion of all initiatives in these fields. Both the SPD and FDP made a priority of environmental and transport issues, whilst the CDU emphasised the importance of cultural and transport matters and placed only a low level of significance upon the environmental category.

The second question to be addressed was that local politics has become more conflictual as a result of the Greens' presence in Germany's local parliaments. This was shown to be the case in Mainz. Whilst the period preceding the election of the Greens had been marked by high levels of unanimity, with almost 90 per cent of motions being supported by all the council groups, that following the Greens' election saw only 73.3 per cent of motions gaining such backing. It was possible to identify three main factors underlying variations in the levels of conflict witnessed over the course of the analysis. Not only were political events in Mainz, such as the election of new members of the council executive, judged to exert an influence upon the course of council meetings, but also the council group responsible for initiating motions and the subject areas of the motions affected the nature of the decision. Green motions with a military subject area introduced at a time marked by tension over other political events were more likely to lead to conflict than FDP motions with an environmental subject area initiated at other times. However, the difficulties with regard to the identification of New Politics issues could not be bridged by means of a quantitative analysis alone. For this reason, it is now necessary to examine the content of the initiatives introduced by the Mainz council groups in more qualitative terms.

10
The Local Political Agenda in Mainz: Persistence and Change

In Chapters 8 and 9 changes in the style and content of Mainz's local politics between 1984 and 1987 were addressed. It was shown that both the agenda and the consensual style of local politics in the city had changed to a certain degree during this period. However, in the context of the New Politics debate, a number of difficulties were raised with regard to the identification of a New–Old Politics dimension. Two major limitations characterised the quantitative analysis applied in Chapter 9. Firstly, difficulties inherent in attempts to classify motions according to a New or Old Politics subject area could not be overcome. Secondly, an analysis of the resolutions tended to mask over the nature of conflict witnessed in the Mainz city council. This chapter aims to overcome some of the these difficulties by using more qualitative techniques. This was achieved with reference to two main sources. Firstly, the texts of the relevant motions introduced by the Mainz council groups between 1984 and 1987 were examined. This allowed judgements to be made about stylistic and contextual differences between the initiatives of the Mainz council groups. Secondly, recourse was had to the minutes of the council meetings in which the motions were debated. Extracted minutes of council meetings are produced after each session by the Mainz city authorities which summarise the principal contributions made by the participants of each council group to the debate. In addition to such condensed reports, full transcripts of the proceedings were made available on particularly important occasions. An examination of the contributions of the four council groups to the debate on individual topics allows a better understanding of differing interpretations accorded to the role of local politics by the parties.

In Chapter 3 the main elements of the New Local Politics were identified in terms of its broad interpretation of the scope of

Article 28.2 of the Basic Law, the conflictual nature of its agenda and its influence upon the politicisation of all spheres of local council activity. Subsequently, it was shown that the Greens' approach to local politics fundamentally differs from that of the established German political parties. By addressing the content of the issues under discussion in the Mainz city council in conjunction with the debate regarding them, the extent to which the New Local Politics played a role in the city will be discussed at two levels. Firstly, the system level at which the Mainz council groups' motions were directed will be assessed. The traditional, Old Local Politics view is that the agenda of local councils should only address issues of immediate relevance to the local level, whilst the New Politics approach places local issues in a much wider context. Secondly, the content and style of the initiatives with a local orientation will be addressed. The aim of this analysis is to judge the degree to which the Greens' local level motions differ from those of the established parties.

Supra-Local Issues in Mainz

By concentrating upon two particular themes, international issues and nuclear-free zones, in this section attention is to be focused upon motions initiated by the Mainz council groups between 1984 and 1987 which contained either an international or a national dimension. These supra-local issues can, by their very nature, be regarded as belonging to Germany's New Local Politics agenda. With the strict exception of the FDP, all council groups in Mainz were responsible for introducing motions with a supra-local dimension at some time during the period under review. An analysis of the motions' texts and of the ensuing debate will provide an indication of the changing scope of German local politics.

Global Politics at Local Level: The Discussion of Town Partnerships

One obvious example of an international issue to which every locality can legitimately address itself without fear of transcending the competences of local authority self-administration is that

of town partnerships. This is a long-established area of local politics in the Federal Republic, although its recent treatment serves
to illustrate the means by which the Greens have contributed
towards a politicisation of German local politics. Traditionally,
town-twinning arrangements were made by German local communities as a gesture of reconciliation, as a means of re-establish-
ing contact between the citizens of countries which had previously been at war or simply to reduce tension between citizens
of different countries. In this respect, partnerships are normally
made with reference to the commonalities of the respective
towns. Similarities can be sought in either historical, industrial,
political or geographical terms. Mainz, for example, enjoys a
long-standing partnership with Watford (UK), both localities
having well-established printing industries. Before the election
of the Greens to the city council in 1984, further partnerships
existed between Mainz and Dijon (France), Zagreb (Yugoslavia),
Valencia (Spain) and Haifa (Israel). However, a major feature of
all town-twinning arrangements was their foundation upon the
unanimous support of all council groups at their inception. To
this extent, town partnerships were largely uncontroversial in
post-war Mainz.

As has already been noted in Chapter 5, the Greens tend to
regard the function of town partnerships in rather different
terms from other political parties. For the Mainz Greens, partnerships occupied an important political function, since they provided a means of expressing solidarity with the citizens of the
partner towns and countries and of drawing public attention to
the North–South divide. In contrast to the formal links maintained by the respective towns' authorities the Greens sought to
establish direct contact with the inhabitants of the twin town,
preferably with people who shared the Greens' ideology. Regular links existed, for example, between the Mainz Greens and
local peace groups in Watford, extending to the partial funding
by the Greens of the visits of peace activists from Watford.[1]

In order to demonstrate their feelings of solidarity with the
citizens of countries threatened by US foreign policy, most
notably with the population of Nicaragua, the Mainz Greens
acted in conjunction with a local initiative group to support

---

[1] A subsidy of DM 900 was set aside for the visit in July 1985.

efforts to establish a partnership with the Nicaraguan town of Diriamba.[2] However, it would be wrong to assume that the Greens were alone in supporting such a link, since the partnership was also approved by a number of left-wing SPD councillors and local party wards. Significantly, the majority of the SPD council group and their representatives on the council executive in particular were more lukewarm about the proposal.

The Green council group sought financial backing for projects in Diriamba and the establishment of a full twinning arrangement in a number of motions. The text of an initial motion identified the underlying reasons for seeking such an arrangement: 'A letter to the US forces based in Mainz will unambiguously point out that the city of Mainz severely opposes the aggressive and imperialistic policies of the US government towards Nicaragua' (M147/1984). Falling within an initial period marked by a certain *rapprochement* between the Greens and the SPD, both parties agreed to withdraw their own initiatives in favour of a joint initiative. Acting upon a request from the local initiative group, keen to avoid any splits on this topic,[3] both parties agreed upon the wording of a joint motion which reflected the more moderate approach of the SPD council group: 'The city of Mainz declares its solidarity with the people of Nicaragua in their efforts to achieve sovereignty and peace' (M23/85).

Nevertheless, even in its more moderate form, such a proposal caused controversy when debated in the council session of 26 February 1985. A portrayal of the course of the debate serves to illustrate the varying interpretations accorded to the role of local councils by the individual council groups in Mainz. The debate operated essentially on two levels. Whilst the FDP disputed the legitimacy of debating matters of international relevance in the local arena, the CDU was more willing to express its reservations in substantive terms. Green councillor Günter Beck's speech opened the debate by placing the initiative into its broad international context:

---

[2] The initiative group in question is the *Verein zur Föderung der Städtepartnerscharft Mainz/Diriamba (STP-Verein)*.

[3] Letter of 7 December 1984 from Charles Franck, chairman of *STP-Verein* to SPD and Green council groups.

Five years ago ... the people of Nicaragua used armed force to chase the dictator Somoza from the country. In close collaboration with the USA, whose governor he was, he plundered the country and its people, laid waste to the land and terrorised the people. The Sandinistas introduced a comprehensive literacy campaign and reformed the health service and agriculture. The successes to date have been considerable. But since the start of these revolutionary changes the Reagan Administration has inflicted war upon Nicaragua ... by means of the Contras and other so-called opposition groups; by laying mines off its coast, by the threatening manoeuvres of America's military might, linked to the promise that an invasion cannot be ruled out (council minutes, 26 February 1985).

Councillor Ebsen argued along similar lines for the SPD, criticising US foreign policy and drawing parallels between events in Nicaragua and those in Chile in 1973, which saw the Allende government replaced in a US-backed coup by the military dictatorship of General Pinochet:

Solidarity with the people of Nicaragua is an element of this motion today. What does that mean? Solidarity with the people of Nicaragua means protecting them from the fate of the Chilean people. What can we do about it? We certainly cannot directly affect foreign policy. But other than the necessary admonitions to and criticisms of our allies, the United States, we can also help in a practical way ...

Today we are discussing a concrete measure with which we can express our solidarity in practical terms as well as foster the development of the country ... (council minutes, 26 February 1985).

Significantly, CDU councillor Armin Korn entered into the debate at the same international level as the SPD and Greens. No doubts were raised by him of the legitimacy of debating such a matter at local level; indeed, Third World aid was regarded by him as being a relevant part of local council activity. Dr Korn's only difficulty lay in the choice of Nicaragua as a worthy recipient of such aid:

With this motion we ask ourselves ... why this particular country at this particular time? Why not Afghanistan or Rwanda or another African country governed by hunger and death ...? We believe that this country was chosen for the sole purpose of satisfying anti-American feelings of resentment.

... I ask my respected colleagues in the SPD council group: Is it really truthful and just to accuse our most important ally – the USA –

213

of always having the most sinister intentions, despite the fact that for forty years we in Germany have on the whole had positive experiences with the Americans? (council minutes, 26 February 1985).

Only FDP group leader Günter Storch expressed fundamental reservations about the discussion of international affairs in the city council. His response exemplified the FDP's restrictive interpretation of the role of local councils:

> Once more we are experiencing a great hour of German foreign policy in the Mainz city council. Once again we are dealing with a subject which does not belong here, as we have done so often since the Greens have a voice in this city council. In our view the motion of the SPD and the Greens has only a superficial humanitarian aim. In reality its sole purpose is to make a political statement, a declaration of solidarity which does not belong in the Mainz city council. This is an issue of German foreign policy and according to the Basic Law the federal level is responsible for foreign policy. ... Whoever is in disagreement with German foreign policy, as it is practised by the current government, must take this up at the responsible location, namely the Federal Parliament, and not in city councils and local parliaments (council minutes, 26 February 1985).

Despite the orientation of the original motion towards providing financial assistance to Diriamba, it was evident in this case that the debate revolved more about issues of international politics than about affairs of specific relevance to Mainz. Indeed, the contributions of the Green, SPD and CDU councillors quoted above could easily have emanated from the Federal Parliament in Bonn. In terms of the New–Old Local Politics dimension, it is possible to identify clear differences between the respective parties. The FDP is firmly rooted in the Old Local Politics, whilst the remaining parties are open to the discussion of New Local Politics topics.

On all subsequent occasions on which the possible town partnership with Diriamba was discussed by the Mainz council conflict emerged. In June 1985, for example, acting upon a request from the initiative group,[4] the Greens sought to grant the mayor of Diriamba permission to address the council on the latest developments in Nicaragua (M119/1985). The response of the

---

[4] Letter of 7 June 1985 from Charles Franck, chairman of *STP-Verein*, to SPD and Green council groups.

city administration and the other council groups, including the SPD, was to remove the motion from the agenda. The formal reason for their resolution was that they did not wish to set a precedent by allowing one foreign dignitary to address the council. It later emerged that SPD support for the motion was withdrawn in the face of CDU threats to remove its councillors from the session in which the mayor of Diriamba was to speak. This was judged to harm the prospects of a possible partnership arrangement, normally agreed with all-party support.

Not only were the Green and SPD council group responsible for initiating motions relating to Nicaragua, but even the CDU group raised the subject in its own right, seeking to redress the balance somewhat in favour of the US administration. In a 1986 motion, the CDU council group drew attention to perceived civil rights violations by the Sandinista government in Nicaragua and sought council funding for an exhibition on the country in the foyer of the city hall:

> According to reports by the independent Permanent Committee on Human Rights in Nicaragua (CPDH), which have on the whole also been confirmed by 'amnesty international (ai)', there are currently over 3,500 political prisoners in Nicaragua. Torturing by state security services and terror judgements passed by so-called 'anti-Somozan special courts' against alleged opponents of the Sandinista regime are the order of the day. Since the city of Mainz is granting financial aid to the city of Diriamba and attempts are also under way to establish partnership arrangements, such events are of great political interest to the population of Mainz (M233/1985).

Whilst the exhibition was intended to present an 'independent' view of events in Nicaragua, the CDU's strategy was clearly to delay any decision which might have led to the realisation of the proposed partnership between Mainz and Diriamba. Despite Green and SPD opposition to the CDU proposal and the inevitable FDP reservations about whether Nicaragua should be a subject for debate at local level, the Christian Democrats were successful in having their motion referred to committee. Ultimately, the CDU's delaying tactics with regard to the Mainz–Diriamba link succeeded. By the end of the period under analysis, despite a resolution passed in the council meeting of December 1986 by the Greens and SPD, the link had not been formally agreed. Indeed, this was one of many Green initiatives which suffered as a result of the collapse of budget negotiations with the SPD in the winter of 1985/6. Without financial backing, the success of this initiative could not be guaranteed.

With regard to partnership issues, Nicaragua was not the only foreign country to be placed upon the agenda of the Mainz council between 1984 and 1987. The CDU, for example, was responsible for initiating a motion calling for the provision of financial support by the city for a project in the Rwandan town of Kigali (M100/1985). This move can be viewed within the context of the Rhineland Palatinate's unique twinning arrangement with Rwanda. It can also be regarded in terms of being a CDU response to the support provided by the Greens and SPD for Nicaragua. This derives from the fact that the amount of financial aid requested for Kigali (DM 35,000) was identical to the sum agreed for a similar project in Diriamba. Nevertheless, all council groups lent their support to the CDU initiative. Again the nature of debate on the issue provides an insight into changes in Mainz's local politics. The reasoning behind the CDU motion was expressed by Councillor Korn, who drew parallels between poverty and damage to the environment in Rwanda, stating: 'that Rwanda is one of the world's poorest countries. The country faces an ecological catastrophe caused by deforestation.'[5] The SPD response also touched upon similar global issues, with attention being drawn to the North–South divide: 'Councillor Vehof notes that Rwanda once belonged to the German colonies. Since the putsch of 1973 it has been led by a pro-western military government. The SPD council group sees today's motion by the CDU within the perspective of the North–South conflict and in the contrast between poor and rich' (council minutes, 29 May 1985). However, bearing in mind the opinion expressed by its representatives in successive debates on Nicaragua, the most revealing response came from the FDP:

> Council group chairman Dr Storch argues that basically it is not the duty of a local authority to grant development aid. This is the duty of the federal and regional levels. In the present case, the state of Rhineland Palatinate has entered into a true partnership with Rwanda. In this respect it appears right and necessary that the regional

---

[5] From council meeting minutes of 29 May 1985.

capital Mainz should make an appropriate contribution (council minutes, 29 May 1985).

FDP objections to the principle that local councils should be discussing problems of international relevance at all were balanced by support for initiatives which did not run counter to their party's foreign policy. On the one hand, the Mainz FDP forcefully sought to resist the trend towards the discussion of global issues. On the other, it found itself forced to express an opinion on the issues under debate in order to appear politically competent. This suggests that the dynamic affecting the issues of the New Local Politics cannot be resisted by more traditional political forces at local level.

Other International Issues

Town-twinning arrangements undeniably fall within the accepted scope of German local authorities' competences. However, it proved much more difficult for the Mainz Greens to express their opposition to the internal and foreign policies of other countries for which no partnership link existed. In these instances a local relevance often had to be contrived. One such case in which the Mainz Green council group initiated a motion with an international dimension and a contrived local applicability regarded events in Turkey. In order to criticise Turkey's human rights record, the city authorities were requested not to send a representative to a reception held by the Turkish Consul in Mainz: 'In view of the persecution of democratic forces in Turkey, the denial of human rights, the torture in Turkish prisons, participation in the reception equates to an approval of the current balance of power.'[6]

Such a motion is indicative of the Greens' attempts to politicise all aspects of local political life. This also pertains to the actions of the city administration. The party's aim was to make it increasingly difficult for city representatives to maintain links with foreign governments with poor human and civil rights records. Although this particular motion was rejected by the

---

[6] Emergency motion submitted by Greens to *Hauptausschuß* meeting of 23 October 1984.

council, this did not end the debate on Turkey. A bitter and somewhat abusive confrontation between Green councillor Alf Haenlein and SPD executive member Herman-Hartmut Weyel at a demonstration in front of the consulate became the focus for further discussion. Haenlein's choice of words on this occasion was particularly extreme, indicating the depth of feeling with which the Greens tend to treat issues regarding the international arena. When one considers that Weyel was to become mayor of Mainz in 1987, such an exchange would inevitably affect his subsequent relationship with the Greens. It was left to Mayor Fuchs to re-establish the ground rules by which local politicians normally operate: 'Mayor Fuchs holds the view that this event should perhaps give grounds for discussing how one can observe mutual human respect, despite protests and differing opinions' (council minutes, 7 November 1984).

The Greens' opposition to apartheid in South Africa was also debated in a series of council meetings in Mainz. Again an element of local relevance was contrived by the Green council group in order to discuss the topic. In reaction to the state of emergency declared by the South African government in July 1985, for example, the Greens introduced a motion calling for 'practical solidarity against apartheid', the focal point of which was an attempt to restrict sales of the Krugerrand by the Mainz savings bank (*Sparkasse*). This was to be achieved by influencing the city's representatives on the institution's board. Three measures were demanded by the Greens:

— The Mainz savings bank will cease advertising the South African gold Krugerrand. The Mainz savings bank will stop selling these gold coins.
— The Mainz savings bank will prepare an information leaflet for potential borrowers or Krugerrand customers which will inform them of the racist regime in Pretoria and its contempt for mankind and of the significance of foreign gold sales.
— The employees of the Mainz savings bank will be put in a situation by means of instruction and information in which they can objectively explain these measures to the savings bank's customers and can offer appropriate alternatives to the Krugerrand (M139/1985).

The Greens' motion was unacceptable to the other council groups in the form in which it was presented, given the council's lack of controlling powers over the activities of the *Sparkasse*, which is jointly administered by the district adjacent to Mainz (Mainz-Bingen). Instead, the SPD and Greens ultimately accepted an amended form of the motion, issued as an appeal to those responsible in the savings bank's administration to halt sales of the coins. Both the CDU and FDP objected to the motion for formal reasons. The CDU opposed the initiative on the grounds that the savings bank was a 'competitive business which does not have the duty to conduct world politics', the FDP for purely formal reasons: 'Although the FDP is against apartheid, it must reject the motion in its current form since the city council is not responsible for the matter' (both quotes from council minutes, 4 September 1985).

This motion exemplifies the Greens' radical approach to local politics. Not only does the initiative fail to take account of the limitations placed upon local council activity by Article 28.2 of the Basic Law, it would also be difficult to implement in its given form. The fundamentalist strategy adopted by the Mainz Greens regarded constitutional considerations as being of secondary importance. Whilst the Greens recognised the impracticality of some of their proposals, they were willing to take this into account in their efforts to broaden the horizons of local politics. In these cases evidence suggests that the Greens are less interested in initiating practical reforms than in making political statements about events in the international arena. In this sense, it is important for the Greens to seek evidence of conflict. This stems not only from the Green council group's inability to gain majority support for its radical proposals in Mainz, but also from the party's specific relationship with the new social movements. Such measures often originate within the extra-parliamentary sphere and are transported by the Greens into the respective legislature. The outcome of the motion is often immaterial to the group which proposed it (unless financial support is requested), failure tending to confirm a widespread belief in the inadequacy of the parliamentary approach. The main benefit of the exercise simply arises from the fact that the question has been debated and the response of all council groups recorded. These responses can then be used to support further attempts to achieve the groups' aims, particularly in those cases in which the SPD council group has been shown to be acting contrary to some part of its election programme. This attitude also marked the budgetary debate between the Greens and SPD in Mainz in the winter of 1985/6.

The difference between the Greens' internationally oriented motions and those of the SPD and CDU primarily existed in the nature of the demands laid out. Whilst the larger council groups tended to restrict themselves to practical and established means of drawing attention to relevant international issues, such as the holding of exhibitions in the foyer of the city hall, the Greens' demands were of a more substantive nature. This inevitably affects the possible outcome of the relevant motions. The chances of success of Green motions calling for radical solutions to problems in the international arena are likely to be significantly lower than those of CDU or SPD motions which identify practical local means by which they can reach their goal.

A final measure which well illustrated the New–Old Politics divide in the Mainz city council regarded a Green initiative which was introduced in the wake of America's bombing raid on two Libyan cities in April 1986. The raids were carried out in response to Colonel Ghaddafi's alleged role in international terrorist activities. Although the Greens sought to identify a local relevance for their motion, based upon the annual German–American Friendship weeks to be held in Mainz shortly after the attack, the overriding aim of the initiative was to make a statement about events in the international arena: '... With this act of aggression the US government has consciously and deliberately destroyed human lives. It has consciously and deliberately adopted a confrontational path, whose result is an unbearable heightening of the danger of war around the world, but in particular for the people and states of North Africa and Europe' (M66/1986). This initiative exemplifies the Greens' approach of thinking globally and acting locally. The speech prepared by Green councillor Hans-Jörg von Berlepsch, but which could not be made, shows the manner in which a relevance to Mainz was to be contrived from events in North Africa:

> Please don't tell anyone that the US Army in Mainz is an army of peace, which is only protecting us and has nothing to do with the fact that bombs were dropped on two peaceful, defenceless cities in Libya. The US Army in Mainz is one part of that war machine, which is currently being warmed up by the Pentagon.

... Can one rule out in all certainty the possibility that the US Army in Mainz will either indirectly or directly be drawn into the next military strike?

... Is it possible this year that representatives of this city and in this capacity will ceremonially receive the leaders of the US Army in Mainz with the usual set-phrases of friendship ...? – Whilst in Tripoli and Benghazi the earth over the graves of the victims of the US air-raid is still fresh?[7]

In Mainz a motion of this nature had little chance of success between 1984 and 1987. Not only was it is beyond the accepted jurisdiction of the local level, it also ran counter to the political will of the established council groups. In all instances on which the relationship between Mainz and the US forces stationed around the city was problematised by the Greens, the level of conflict within the city council was at its most extreme. The minutes of the meeting in which the Libyan motion was discussed illustrate this point. Whilst the SPD sympathised with the motives underlying the Greens' motion, they did not wish to see the German–American Friendship Weeks used as a 'tribunal' against their allies. Instead, they supported a formal move to prevent discussion of the initiative. With the CDU expressing similar reservations, Green councillor von Berlepsch responded by objecting to the formal approach adopted by the major parties: 'Council group spokesman von Berlepsch declares that he is amazed, even outraged by the motion on the point of order and the attitude of the two large council groups, since it results in an important local political issue being swept under the carpet by the majority's "steamroller"' (council minutes, 30 April 1986). Following a brief interruption of proceedings by spectators, FDP council group leader, Günter Storch, was able to make his contribution to the debate: 'Council group chairman Dr Storch expresses the view that this motion, like many other motions coming from the Greens, also concerns a subject which does not belong to the local political responsibilities of the council. It must be stressed again and again that the city council cannot deal with foreign policy matters. He took note with pleasure of the point of order motion' (council minutes, 30 April 1986). After the removal

[7] From manuscript of speech prepared by Hans-Jörg von Berlepsch for council session of 30 April 1986.

221

of the Greens' motion from the agenda and the council group's subsequent withdrawal from the council chamber, Mayor Fuchs felt obliged to make a statement in support of local US forces: 'Mayor Fuchs points out that in Mainz it is natural to live together with foreign citizens in a sensible way. This also applies to the soldiers and civilians of the forces stationed locally ... . With the Americans, the allies of the Federal Republic, one should talk openly about all sensitive questions' (council minutes, 30 April 1986).

The debate surrounding this motion reveals the limits of what the established parties are willing to accept as being of relevance to the local level. It also indicates the Greens' dependence upon the SPD's granting its support to the discussion of such matters, a recurrent feature throughout the period under analysis.

National Politics at Local Level: Atomwaffenfreie Zone Mainz

Having shown how the Mainz city council increasingly debated international issues following the election of the Greens in 1984, the manner in which further initiatives addressed by the council breached a strict interpretation of the scope of local politics will now be addressed. One area which accounted for a significant proportion of motions with a supra-local focus in Mainz was that relating to military matters. In this respect, an initiative introduced jointly by the SPD and Green council groups in November 1984, seeking to declare Mainz a nuclear weapon-free zone (*Atomwaffenfreie Zone*) was indicative of motions with a national dimension. The motion was important for three reasons. Firstly, it acted as a test case for future agreements between the Greens and the SPD. Secondly, the initiative had a certain historical tradition in Mainz. Thirdly, the subsequent course of resolution agreed by the Mainz council through the legal system proved typical of the increasing levels of conflict affecting local politics in the city.

In certain respects, there was little fundamentally new about the discussion of the question of a nuclear-free zone in Mainz. The discussion of this question had exercised the city council on a number of occasions prior to the election of the Greens in June 1984. As early as April 1958, for example, against the background of Federal Government proposals to allow the presence of atomic weapons on German territory for the first time, the Mainz council had passed two resolutions on the subject. The first called upon the city authorities to prevent the stationing or storage of nuclear weapons within the city's boundaries and to resist demands to provide land for such purposes (M25/1958). The second sought to carry out a plebiscite in Mainz in order to assess the local citizens' views on the issue of the stationing of atomic weapons in Germany: 'Should military forces armed with atomic explosives and atomic launch pads be located on German soil?' (M26/1958).

The debate in 1958 surrounding the legality of the proposed resolutions was essentially the same as that which took place when the issue was discussed again in the 1980s. For this reason it is worth recording some of the comments made by participants in the debate on 28 April 1958. As an indication of the extent of conflict surrounding the issue, the CDU council group had remained away from the council chamber for the session. This left the SPD, as the group responsible for initiating the motion, the FDP and members of the council executive to reach a decision. Commenting upon the nuclear rearmament of the German army in general terms, SPD councillor Distelhut expressed the following opinion: 'This is the start of an extremely dangerous development, against which we must arm ourselves with all decisiveness. We believe that the German people have a right to express their opinion on whether they agree with such a development. In particular, however, the population of the so badly affected city of Mainz has a right to express this opinion' (council minutes, 28 April 1958). This view was not shared by the executive committee member responsible for legal matters, who strongly contested the legality of the second motion, arguing that it lay beyond the competences of the local legislature: 'This motion ... quite clearly falls within the competences of the federal level. When all is said and done, therefore, it is the Federal Parliament which could decide this matter, but not a local legislature, and not the city council of Mainz either' (council minutes, 28 April 1958). In the vote, the first initiative seeking to prevent the local storage of nuclear weapons was passed unanimously, whilst the second calling for the plebiscite was subject to a majority decision, with the FDP voting against. This resolution was technically still in force some twenty-five years later in 1983, during the height of a second phase of the Peace Movement in Mainz. Before the 1984 election of the Greens, local peace groups had already petitioned the council to declare the city a nuclear-free zone. In doing so they made use of a mechanism included within the local constitution of the Rhineland Palatinate which allows for the direct participation of citizens in local council affairs. According to Paragraph Seventeen of the constitution, once certain formal stipulations have been met by the initiating group, the council is obliged to debate the issue in its next session. Following the collection of sufficient signatures by petition organisers, the city council debated the question of whether Mainz should be declared nuclear-free. The CDU council group opposed the petition for formal, legalistic reasons, based on their belief that local authorities are not competent to discuss matters of national security:

> Whilst the communities are in their areas and under their own responsibility the sole carriers of the entire local administration, the competences of the communities are not without limitations. The local sphere of activity only regards duties which are rooted in the local community and which specifically refer to the local community. ... The city of Mainz is not competent to deal with the general defence policy question under debate here. This is not altered by the fact that artificial attempts have been made to establish a local relevance ... by trying to discuss a nuclear-weapon-free zone in Mainz (council minutes 23 March 1983).

Though they had succeeded in ensuring that the petition was discussed in the council, the peace groups' proposal was ultimately rejected when an SPD resolution was unsuccessful in the final vote, with the combined strength of the CDU and FDP council groups matching that of the SPD.

The SPD–Green motion of November 1984 should be viewed within this broad context. Given the existence of a red–green majority in the new council chamber, the chances of this initiative's succeeding were much greater than on previous occasions. Indeed, the success of the nuclear-free zone proposals was regarded in some ways as a further test for a possible long-term alliance between the Greens and SPD in Mainz. Yet even before the motion was introduced it was recognised by the initiating council groups that any new resolution in favour of establishing

Mainz as a nuclear-free zone would meet with the disapproval of the body which supervises the legality of decisions made in the Mainz council chamber, the *Bezirksregierung Rheinhessen-Pfalz*. In order to avert the attentions of the supervisory body, it was regarded as essential for the Greens and SPD to adopt a form of wording in their initiative which specifically applied to Mainz and which could not be interpreted as being beyond the city council's competences. For this reason both council groups withdrew their own initiatives on the subject in preference for a joint motion which would have a greater chance of success.

The joint motion proposed a series of measures. Firstly, Mainz was to declare its support for an international programme, initiated by the Japanese cities of Hiroshima and Nagasaki, which sought to abolish nuclear weapons throughout the world. Secondly, the 1958 decision was to be reactivated on the grounds that it was still relevant, with the rider that the authorities should seek its realisation 'within the framework of its legal possibilities'. Thirdly, the peace groups' petition of March 1983 was to receive further support on the basis that their initiative 'has a concrete meaning for all citizens, especially in Mainz with its exposed situation caused by the military bases in its near vicinity'. Further clauses of the motion sought to publicise the measure through signs posted at entry points to the city, to establish which measures had been taken by the city authorities in the wake of the 1958 resolution and to identify the extent to which Mainz was affected by the stationing of nuclear weapons. The motion represented a serious attempt to by-pass problems of legality by contriving a relevance specific to Mainz.

Despite these attempts at avoiding possible intervention from the supervisory body, the initiative continued to be highly controversial. Prior to the inevitable objections of the supervisory body, both the CDU and FDP council groups outlined their disapproval of the measure in the session of 28 November 1984. The debate on the initiative essentially followed the same course as that held on previous occasions in which the issue was discussed. The only new feature was the contribution made by the Greens, which succeeded in heightening the level of conflict already present by criticising the role of the administration on previous occasions in which the issue had been discussed. Green councillor Alf Haenlein struck an antagonistic tone from the outset, stating:

> that the local activities of the peace movement manifest the desire to save the democratic content of the constitution, by subjecting it to a reappraisal by active citizens. The initial symbolic declaration of the nuclear-weapon-free Mainz should give a signal to those holding political responsibility that the citizens of this country no longer want to see themselves treated simply as objects by the state's thoughts of prestige, economic interests and technocratic crisis management (council minutes, 28 November 1984).

Despite the fact that the motion under debate was initiated by both the SPD and Green council groups, Haenlein still succeeded in adopting a position generally critical of the Social Democrats, most particularly of SPD Mayor Fuchs, whose casting vote could have led to the acceptance of the 1983 petition: 'The citizens' initiative's petition of 1983 failed on a tied vote, with the vote of the Mayor being the decisive factor. Today there is an opportunity of correcting this set-back' (council minutes, 28 November 1984). Following the Green councillor's remarks, Mayor Fuchs felt obliged to respond in similarly belligerent fashion: 'With reference to the comments of Mr Haenlein, Mayor Fuchs states that he requires no lectures from the Greens about his behaviour. As a Social Democrat he knows on the basis of long years in the war and in imprisonment what it means to fight for peace' (council minutes, 28 November 1984).

Whilst the SPD–Green motion was ultimately accepted, against the opposition of the CDU and FDP council groups, in the months that followed the supervisory body insisted that the city overturn its resolution and withdraw signs posted at city boundaries declaring Mainz a nuclear-free city. Their criticism was essentially that expressed by the FDP and CDU council groups during the debate over the issue in the council meetings of 1958, 1983 and 1984. The principal difference was that the supervisory body actually possessed the authority by which the resolution could be overruled. Its first objection stemmed from the belief that the issue lay beyond the competence of the local level:

> Duties of military defence have neither a reference to the local community nor can they be dealt with by them under their own responsi-

bility and independently. By their very nature, defence measures are assigned to the state.

City councillors who use their role as representatives to express general opinions on the problems of military defence and pass resolutions linked to this are overstepping their mandate, since they are dealing with issues with which other representatives of the people, namely the members of the Federal Parliament, have been appointed to deal.[8]

A second, somewhat more tenuous criticism affected the signs declaring Mainz nuclear-free. Given that the signs were posted at strategic entry points to the city, it was claimed that their purpose was not so much to advertise the new policy to the citizens of Mainz, but to draw it to the attention of visitors to the city. As a result, a series of regulations governing the location of road signs were contravened. In the event, however, the majority of the signs in question were spirited away from their posts by collectors, leaving only three in the hands of the city authorities. As a final point, the supervisory body also insisted that the 1958 resolution, restricting the movement of atomic weapons within the boundaries of Mainz, be declared null and void. This was despite the fact that there had been no objections to the decision in the intervening twenty-six years.[9]

In this case, the motion was ultimately unsuccessful from a practical point of view. However, it could be argued that events surrounding its course served to concentrate public attention upon the issues involved in the deployment of new missiles in the Federal Republic and thereby to assist in the formation of opinions on the matter. This was essentially the opinion of Green fundamentalists in Mainz. More significant was the fact that this initiative symbolised the increasingly controversial nature of local politics in Mainz during the period under review. This conflict was not only to be found within the council chamber itself. It also affected the relationship between the council, the city authorities and its supervisory body.

---

[8] From letter sent by *Bezirksregierung Rheinhessen-Pfalz* to Mayor Fuchs, dated 24 June 1985.
[9] From letter sent by *Bezirksregierung Rheinhessen-Pfalz* to Mayor Fuchs, dated 24 June 1985.

Summary: Supra-Local Issues in Mainz

Between 1984 and 1987 supra-local themes were regularly under discussion in the Mainz council, and evidence suggests that they now represent an established area of local political debate in the city. With regard to international issues, not only were the traditional town-twinning arrangements the source of debate, but more controversial issues such as US foreign policy in Central America and North Africa and apartheid in South Africa also appeared on the council agenda. A discussion of the treatment of national topics, exemplified by the initiative to create a nuclear-free zone in Mainz, demonstrated the extent to which the local political agenda has changed in the city. Despite the fact that questions relating to national defence had been discussed on previous occasions by the city council, it must be stressed that this tended to occur in an isolated fashion. Between 1984 and 1987 such questions consistently appeared on the agenda of the Mainz city council.

The contribution of the Greens to the prevalence of supra-local issues was of particular significance. Moreover, the nature of the Greens' supra-local motions symbolised the party's role in politicising all aspects of local council activity in Mainz. Both the Libyan motion and that relating to the Turkish Consul illustrated the degree to which all local authority tasks, including its purely representational duties, assume a political role for the Greens and thereby for the council as a whole. The Green council group rarely missed the opportunity of drawing public attention to events beyond the boundaries of Mainz. The direct relevance of such motions to Mainz was often contrived, if existent at all. As a result, the chances of success for these particular motions were relatively limited and totally dependent upon the willingness of the SPD council group to agree to a discussion of the measures in the first place.

However, the fact should not be overlooked that the Greens were not alone in introducing motions of a supra-local relevance. Both the SPD and CDU introduced and debated motions with either a global or a national dimension. The principal difference between the motions of the Greens and those of the CDU and SPD was that the latter motions tended to be of a more practical nature than those of the Greens. Only the FDP sought to resist pressures to discuss supra-local events in Mainz. Nevertheless, the principle that local politicians should only discuss issues of direct local relevance is for the case of Mainz clearly a feature of the past. It is evident that the greatest gulf exists between the Greens and the FDP, which remained rooted in traditional patterns of behaviour.

Motions Specific to Mainz

It has been shown that the Mainz city council increasingly discussed matters which breached the traditional scope of German local politics between 1984 and 1987. The presence of supra-local issues on the city's local political agenda provides evidence of the existence of a New Local Politics dimension in Mainz. However, by no means did all initiatives introduced by the city's council groups transcend the established limits of local political activity. In order to place the supra-local motions into context, it is necessary to address initiatives which were specific to Mainz. In this respect, two types of issue are to be examined. Firstly, attention is to be drawn to initiatives which belonged to the traditional, Old Politics agenda in Mainz. Secondly, locally oriented motions which belonged to a New Local Politics agenda will be discussed.

The Persistence of the Old Local Politics

The overwhelming majority of motions introduced by the Mainz council groups between July 1984 and June 1987 had a specifically local orientation. The issues of the Old Local Politics still accounted for the greatest proportion of the city council's time. This is an important point to make when one considers the likely impact of local political activity upon the Greens. Despite the party's intent to politicise all aspects of such activity, there is very little the Greens can do to resist the discussion of 'unpolitical' matters. The volume of papers presented to councillors by the city administration before each council meeting acts in its own right as a major integrating factor in German local political life.

It is not necessary to enter into great detail about the mundane nature of much local council activity. This has not changed, even under the influence of the Greens. Councils still need to discuss building regulations, planning proposals, local by-laws and budgetary matters irrespective of the political complexion of their representatives. However, it is still useful to draw attention to some typical initiatives discussed by the Mainz council between 1984 and 1987 in order to maintain a sense of perspective. The initiatives of the FDP were exemplary in this respect, contrasting markedly with those of the Greens. The approaches of these two parties towards local politics was the most polarised in terms of the Old–New Local Politics dimension. Whilst the Mainz Greens' broad strategy was to introduce themes of general political relevance and thereby encourage political debate, the FDP remained rooted in more established forms of behaviour. The analysis of supra-local issues showed that both the CDU and SPD council groups went some way towards accommodating New Local Politics themes in their repertoires.

Among the FDP initiatives which serve to illustrate the conflicting approaches witnessed in Mainz between 1984 and 1987 were several which referred to purely administrative measures. Issues such as the number of motions introduced in individual council sessions (M103/1985), public house opening times (M20/1987), or the fouling of public footpaths by dogs (M13/1985) were characteristic of the FDP's activities. A typical example of an 'unpolitical' FDP motion called for improved measures to be adopted to ensure the prompt return of books to municipal libraries:

> The constant reminding of overdue borrowers in the city and public libraries results in considerable administrative and financial costs. At the same time, the attraction of the libraries is reduced by large numbers of overdue books. Although warnings subsequent to a free first warning are linked to fines, these are apparently not high enough to cause the increasing number of thoughtless borrowers to return their books according to the rules (M50/1985).

Given the limited focus of this initiative it was unlikely to lead to any form of conflict in the council session for which it was intended. The debate on the measure was indicative of the sheer banality and lack of political content which applied to most of the activities of the Mainz city council. The executive member responsible for local library services lent his support to the FDP proposals: 'The administration also has the intention of dispensing with the first free warning, although the opportunity should remain of lengthening the loan period for a further four weeks by contacting the library administration in advance. However, the administration also sees the necessity of introducing a more rigorous system of reminders.' The CDU response was essentially the same: 'In the interest of other users, negligent borrowers must be obliged through appropriate measures to keep to the library regulations' (council minutes, 19 March 1985). Whilst the Greens felt compelled to welcome the initiative, the SPD opted not to express an opinion on the FDP's motion, presumably on the grounds that nothing new could be added to the debate. As a result, this initiative followed the course of the vast majority of other motions introduced by the (established) Mainz parties. Under such circumstances, it is hardly surprising that three-quarters of all initiatives were referred unanimously to council committee during the period under review.

Even on occasions on which the FDP's motions led to conflict, the subject area of their initiatives was highly localised. An example was provided by a motion calling for the establishment of a working group comprising representatives of the council, administration and local business 'whose duty it should be to work out measures to raise the attraction of Mainz as a shopping city' (M80/1984). At surface level such an initiative might appear uncontroversial. A political aspect to the motion emerges when it is placed into the context of the FDP's underlying wish to gain public support for its aim of seeking improvements in local roads and the construction of new car-parking facilities in the city centre. Not surprisingly, the Greens' attitude towards the FDP motion was unfavourable. Councillor Ute Schmailzl objected to attempts to develop the city centre as a site purely for business and commercial interests: 'It is to be feared that the FDP motion will lead to a more hectic pace in the city centre, that people will be tempted to consume more, that the cityscape will become more anonymous and that more advertising will dominate.' Whilst the SPD essentially sympathised with this attitude, the CDU exploited the opportunity to criticise the Greens' anti-business stance: 'There is no need to consider the arguments put forward by the Greens since the question arises here of how

231

the affected people should earn their living if the plans of the Greens were realised' (council minutes, 3 October 1984).

The two motions cited above exemplify the traditional approach of the FDP to local politics in Mainz. It should be recognised, however, that the FDP was not the only party responsible for introducing motions of a traditional orientation between 1984 and 1987. Each of the other council groups was also active in this respect. CDU motions seeking to establish a regular ceremony in the city hall during which naturalisation documents would be handed over to new citizens of Mainz (M209/1985) or demanding a new type of street lighting for a local thoroughfare (M8/1986) also fell within this category. Significantly, despite the fact that the Greens set great store by their slogan *global denken, vor Ort handeln*, on a significant number of occasions the party introduced motions of relevance to Mainz alone. One initiative, for example, had as its subject area the fouling of footpaths by dogs (M79/1985). Despite the fact that the problems caused by dogs are of great importance to a large proportion of the local citizens, it might still appear surprising to find the Greens addressing an issue which so clearly belongs to the Old Local Politics agenda: 'Streets, paths and public squares and spaces must be kept free from dog excrement by the dogs' owners. For this purpose, the city will make available paper bags and cardboard scoops, made from recycled paper of course, which will be offered for sale in newsagents, kiosks, grocery shops and supermarkets' (M79/1985). In the council session of 29 May 1985 this motion was unanimously referred to the environment committee for further deliberation. This was the typical response of a local council dealing with a traditional local issue.

This discussion would tend to support the contention that whenever the Greens introduce motions of a specifically localised nature which relate to traditional local politics issues, they will not give rise to conflict. As a result, the finding of the quantitative analysis which showed that Green initiatives were more conflictual than those of the established parties' council groups needs to be qualified. The initiatives were obviously not conflictual simply because they had originated from the Green council group. Of greater significance was the content of the relevant initiative and the practicalities of implementing its proposals. Again, the conclusion is to be drawn that the conflict arising from the Greens' initiatives was linked to the ideological factors underlying them and to the fact that the party openly sought evidence of conflict at local level.

The Discussion of New Local Politics Issues

Whilst it would be misleading to underestimate the strength and persistence of established forms of local politics, it is still necessary to identify issues which are relatively new to German local politics. It is also important to examine the party-political origins of such issues. In this section local issues with a New Politics dimension will be addressed. Supra-local motions have already been assigned to the New Local Politics agenda in Mainz. However, a significant number of initiatives with a purely local orientation must also be regarded as belonging to this agenda (see Baker *et al.* 1981; Bürklin 1984; Schmitt 1987). In general, initiatives relating to 'quality of life' issues form the basis of the newly emerging agenda. Motions dealing with environmental protection, with urban planning, with improvements to the local transport system, with social minority groups or with the implications of military activity in and around Mainz are all representative of a new dimension of local politics in Mainz.

The nature of this new agenda is best illustrated by means of example. Difficulties arising from a treatment of all environmental issues as 'new' have already been addressed in Chapter 9. Whilst this complex area requires further analysis, one obvious case of a 'new' theme increasingly under debate in the Mainz city council following the election of the Greens was that of women's affairs. As indicated above, such issues were not debated frequently enough to justify the creation of a specific 'women's issues' category in the quantitative analysis. Nevertheless, it is still worth examining the means by which women's topics were addressed by the Mainz city council groups between 1984 and 1987.

Attention has already been drawn to the manner in which the Greens sought to politicise the role of the city authorities and their representatives in Mainz with regard to supra-local topics. The same strategy was adopted in motions introduced by the Green council group with a purely local orientation. In one initiative, for example, the Greens protested about the participation of the executive member responsible for cultural affairs at a reception for competitors in a Miss Europe pageant held in Mainz. The Greens proposed that the city should withdraw its financial and organisational support from such competitions in the future on the grounds that such competitions demean the role of women in society:

> It is the aim of such events to assign to women a role which exclusively measures the value of a woman according to her physical merits. Women should meet an ideal of beauty created by men and satisfy male desires for prestige. In this way young girls are shown early on their destiny as objects for sale. Competition is stirred up with less conformist women.
>
> ... Such a competition has nothing to do with culture, but in the face of undiminished acts of violence against women and the often futile fight for equality represents a slap in the face of independent women' (M129/1985).

Such Green motions seek to provoke a critical response from both the other council groups and the council executive. The motion distinguishes the Greens' attitude to local politics from that of the other council groups. On the basis of the findings of previous sections, for instance, it would be highly unlikely for the FDP to support let alone be responsible for initiating similar proposals. Consequently, the Green proposal divided the opinions of the other council groups when debated in the council session of 4 September 1985. SPD councillor Gisela Thews suggested that the city authorities should develop a greater sensitivity for the problems of women, yet failed to commit her council group to the measure. The FDP response to the discussion of such new topics in the city council was characteristically antagonistic: 'If the beauty competitions denounced in the motion have been enhanced, then this has only occurred by virtue of the fact that the Mainz city council is dealing with them ... '. However, the CDU was willing to discuss the Greens' initiative on its merits, with councillor Rainer Martin Laub regarding the motion as posing a fundamental threat to the practice of local democracy: '... Bans of the proposed nature cannot be reconciled with the democratic system. Nor can it be accepted that city representatives are kept tied to their mothers' apron-strings by restrictions of the type sought.' Even Mayor Fuchs expressed reservations about the practicability of the Greens' proposed restrictions, arguing on purely formal grounds: 'that to represent the city is the duty of the mayor, who can also assign the task to members of the executive committee. No case is known to him in which official representatives of the city failed to observe proprieties' (council minutes, 4 September 1985). In the ensuing vote the Green motion was rejected. However, it is unclear how the individual council groups voted. Given that thirty-four votes were registered against the motion and that the FDP and CDU council groups had twenty-seven representatives between them, it can be inferred that a number of SPD councillors also rejected the proposal. Other Social Democrats must have either abstained or supported the Greens' initiative. The outcome of this motion illustrates well the differences of opinion which exist within the SPD council group over the issues of the New Politics at local level. It also serves to portray the Greens' strategy of seeking to bring divisions within the SPD council group to light.

A more radical proposal by the Greens, certain to raise conflict in the council, was provided by a call to establish a night-taxi service for the sole use of women. The service was to be charged at the rate of a local bus ticket. This particular motion should be viewed in the context of similar proposals introduced by the Greens throughout the Federal Republic (see *Taxi* 1985). The initiative in Mainz was perceived less in terms of providing a permanent solution than as a means of drawing attention to the problem of violence against women. In the Greens' opinion a widespread fear amongst Mainz women of venturing out after dark imposes severe restrictions upon their ability to participate fully in the social, cultural and political life of the city:

> Despite the equality rules laid down in the Basic Law, women are unable to move freely at night in public. Especially when they are on their own, they must reckon with being molested, pestered, followed or raped. This also applies to the route to and from the bus stop or parking place. For this reason, many women do not leave their homes in the evening and are thereby excluded from social, cultural and political life (M205/1985).

The Green's motion gained the backing of the SPD council group in the session of 13 November 1985 in which it was debated, albeit with a number of qualifications governing the financing of the proposed scheme. In this sense, the Social Democrats' backing for the night-taxi motion should be regarded within the context of the then impending debate on the 1986/7 city budget. Although not one of the Greens' minimum demands, the night-taxi project was still a focus for discussion in the budget deliberations. Both the CDU and FDP council groups rejected the measure. The CDU maintained that other sections of the population could be disadvantaged by the scheme, particularly elderly or disabled men. For the CDU the question of violence against women was purely a matter of public safety and therefore for the police. This opinion was also shared by the FDP, who rejected the proposal outright on the grounds of the significant costs involved. In the vote on motion M205/1985, the Greens' proposal was referred to council committee by a majority of Green and SPD councillors, against the opposition of the CDU and FDP groups.

Despite this initial success, by June 1987 the night-taxi service had still not been implemented. Nor was their any prospect of its being introduced by the Mainz authorities. The main difficulty lay in the absence of funding for the project and the diminishing political will of the SPD council group to cooperate with the Greens. When the two parties failed to agree on the 1986/7 city budget, the night-taxi service for women became one of several Green proposals which could no longer be realised. This serves to emphasise once again the lack of political consideration which characterised the Greens' budget negotiations of the winter of 1985/6. Not only did the party lose all influence over the selection of executive personnel, they also lost the opportunity of implementing their more radical proposals. For the night-taxi to have stood a chance of success, it would have been necessary for the Greens not only to assist in the passing of the 1986/7 budget, but also to be able to exert influence over the subsequent 1988/9 budget.

Summary: Continuity and Change in Mainz's Local Politics

The aim of this chapter has been to complement the quantitative study conducted in Chapter 9 by means of a more qualitative analysis of the topics under discussion in the Mainz city council between 1984 and 1987. The qualitative study allows additional conclusions to be drawn about the extent to which the Mainz city council's activities were characterised by a New Local Politics dimension in the period under scrutiny. These conclusions pertain to both the agenda and style of local politics in Mainz.

Firstly, the analysis supported the contention made in the previous chapter that the agenda of Mainz's local politics changed in a number of respects in the period following the election of the Greens to the city council. Most noticeably, the council was increasingly drawn into the discussion of supra-local topics. This provides additional evidence of the development of a more liberal interpretation by the Mainz council groups of Article 28.2 of the Basic Law, which restricts the competences of local authorities to address matters relevant only to the local citizens. Significantly, whilst the Greens were most active in this area, both the CDU and SPD also introduced motions with either a national or an international dimension. Only the FDP remained fundamentally opposed to the discussion of such topics in the Mainz local council. The important point was also made, in the discussion of the agenda of local politics in Mainz, that, despite the emergence of issues related to the New Politics agenda, the great majority of council duties corresponded to traditional, Old Local Politics issues. Even the Greens were obliged to discuss the granting of planning permission or changes in local by-laws. This reinforces the suggestion that the local level acts as an integrating force upon the Greens. With regard to the changing agenda of Mainz's local politics, it is apparent that the city is in a period of transition. Whilst the Old Politics issues continue to dominate the local agenda, the topics of the New Politics are gradually becoming more common (for example women's affairs). This is of direct relevance to the second area addressed in this chapter.

A second feature of the qualitative analysis was the discussion of the manner in which the New Local Politics issues were debated by the Mainz council. The statistical analysis of the initiatives of the Mainz council groups found that the Greens' motions were much more likely to lead to dissent than those of the established parties. In this chapter it was possible to show that the New Politics orientation of the Green council group's motions represented a significant factor underlying the high levels of conflict affecting the initiatives. Thus all issues with a national or an international dimension were conflictual. Since the Greens were more active in this field, it was inevitable that the party's initiatives would be more conflictual than those of the other council groups. However, it needs to be stated that not all new issues necessarily gave rise to conflict. Initiatives aimed at the local level and belonging to certain subject areas proved less confrontational than the more global proposals.

Conclusion: The German Greens and the New Local Politics

This study has set out to examine both the impact of the Greens upon a changing local politics in Germany and the effect of local political activity upon the Greens themselves. Against a theoretical background which linked party system change at local level to changes registered at higher levels of the German political system, it has been shown that the local level does not remain immune from the various interconnecting factors which have precipitated a growing instability at the federal and regional levels. The main source of the declining stability of all German party systems is to be found in the process of socio-economic modernisation, which has served to reduce the relevance of the principal socio-structural cleavages which underpin the Federal Republic's traditional party systems. On the one hand, there has been a marked decline in the relative strength of the traditional social groups, which in the past have represented the core source of support for the country's established political parties. The fact that religion continues to be a good indicator of electoral preference is tempered by the continuing loosening of the links between individuals and their churches. On the other hand, new social groupings such as the new middle class are continuing to develop. These groups are no longer bound to the established political parties by social structural ties, and their members share values fundamentally distinct from those of people belonging to the traditional social groups, such as the old middle class and blue-collar workers. The rise of the New Politics, with its unique agenda and its unconventional forms of political expression, also has its origins in the Federal Republic's changing social structures.

Factors which underpin party system change at the federal and regional levels in Germany clearly have a significant bearing upon the development of the Federal Republic's local party systems. In this respect, Germany's distinct local council constitutions appear to play only a minor role in the receptiveness of local party systems to political change. While the potential for the emergence of conflict at local level tends to be greater in those regions in which executive powers are divided between different organs of local government (Northern Germany) than in regions in which such powers are held by a single person (Southern Germany), other factors are noticeably more important in explaining the spread of the New Local Politics. Simply stated, variations in the rates of social and economic change have resulted in the non-uniform development of local party systems in Germany's communities. With regard to the discussion of the impact of the New Politics at local level, the party systems of localities in which the rate of socio-economic change has been most pronounced are more susceptible to the New Politics agendas, ideologies and forms of political action than the party systems of communities in which change has occurred more gradually. For this reason, change can be expected to occur initially in Germany's urban service-sector centres before gradually spreading to the traditional (heavy) industrial areas and the countryside.

While social structural factors provide the basis against which political change occurs at local level, it would be misleading to suggest that such changes are inevitable once the necessary socio-economic conditions prevail. There is also a need for political agents to implement change at local level. In Germany this has occurred initially in the form of the SPD new left and subsequently of the Greens. An examination of the changing nature of German local politics prior to the rise of the Greens in the second half of the 1970s provided initial evidence of the emergence of a New Politics dimension at local level, which was in stark contrast to more established local political practices. These remained rooted in and still persist in consensual and essentially 'unpolitical' forms of behaviour. The New Local Politics represents more than just an extension of the New Politics agenda to the local level. In addition to new issues, the New Local Politics is characterised by its parliamentary styles, its conflictual orientation, its broad definition of the powers of local decision-makers and its preference for open decision-making practices. The Old Local Politics conforms to a more traditional approach to local political behaviour. It can be identified in consensual decision-making structures, a strict adherence to narrow interpretations of the function of local authorities and a clear preference for representative democratic decision-making forms. Signs of an emergent Old–New Local Politics dimension at local level could be witnessed by the mid-1970s in cities such as Frankfurt, yet only with the rise of the Greens did the New Local Politics become a more universal phenomenon in the Federal Republic.

The contrasting New Local Politics and Old Local Politics approaches presented the basis for a general analysis of the role of the Greens in Germany's local politics, with discussion focusing upon the extent to which the Greens, as a party of the New Politics, have influenced and in turn been influenced by the country's local politics. The relevance to the Greens of the communal level of the German political system extends beyond the local origins of the first ecological lists and the ability of the Greens to maintain a distinct and heterogeneous profile in the Federal Republic's local councils. The Greens certainly conform to the characteristics of the New Politics party model at local level. This applies in three respects. Firstly, the Green electorate at local level comprises the same core groups belonging to the young, urban new middle class that tend to support the party at elections to higher levels of government. Secondly, since the Greens' ideology does not draw distinctions between levels of the political system, it is necessarily similar at local level to that which prevails at the national and regional levels. The fact that the Greens' agenda consciously seeks to transgress the traditional boundaries of local authority competences is itself indicative of the party's New Local Politics approach. It is in this respect that the Greens most often come into conflict with the established political actors at local level. Finally, the Greens' New Politics organisational structures are also relevant at local level. However, a study of the extent of Green representation at local level points to the existence of a severe structural problem for the Greens, which derives from their low membership figures and the difficulties associated with maintaining links with a loosely defined and constantly changing *Basis*. The pervasive lack of interest of party and movement activists in local political affairs means that Green and alternative council groups are commonly condemned to become totally self-reliant and act without a grassroots. Since there are no adequate means by which party representatives can be controlled, this often renders irrelevant the grassroots democratic structures adopted by the majority of local Green parties.

The general discussion in Part I of the Greens' origins, electorate and representation at local level provided a framework for a further, more detailed analysis of the impact of the party's ideology at local level. The heterogeneous nature of the Greens at local level and the fact that the party has undergone a significant amount of internal change during the course of their period of local council representation make attempts to generalise about their activities at local level rather difficult. This problem is aggravated by the absence of objective source materials on many aspects of Green local politics. As a result, a case-study method of analysis was adopted in Part II. This was undertaken in the city of Mainz, which, in terms of its social and economic structures and its traditional party system prior to the emergence of the Greens, can be regarded as being typical of medium-sized cities in Germany. The characteristics of the Mainz party system lent themselves particularly well to a study of the impact of the Greens upon established forms of local political behaviour in the Federal Republic and to an examination of the issues raised in the analysis of general features of Green local politics.

On the basis of the experiences drawn from the participation in local politics of Green groups throughout the Federal Republic, two broad areas were subjected to a more detailed analysis in the case study. Firstly, an assessment was made of the extent to which established local political practices have been affected by the Greens' openly ideological approach. In this context, the degree to which the Greens' adoption of unconventional parliamentary styles at local level runs counter to established forms of political behaviour and serves to politicise all aspects of local council activity was also investigated. Clarification was then sought of whether the Greens have been responsible for the rising levels of conflict which have been witnessed in Germany's local councils and, if this is the case, whether this has occurred largely as a result of their New Local Politics approach. Having examined the effect of the Greens upon Germany's local politics, the second area to be covered in the case-study analysis was the possible effect of local political activity upon the Greens themselves. This issue was addressed in terms of the question of whether or not the participation of the Greens in local politics inevitably leads to their integration into the established political system.

That German local politics has become much more conflictual as a result of the Greens' ideological approach was demonstrated in a number of respects for Mainz. The established consensual patterns and styles of local politics were shown to have been undermined by the Greens' presence. Events surrounding the appointment of new council executive members in Mainz, for example, were indicative of the extent to which areas traditionally regarded as being uncontroversial became politicised following the election of the Greens to the city council. The Greens represented the most vocal source of opposition to the consensual practices which had characterised Mainz's local politics for the preceding thirty years. Further signs of politicisation were evident in the Greens' attempts to exert influence over the representative duties of executive members. Signs of an emergent cleavage along a New–Old Local Politics divide could be discerned during the course of the 1986/7 budget negotiations between the Greens and the SPD in Mainz. The two parties operated at cross purposes throughout their discussions. While the Greens' overriding interest was in the implementation of their policy proposals, the SPD continued to lay greatest emphasis upon the confirmation of party representatives in key executive positions. The contrasting approaches of the Greens and the SPD could not be reconciled and ultimately led to the reinstatement of a Grand Coalition administration in Mainz for the remainder of the electoral period. This had the effect of excluding the Greens from all future influence over the development of Mainz's local politics until 1989. In the end, it proved more straightforward for the SPD to accept the tried and tested forms of cooperation with the CDU than to risk making a deal with the Greens.

The fact that the Greens have been responsible for an increase in expressions of political disunity at local level was perhaps most starkly portrayed in the analysis of the initiatives of the Mainz council groups. The Greens were responsible for more conflictual initiatives than the three other council groups combined. While the period preceding the election of the Greens had been marked by high levels of unanimity, with almost 90 per cent of motions being supported by all the council groups, that following the Greens' election saw only 73.3 per cent of motions gain such backing. When the Greens were removed from the analysis, it became clear that the level of consensus affecting the motions of the established parties' council groups had not changed substantially from one council period to the next. The Greens most clearly represented the source of growing conflict in Mainz, with only 56.1 per cent of their initiatives gaining all-party backing.

With regard to the agenda of local politics, the qualitative analysis of the initiatives of the Mainz council groups between 1984 and 1987 showed that the council was increasingly drawn into the discussion of topics linked to the New Local Politics agenda. Although difficulties were identified with regard to the location of specific topics on a New–Old Local Politics dimension, not only were international issues increasingly under discussion in Mainz, but a number of issues with a national orientation became the focus for council attention. This served to provide evidence of the development of a more liberal interpretation by the Mainz council groups of Article 28.2 of the Basic Law, which restricts the competences of local authorities to address matters relevant only to the local citizens. Significantly, while the Greens were most active in this area, both the CDU and SPD also introduced motions with either a national or an international dimension. Only the FDP remained fundamentally opposed to the discussion of such topics in the Mainz local council.

With regard to the changing styles and agenda of its local politics, it was apparent, therefore, that the city of Mainz was located in a period of transition. While the Old Local Politics issues continued to dominate the local agenda, the topics of the New Local Politics were of increasing relevance.

With regard to the effect of local political activity upon the Greens, a number of factors supported the contention that they are unable to resist pressures which have led to their rapid integration into the political system at local level. The parliamentary styles adopted by the Green council group were evident in the very high level of activity maintained during the period under review. Over one-third of all motions were introduced by the Greens between 1984 and 1987. On the one hand, this demonstrates that the Greens do not differentiate between the levels of the German party system in terms of their desire to implement policy changes. On the other, despite the emergence of a New

Politics agenda, the fact that the great majority of council duties are of the traditional, Old Local Politics variety ultimately had a bearing upon the Greens. Even the Greens were obliged to discuss mundane topics such as the granting of planning permissions or changes in local by-laws. This demonstrated the extent to which the local level acts as an integrating and reforming force upon the Greens, a factor backed up by the sheer volume of initiatives introduced by the party. The absence of a large source of extra-parliamentary support meant that the Mainz Green *Fraktion* was obliged to conduct most of the tedious council duties itself, leaving little time free for other forms of political activity.

Political events in Mainz between 1984 and 1987 were symbolic of a growing conflict between the Greens' New Local Politics and the traditional Old Local Politics of the established political parties. Without doubt, the Greens have changed Germany's local politics since the late 1970s in a quite radical manner. This has occurred with respect to both the agenda and style of local council activities in the 1980s. In some ways, the Greens picked up at the point at which the SPD new left was unable to realise its goal of establishing local politics as *Gesellschaftspolitik*. Given the widespread representation of the Greens at local level, it must be contended that local party systems throughout the Federal Republic of Germany will increasingly be marked by a New–Old local politics dimension. However, if the Greens were to continue to fade from German politics, it is possible that at least some of the more traditional forms of local politics would return. In particular, the tendencies towards consensual forms of political behaviour are strongly represented in all the major political parties and are positively encouraged by council administrations.

The Future of the German Greens

While this study has primarily sought to establish a picture of the role of the Greens at local level in the Federal Republic, on the basis of the discussion it is possible to draw some further conclusions regarding the future of the Green Party as a whole in post-unification Germany.

At one level, the future of the Greens would appear to be assured. The changing social structures of the Federal Republic, which gave rise to the Greens in the first place, will continue to change in the years ahead. The highly educated new middle class will continue to expand, and the process of secularisation will further weaken the links between population groups and the churches. The social milieux which favour support for the Greens and are to be found in Germany's large towns and cities will not disintegrate overnight. However, social structures and social milieux are not the sole determinants of electoral outcomes. Issues also play an important role in deciding how voters cast their ballots. The issues highest in voters' minds at the 1990 Federal Election, when the political agenda turned once more to the Old Politics issues of security and economic growth, did not favour the Greens. Nor was the Greens' campaign assisted by the impression given to voters that they were a party divided between its various factions and holding ambiguous policy goals. In many ways, therefore, the future of the German Greens will depend upon their ability to appear once more a creative force in the Federal Republic's politics. In this respect, much will depend upon the success of those Greens who are involved in alliances and coalitions with the SPD at regional and local level.

However, there are also signs that the Greens have reached the limits of their capacity to be creative. Above all, one should not underestimate the amount of change witnessed within the Green movement itself since the early 1980s. It is no longer the case that the Greens simply represent the parliamentary arm of the extra-parliamentary protest movement. Instead, notwithstanding their ambivalent attitude towards representative democratic institutions, the Greens are essentially a party of Germany's parliaments at all levels of the political system. The swift integration of the active core of the Green movement into the Federal Republic's local councils, where their energies are spent in the day-to-day discussion of administrative matters, affects the ability of the Greens to maintain their radical edge. Since the Greens will never be a mass-membership party, it might become necessary for them to think twice before committing themselves so wholeheartedly to such an intense form of political involvement at local level. While access to the decision-making process is easiest at local level, this is not the level at which the political system of the Federal Republic as a whole can best be reformed according to Green wishes. Despite the attempts of Green groups to raise new and often controversial topics at local level and to politicise administrative processes, there are limits to the extent to which this strategy can be pursued on a long-term basis. In any case, as was shown in Mainz, the established political parties have themselves succeeded in at least partially addressing the issues of the New Politics agenda.

A further question mark which hangs over the future of the Greens concerns their ability to develop a basis in eastern Germany. Despite the relative success of the *Bündnis 90*/Greens in the new federal states at the 1990 Federal Election, where they secured 5.9 per cent of the vote and eight seats, there must be doubts about the Greens' long-term chances of maintaining this level of support in eastern Germany. This is important because future elections will require political parties to secure 5 per cent of the vote across the whole of Germany in order to gain representation in the Federal Parliament. Two factors suggest that the Greens might have problems in finding a constituency in eastern Germany. Firstly, the social structures of the eastern regions do not tend to favour support for the Greens. Secondly, the issues which will continue to dominate the political agenda in the East will concern the material well-being of the German citizens who are living in the difficult post-unification economic climate. While the Greens have been able to establish a basis at local level in western Germany from which they can expand, it will be much harder for them to do so in the East. Not only will the Greens' resources necessarily be thinly spread, pending the reorganisation of local government, but it is unlikely that there will be much resonance for the ideological, conflict-oriented New Local Politics approach in an area of the Federal Republic which is facing the difficult task of rebuilding. The Old Local Politics will inevitably dominate in eastern Germany for a number of years to come.

The future of the German Greens is, therefore, hanging in the balance. Nevertheless, while it is unlikely that the Greens will achieve the same level of success witnessed in the 1980s in the future, there is still room in the German political system for a party which is distinctly to the left of the SPD. Whether the Greens will make the most of this opportunity will depend upon their ability to become recognised as a radical reforming party and to make best use of their limited organisational resources.

Bibliography and References

For the sake of simplicity, references have been divided into three separate sections. The first section contains references to academic works (for example Alber 1985). The second section encompasses works which are predominantly of a statistical nature and are most commonly referred to in terms of a citation of the region or locality to which they pertain (for example Frankfurt 1989a). The final section of references covers all other non-academic and non-statistical sources referred to in the text and, on the whole, comprises publications which have emerged from within the Green and Alternative spectrum of the Federal Republic. In order to distinguish such materials clearly from the statistical sources included in the second section, they are identified by means of an italicisation (for example *Geseke* 1987).

Books and Articles

Alber, J. (1985) 'Modernisierung, neue Spannungslinien und die politischen Chancen der Grünen', *Politische Vierteljahresschrift* 26, No. 3:211–26

Almond, G.A. and Verba, S. (1963) *The Civic Culture. Political Attitudes and Democracy in Five Nations*, Little and Brown, Boston. Reprinted 1965

Andersen, U. (ed.) (1984a) *Kommunalpolitik und Kommunalwahlen in Nordrhein-Westfalen*, Landeszentrale für politische Bildung Nordrhein-Westfalen, Düsseldorf

——, (1984b) 'Die Stellung der Gemeinden in Nordrhein-Westfalen', in U. Andersen (ed.) *Kommunalpolitik und Kommunalwahlen in Nordrhein-Westfalen*:9–31

——, (ed.) (1987) *Kommunale Selbstverwaltung und Kommunalpolitik in Nordrhein-Westfalen*, Schriften zur politischen Landeskunde Nordrhein-Westfalens 3, Landeszentrale für politische Bildung Nordrhein-Westfalen, Kohlhammer, Cologne

Anon. (1985) 'Liebe Leute – ich höre mit dem Parlamentskram auf', in R. Rohr and W. Hoss (eds.) *Grüne und andere Listen*:97–102

Arndt, R. (1983) 'Am Beispiel Frankfurt: Die Regierbarkeit der Städte', in P. Klein (ed.) *Sozialdemokratische Kommunalpolitik im Schatten Bonns*:24–46

References

Arzberger, K. (1980) *Bürger und Eliten in der Kommunalpolitik*, Kohlhammer, Stuttgart, Berlin, Cologne and Mainz

Ausschuß Wahlforschung (1984) *Kommunalwahlen 1984 in Nordrhein-Westfalen. Materialien zur kommunalen Wahlforschung*, Ausschuß Wahlforschung, Verband Deutscher Städtestatistiker, Duisburg

——, (1987) *Politische Wahlen in 65 Großstädten und in den Bundesländern 1949–1987*, Arbeitsheft 9, Verband Deutscher Städtestatistiker, Duisburg

——, (1989) *Kommunalwahlen 1989 und 1984 in Nordrhein-Westfalen. Kommunale Wahlstatistiken nach Alter und Geschlecht*, Arbeitsheft 11, Verband Deutscher Städtestatistiker, Duisburg

Baker, K.L., Dalton, R.J. and Hildebrandt, K. (1981) *Germany Transformed. Political Culture and the New Politics*, Harvard U.P., Cambridge MA and London

Behr, A., Breit, G., Lilge, H. and Schissler, J. (1986) *Wahlatlas Hessen: 1946 bis 1985*, Höller und Zwick, Brunswick

Bensch, G. (1985) 'Ökonomisch bedingte Antriebskräfte und Begrenzungsfaktoren der urbanen Entwicklung', in Verband Deutscher Städtestatistiker (ed.) *Neue Perspektiven der urbanen Entwicklung*, Amt für Statistik und Stadtforschung, Duisburg:16–35

Berg-Schlosser, D. and Schissler, J. (eds.) (1987) *Politische Kultur in Deutschland. Bilanz und Perspektiven der Forschung*, Politische Vierteljahresschrift, Sonderheft 18

Berger, M., Gibowski, W.G., Jung, M., Roth, D. and Schulte, W. (1987) 'Die Konsolidierung der Wende. Eine Analyse der Bundestagswahl 1987', *Zeitschrift für Parlamentsfragen* 18, No. 2:253–84

Betz, H.-G. (1991) *Postmodern Politics in Germany: The Politics of Resentment*, Macmillan, London

Beyer, A. (1983) *Verfassung und Taktik: Vorraussetzungen, Folgen und Ergebnisse der Hamburger Bürgerschafts- und Bezirksversammlungswahlen im Juni und Dezember 1982*, Landeszentrale für politische Bildung, Hamburg

Beyer, J. and Holtmann, E. (1987) '"Sachpolitik", Partizipation und Apathie in der Nachkriegsgesellschaft', in D. Berg-Schlosser and J. Schissler (eds) *Politische Kultur in Deutschland*:144–53

Beyermann, E. (1986) 'Kommunalwahl 1986. Teil 2: Gemeindeergebnisse der Kreiswahl', *Statistische Monatshefte Schleswig-Holstein*, No. 8/86:164–8

von Beyme, K. (1979) *Das politische System der Bundesrepublik Deutschland: Eine Einführung*, Piper, Munich

Bick, W. (1985a) 'Zum Wahlverhalten junger Wähler. Die Grünen auf Erfolgskurs und an ihren Grenzen', in Stadt Duisburg (ed.) *Materialien zur Stadtforschung*, Amt für Statistik und Stadtforschung, No. 5:7–23

249

References

——, (ed.) (1985b) *Städtestatistik und kommunale Wahlforschung – Konzepte und Ergebnisse*, Arbeitsheft 4, Ausschuß Wahlforschung, Verband Deutscher Städtestatistiker, Duisburg

Boch, R., Schiller-Dickhut, R. and Winter, M. (1982) 'Die alternative Wahlbewegung und die Kommunalpolitik – das Beispiel Bielefeld', in R. Schiller-Dickhut *et al.* (eds) *Alternative Stadtpolitik*:9–43

Bockelt, R. (1989) *Die kommunalen Ebenen in Bayern: Kommunal-Ordnungen und Wahlen*, 3rd edn, Bayerische Landeszentrale für politische Bildungsarbeit, Munich

Bolaffi, A. and Kallscheuer, O. (1983) 'Die Grünen: Farbenlehre eines politischen Paradoxes. Zwischen neuen Bewegungen und Veränderung der Politik', *Prokla* 13, No. 51:62–105

Borchmann, M. (1982) 'Gemeindlicher Aufgabenkreis und Tagesordnung der Vertretungsköperschaft. Zugleich ein Beitrag zu Erscheinungsformen "grüner" Kommunalpolitik', *Der Städtetag* 35, No. 10:648–51

Brand, K.-W. (1982) *Neue soziale Bewegungen: Entstehung, Funktion und Perspektive neuer Protestpotentiale; Eine Zwischenbilanz*, Westdeutscher Verlag, Opladen

——, (1987) 'Kontinuität und Diskontinuität in den neuen sozialen Bewegungen', in R. Roth and D. Rucht (eds.) *Neue soziale Bewegungen in der Bundesrepublik Deutschland*:30–44

Brinkmann, H.U. (1988) 'Wahlverhalten der "neuen Mittelschicht" in der Bundesrepublik Deutschland', *Aus Politik und Zeitgeschichte*, No. 30/31:19–32

Bürklin, W.P. (1981) 'Die Grünen und die "Neue Politik". Abschied vom Dreiparteiensystem?' *Politische Vierteljahresschrift* 22, No. 4:358–82

——, (1984) *Grüne Politik. Ideologische Zyklen, Wähler und Parteiensysteme*, Westdeutscher Verlag, Opladen

——, (1987) 'Governing left parties frustrating the radical non-established Left; the rise and inevitable decline of the Greens', *European Sociological Review* 3, No. 2:109–26

——, (1988) 'The Split Between the Established and the Non-established Left in Germany', *European Journal of Political Research* 13, No. 3:283–93

——, and Kaltefleiter, W. (1987) 'Die Bundestagswahl 1987: Streitfragen einer neuen Konfliktdimension', *Zeitschrift für Politik* 34, No. 4:400–25

Bullmann, U. (1985) 'Rot-grüne Politik von unten?', in U. Bullmann and P. Gitschmann (eds) *Kommune als Gegenmacht. Alternative Politik in Städten und Gemeinden*, VSA, Hamburg:178–98

——, (1987) 'Mehr als nur der Unterbau. Die Zusammenarbeit von Sozialdemokraten und Grünen in den Kommunen', in R. Meng (ed.) *Modell Rot-Grün?*:54–90

Chandler, W. and Siaroff, A. (1986) 'Postindustrial Politics in Germany

References

and the Origins of the Greens', *Comparative Politics* 12, No. 3:303–25

Chaput de Saintogne, R.A. (1961) *Public Administration in Germany. A Study in Regional and Local Administration in Land Rheinland-Pfalz*, Weidenfeld and Nicolson, London

Conradt, D.P. (1980) 'Changing German Political Culture', in G.A. Almond and S. Verba (eds) *The Civic Culture Revisited*, Little and Brown, Boston: 212–72

——, and Dalton, R.J. (1988) 'The West German Electorate and the Party System: Continuity and Change in the 1980's', *Review of Politics* 50, No. 1:3–29

Cotgrove, S. and Duff, A. (1981) 'Environmentalism, Values and Social Change', *British Journal of Sociology* 32, No. 1:92–110

Cryns, M. and Hembach K. (1987) 'Kommunalwahlen und kommunales Wählerverhalten in Nordrhein-Westfalen', in U. Andersen (ed.) *Kommunale Selbstverwaltung und Kommunalpolitik in Nordrhein-Westfalen*:109–31

Dalton, R.J. (1981) 'The persistence of values and life cycle changes', *Politische Vierteljahresschrift* 22, Sonderheft 12:189–207

——, (1984) 'Cognitive Mobilization and Partisan Dealignment in Advanced Industrial Democracies', *Journal of Politics* 46, No. 1:264–84

Datenreport (1987) *Zahlen und Fakten über die Bundesrepublik Deutschland*, Statistisches Bundesamt (ed.), Bundeszentrale für politische Bildung, Bonn

——, (1989) *Zahlen und Fakten über die Bundesrepublik Deutschland*, Statistisches Bundesamt (ed.), Bundeszentrale für politische Bildung, Bonn

Derlien, H.-U., Gürtler, C., Holler, W. and Schreiner, H.J. (1975) *Kommunalverfassung und kommunales Entscheidungssystem*, Anton Hain, Meisenheim am Glan

Deutscher Städtetag (1987) *Volkszählung 1987: Ausgewählte Ergebnisse für Städte mit mehr als 100,000 Einwohnern sowie für kreisfreie Städte unter 100,000 Einwohner*, Deutscher Städtetag, Cologne

Ebermann, T. and Trampert, R. (1985) *Die Zukunft der Grünen. Ein realistisches Konzept für eine radikale Partei*, Konkret, Hamburg

Engel, A. (1984) 'Wahlergebnis und Wählerverhalten in Rheinland-Pfalz. Eine Analyse der Bundestags- und Landtagswahlergebnisse 1983', *Analysen und Berichte* 8, Forschungsgruppe Parteiendemokratie, Coblenz

Erfurth-Hirtz, M. (1985) *Sozialstrukturanalyse der Mainzer Neustadt: Eine Sekundäranalyse*, Materialien zur Jugendhilfeplanung Mainz 7, Mainz

Ernst, E. (1982) *Der Streit um den Ausbau des Frankfurter Flughafen, Zum Nachdenken*, Informationsdienst der Hessischen Landeszentrale für politische Bildung, Wiesbaden

Fabritius, G. (1975) 'Wie mächtig ist der Bürgermeister in Baden-Württemberg? Die süddeutsche Ratsverfassung im Vergleich mit den

References

Gemeindeverfassungen anderer Bundesländer', *Der Bürger im Staat* 25, No. 1: 39–44

Feist, U. and Krieger, H. (1985) 'Die nordrhein-westfälische Landtagswahl vom 12. Mai 1985. Stimmungstrend überrollt Sozialstrukturen oder: Die Wende ist keine Kaffeefahrt', *Zeitschrift für Parlamentsfragen* 16, No. 3:355–72

——, and Krieger, H. (1987) 'Alte und neue Scheidelinien des politischen Verhaltens. Eine Analyse zur Bundestagswahl vom 25. Januar 1987', *Aus Politik und Zeitgeschichte*, No. 12/87:33–47

Fischer, J. (1989) 'Rot-Grün oder Wallmann', interview with J. Fischer, *Stichwort GRÜN*, No. 11:27

Flanagan, S. and Dalton, R. (1984) 'Parties under stress: realignment and dealignment in advanced industrial societies', *West European Politics* 7, No. 1:7–23

Fogt, H. (1983) 'Die Grünen in den Parlamenten der Bundesrepublik: ein Soziogramm', *Zeitschrift für Parlamentsfragen* 14, No. 4:500–17

——, (1984) 'Basisdemokratie oder Herrschaft der Aktivisten? Zum Politikverständnis der Grünen', *Politische Vierteljahreschrift* 25, No. 1:97–120

——, (1986) 'Die Mandatsträger der GRÜNEN. Zur sozialen und politischen Herkunft der alternativen Parteielite', *Aus Politik und Zeitgeschichte*, No. 11/86:16–33

——, (1987) 'Zwischen Parteiorganisation und Bewegung. Die Rekrutierung der Mandatsträger bei den GRÜNEN', Manuscript, Bonn-Sankt Augustin

——, and Uttitz, P. (1984) 'Die Wähler der Grünen 1980–1983: systemkritischer neuer Mittelstand', *Zeitschrift für Parlamentsfragen* 15, No. 2:210–26

Frankland, E.G. (1988) 'The Role of the Greens in West German Parliamentary Politics, 1980–87', *Review of Politics* 50, No. 1:99–122

Frey, R. (1976) 'Kommunale Selbstverwaltung im Verfassungsstaat' in R. Frey (ed.) Kommunale Demokratie. Beiträge für die Praxis der kommunalen Selbstverwaltung, Verlag Neue Gesellschaft, Bonn-Bad Godesberg

——, and Naßmacher, K.-H. (1975) 'Parlamentarisierung der Kommunalpolitik?' *Archiv für Kommunalwissenschaften* 14, No. 2:193–211

Gabriel, O.W. (ed.) (1979a) *Kommunalpolitik im Wandel der Gesellschaft. Eine Einführung in Probleme der politischen Willensbildung in der Gemeinde*, Sozialwissenschaftliche Studien zur Stadt- und Regionalpolitik 5, Anton Hain, Königstein/Ts

——, (1979b) 'Die politische Stellung der Gemeinden im föderativen Verfassungssystem', in O.W. Gabriel (ed.) *Kommunalpolitik im Wandel der Gesellschaft*:25–61

——, (1979c) 'Strukturen politischer Willensbildung in der Gemeinde', in O.W. Gabriel (ed.) *Kommunalpolitik im Wandel der Gesellschaft*:63–8

References

——, (ed.) (1983a) *Bürgerbeteiligung und kommunale Demokratie, Beiträge zur Kommunalwissenschaft* 13, Minerva, Munich

——, (1983b) 'Gesellschaftliche Modernisierung, politische Beteiligung und kommunale Demokratie. Strukturen, Bedingungen und Folgen bürgerschaftlicher Beteiligung an der kommunalen und nationalen Politik', in O.W. Gabriel (ed.) *Bürgerbeteiligung und kommunale Demokratie*:57–103

——, (1984) 'Parlamentarisierung der Kommunalpolitik', in O.W. Gabriel *et al.*, *Opposition in Großstadtparlamenten*:101–47

——, (1986) *Politische Kultur und Postmaterialismus in der Bundesrepublik*, Westdeutscher Verlag, Opladen

——, (ed.) (1989a) *Kommunale Demokratie zwischen Politik und Verwaltung*, Beiträge zur Kommunalwissenschaft 29, Minerva, Munich

——, (1989b) 'Einleitung: Kommunale Demokratie zwischen Politik und Verwaltung', in O.W. Gabriel (ed.) *Kommunale Demokratie zwischen Politik und Verwaltung*:9–16

——, (1990) 'Demokratische Entwicklung und politische Kompetenz', *Aus Politik und Zeitgeschichte*, No 25/90:15–26

——, Haungs, P. and Zender, M. (1984) *Opposition in Großstadtparlamenten*, Forschungsbericht 42, Konrad-Adenauer-Stiftung, Ernst Knoth, Melle

——, and Jann, W. (1990) 'Rheinland-Pfalz', in F. Esche and J. Hartmann (eds) *Handbuch der deutschen Bundesländer*:345–82

Gawatz, E. and Petri, R. (1989) 'Die Landtags- und Kommunalwahlen im Spiegel der Statistik', in Landeszentrale für politische Bildung Baden-Württemberg (ed.) *Taschenbuch Baden-Württemberg: Gesetze - Daten – Analysen*:135–50

Gibowski, W. and Kaase, M. (1986) 'Die Ausgangslage für die Bundestagswahl am 25. Januar 1987', *Aus Politik und Zeitgeschichte*, No. 48/86:3–19

Graf, P. (1977) 'Die Aufgaben der Städte und Gemeinden und Ihre Funktion im gesellschaftlichen Gesamtsystem', in T. Stammen and H. Rausch (eds) *Aspekte und Probleme der Kommunalpolitik*, 3rd edn, Ernst Vögel, Munich:46–61

Grupp, J. (1986) *Abschied von den Grundsätzen? Die Grünen zwischen Koalition und Opposition*, Edition Ahrens, Berlin

Güllner, M. (1986) 'Der Zustand des lokalen Parteiensystems: Chance oder Ende der Kommunalpolitik?' In J.J. Hesse (ed.) *Erneuerung der Politik "von unten"? Stadtpolitik und kommunale Selbstverwaltung im Umbruch*, Westdeutscher Verlag, Opladen:26–37

——, and Löffler, U. (1981) *SPD und Großstadt. Daten, Fakten und Anmerkungen über die Wählersubstanzverluste der Sozialdemokratie in Großstädten*, SPD-Unterbezirk, Cologne

References

Hallensleben, A. (1984) *Von der Grünen Liste zur Grünen Partei? Die Entwicklung der Grünen Liste Umweltschutz von ihrer Entstehung in Niedersachsen bis zur Gründung der Partei DIE GRÜNEN 1980*, Muster-Schmidt, Göttingen

Heidger, R. (1987) *Die Grünen – Basisdemokratie und Parteiorganisation: eine empirische Untersuchung des Landesverbands der Grünen in Rheinland-Pfalz*, Edition Sigma Bohn, Berlin

Henkeborg, P. (1987) 'Andere Koalitionen oder andere Politik. Verändert rot-grün die politische Kultur?', in R. Meng (ed.) *Modell Rot-Grün?*:91–122

Henkel, G. (1991) 'Brauchen die neuen Bundesländer eine kommunale Gebietsreform?' *Der Landkreis* 61, No. 8-9:501–3

Henning, V. (1986) 'Leute persönlich ansprechen und Vorurteile abbauen', *Alternative Kommunalpolitik* 6, No. 3:34–6

Herbers, H. (1987) 'Grüne Kommunalpolitik. Nahbereich zwischen Rhein und Weser. Wo die Bündnisse kommen – anders als gedacht', *Kommune* No. 8:32–5

Hermann, D. and Werle, R. (1983) 'Kommunalwahlen im Kontext der Systemebenen', *Politische Vierteljahresschrift* 24, No. 4:385–405

Hess, R. (1986) *Rheinland-Pfalz: Unser Land. Eine kleine politische Landeskunde*, Landeszentrale für politische Bildung Rheinland-Pfalz, Mainz

——, and Hundertmark, G. (1987) *Unsere Gemeinde. Eine Einführung*, 5th edn, Landeszentrale für politische Bildung Rheinland-Pfalz, Mainz

Hesse, J.J. (1982) 'Bürger und Parteien auf lokaler Ebene: Die Kommune als Ort der gesellschaftlichen und politischen Integration?', in J. Raschke (ed.) *Bürger und Parteien: Ein schwieriges Verhältnis*, Campus, Frankfurt:235–49

Hildebrandt, K. and Dalton, R.J. (1977) 'Die neue Politik: Politischer Wandel oder Schönwetterpolitik?' *Politische Vierteljahresschrift* 18, No. 2/3:230–56

Holtmann, E. (1990) 'Kommunalpolitik im politischen System der Bundesrepublik', *Aus Politik und Zeitgeschichte*, No. 25/90:3–14

Holtz, P. (1985) 'Wahlverhalten von Geburtsjahrgängen – Möglichkeiten und Grenzen der Umrechnung der repräsentativen Wahlstatistik', in W. Bick (ed.) *Städtestatistik und kommunale Wahlforschung*:133–51

Hoplitschek, E. (1982) 'Partei, Avantgarde, Heimat – oder was? Die "Alternative Liste für Demokratie und Umweltschutz" in West Berlin', in J. Mettke (ed.) *Die Grünen. Regierungspartner von morgen?*:82–100

Huber, J. (1983) 'Basisdemokratie und Parlamentarismus: Zum Politikverständnis der Grünen', *Aus Politik und Zeitgeschichte*, No. 2/83:33–45

Ilien, A. and Jeggle, U. (1978) 'Die Dorfgemeinschaft als Not- und

References

Terrorzusammenhang', in H.-G. Wehling (ed.) *Dorfpolitik*, Westdeutscher Verlag, Opladen:38–57

INFAS (1984) *Nordrhein-Westfalen Kommunalwahlen 1984. Analysen und Dokumente*, INFAS-Report Wahlen, Bonn-Bad Godesberg

Inglehart, R. (1971) 'The silent revolution in Europe: Intergenerational change in post-industrial societies', *American Political Science Review* 65, No. 4:991–1017

——, (1977) *The Silent Revolution. Changing Values and Political Styles Among Western Publics*, Princeton University Press, Princeton

——, (1981) 'Post-Materialism in an Environment of Insecurity', *American Political Science Review* 75, No. 4:880–900

——, (1983) 'Traditionelle politische Trennungslinien und die Entwicklung der neuen Politik in westlichen Gesellschaften', *Politische Vierteljahresschrift* 24, No. 2:139–65

Innenministerium des Landes Nordrhein-Westfalen (1989) *Umfrage zu den Bedingungen der Kommunalpolitik in Nordrhein-Westfalen: Auswertung der Antworten*, Düsseldorf

——, (1991) *Reform der Kommunalverfassung in Nordrhein-Westfalen*, Düsseldorf

Irving, R.E.M. and Paterson, W. (1991) 'The 1990 German General Election', *Parliamentary Affairs* 44, No. 3:353–72

Ismayr, W. (1985) 'Die GRÜNEN im Bundestag: Parlamentarisierung und Basisanbindung', *Zeitschrift für Parlamentsfragen* 16, No. 3:299–321

——, and Kral, G. (1990) 'Bayern', in F. Esche and J. Hartmann (eds) *Handbuch der deutschen Bundesländer*:91–132

Jakob, A. (1975) 'Das Ende der Dorfpolitik. Zur Sozialgeschichte des Dorfes und zur Sozialpsychologie seiner Bewohner', *Der Bürger im Staat* 25, No. 1:26–31

Jesse, E. (1986) *Die Demokratie der Bundesrepublik Deutschland: Eine Einführung in das politische System*, 7th edn, Colloquium, Berlin

Johnsen, B. (1988) *Von der Fundamentalopposition zur Regierungsbeteiligung. Die Entwicklung der Grünen in Hessen 1982–1985*, SP-Verlag, Marburg

Jurtschitsch, E., Rudnick, A. and Wolf, F.O. (eds) (1988) *Grünes und Alternatives Jahrbuch 1988: Grüne Perspektiven*, Kölner Volksblatt, Cologne

Kaack, H. (1971) *Geschichte und Struktur des deutschen Parteiensystems*, Westdeutscher Verlag, Opladen

Kaltefleiter, W. (1991) 'Die Struktur der deutschen Wählerschaft nach der Vereinigung', *Zeitschrift für Politik* 38, No. 1:1–32

Kanitz, H. (1988) *Das Verhältnis zwischen SPD und GRÜNEN auf kommunaler Ebene in Nordrhein-Westfalen. Ein Erfahrungsbericht*, Institut für Kommunalwissenschaften, Konrad-Adenauer-Stiftung, Kommunal-Verlag, Recklinghausen

255

References

Kevenhörster, P. (1983) 'Kommunalwahlen – Instrumente bürgerschaftlicher Einflußnahme auf die Kommunalpolitik', in O.W. Gabriel (ed.) *Bürgerbeteiligung und kommunale Demokratie*:157–72

Kimmel, A. (1985) 'Die saarländische Landtagswahl vom 10. März 1985. Zwei Verlierer, zwei Gewinner, ein Sieger oder: Der Wähler hat den Wechsel gewollt', *Zeitschrift für Parlamentsfragen* 16, No. 3:322–37

Kimminich, O. (1983) 'Die Parteien im Rechtsstaat: Herausforderung durch die "Alternativen"', *Die Öffentliche Verwaltung* 36, No. 6:217–26

Kistler, H. (1985) *Die Bundesrepublik Deutschland. Vorgeschichte und Geschichte 1945–1983*, Bundeszentrale für politische Bildung, Bonn

Kitschelt, H. (1988) 'Organization and Strategy of Belgian and West German Ecology Parties. A New Dynamic of Party Politics in Western Europe?' *Comparative Politics* 20, No. 2:127–54

——, (1989) 'The Internal Politics of Parties: The Law of Curvilinear Disparity Revisited', *Political Studies* 37, No. 3:400–21

Klein, A. (1981) 'Programmatische Orientierung kommunalpolitischer Entscheidungsträger', *Zeitschrift für Parlamententsfragen* 12, No. 3:309–17

Klein, P. (ed.) (1983) *Sozialdemokratische Kommunalpolitik im Schatten Bonns. Eine kommunalpolitische Dokumentation*, Vorwärts, Bonn

——, and Clauditz, U. (eds) (1983) *Ein Arbeitsbuch zur Kommunalpolitik*, Neue Gesellschaft, Bonn

——, and Kirchner, W. (1983) 'Die Bedeutung der Kommunalwahlniederlagen für die SPD', in P. Klein (ed.) *Sozialdemokratische Kommunalpolitik im Schatten Bonns*:47–73

Klingemann, H.-D. (1985) 'West Germany', in I. Crewe and D. Denver (eds.) *Electoral Change in Western Democracies. Patterns and Sources of Electoral Volatility*, Croom Helm, London and Sydney:230–63

Klotzsch, L. and Stöss, R. (1986) 'Die Grünen', in R. Stöss (ed.) *Parteienhandbuch*:1509–98

Koenigs, T. (1988) 'Frankfurt: Die Grüne Stadt am Main', interview with M. Fester and S. Kraft, *Kommunard/inn/en Rundbrief* 4/88, Grüne und Alternative in den Kommunalvertretungen Hessen e.V., Fulda:3–6

Köser, H. (1991) 'Der Gemeinderat in Baden-Württemberg: Sozialprofil, Rekrutierung, Politikverständnis', in T. Pfizer and H.-G. Wehling (eds) *Kommunalpolitik in Baden-Württemberg*:141–61

Köth, A. and Kolmer, C. (1983) *Strukturanalyse der Stadt Mainz: Eine Sekundäranalyse*, Materialien zur Jugendhilfeplanung Mainz 1, Mainz

Kolinsky, E. (1984) *Parties, Opposition and Society in West Germany*, Croom Helm, London and Sydney

——, (1988) 'The West German Greens – a women's party?' *Parliamentary Affairs* 41, No. 1:5–16

——, (ed.) (1989a) *The Greens in West Germany. Organisation and Policy Making*, Berg, Oxford, New York and Munich

References

——, (1989b) 'Women in the Green Party', in E. Kolinsky (ed.) *The Greens in West Germany*:189–221

Kommunalverband Ruhrgebiet (1985) *Wahlen im Ruhrgebiet. Erste Bestandsaufnahme*, Arbeitshefte Ruhrgebiet des Kommunalverbandes Ruhrgebiet, Essen

——, (1989) *Kommunalwahlen NRW 1989*, Aktuell 12, No. 2, Kommunalverband Ruhrgebiet, Essen

Krämer, R. and Winter, M. (1982) 'Haben drei Jahre Bunte Liste im Rathaus die Bielefelder Linke gestärkt?', in J. Reents (ed.) *Es grünt so rot. Alternativen zwischen Mode und Modell*, Konkret, Hamburg:155–75

Kühr, H. (1983) 'Politik in der Gemeinde', *Informationen zur politischen Bildung* 197, Bundeszentrale für politische Bildung, Bonn

Kunz, V. (1989) 'Die Einnahmen und Ausgaben der Gemeinden', in O.W. Gabriel (ed.) *Kommunale Demokratie zwischen Politik und Verwaltung*:59–106

Kuschke, W. and Cryns, M. (1984) 'Kommunalwahlen in Nordrhein-Westfalen', in U. Andersen (ed.) *Kommunalpolitik und Kommunalwahlen in Nordrhein-Westfalen*:59–94

Langguth, G. (1984) *Der grüne Faktor. Von der Bewegung zur Partei*, Edition Interfromm, Zürich

Leder, G. and Friedrich, W.-U. (1986) *Kommunalpolitik und Kommunalwahlen in Niedersachsen*, Landeszentrale für politische Bildung Niedersachsen, Hanover

Lehmbruch, G. (1975) 'Der Januskopf der Ortsparteien. Kommunalpolitik und das lokale Parteiensystem', *Der Bürger im Staat* 25, No. 1:3–6

Lilge, H. (1966) *Der Staatsbürger 1: Peter wird Minister*, Carl Ueberreuter, Vienna and Heidelberg

——, (1986) *Hessen in Geschichte und Gegenwart*, Steiner-Verlag-Wiesbaden, Stuttgart

Lipset, S.M. and Rokkan, S. (1967) 'Cleavage Structures, Party Systems and Voter Alignments: An Introduction', in S.M. Lipset and S. Rokkan (eds) *Party Systems and Voter Alignments: Cross-National Perspectives*, Free Press, New York:1–64

Löffler, B. and Rogg, R. (1991) '*Kommunalwahlen und kommunales Wahlverhalten*', in T. Pfizer and H.-G. Wehling (eds) *Kommunalpolitik in Baden-Württemberg*:108–24

Lommer, H. and Rieß, J. (1985) 'Alternative Wahlbewegung und Grüne Kommunalpolitik', in W. Pohl *et al.* (eds) *Handbuch für alternative Kommunalpolitik*:9–16

Loreck, J. (1987) 'Rot-grüne Rathaus-Bündnisse. Szenen einer wilden Ehe', *Vorwärts*, No. 2, 10 January:15–17

Mann, H.-J. (1989) 'Das Kommunalwahlsystem' in Landeszentrale für politische Bildung Baden-Württemberg (ed.) *Taschenbuch Baden-Württemberg: Gesetze – Daten – Analysen*:99–134

References

Maren-Grisebach, M. (1982) *Philosophie der Grünen*, Olzog, Munich

Mattar, M. (1983) 'Formen politischer Beteiligung in den Gemeindeordnungen der Bundesländer', in O.W. Gabriel (ed.) *Bürgerbeteiligung und kommunale Demokratie*:105–25

Meng, R. (ed.) (1987) *Modell Rot-Grün? Auswertung eines Versuchs*, VSA, Hamburg

Metzger, O. (1987) 'Findet der "Ausstieg" 1989 statt?', *Kommunarden-Rundbrief*, No. 4, Grüne und Alternative in den Räten von Baden-Württemberg, Stuttgart:4–8

Meulemann, H. (1985) 'Säkularisierung und Politik. Wertwandel und Wertstruktur in der Bundesrepublik Deutschland', *Politische Vierteljahresschrift* 26, No. 1:29–51

Meyer-Ullrich, G. (1988) *Wie wirksam sind kommunale Gleichstellungsstellen in Bezug auf die Umsetzung GRÜN-feministischer Politik? Projektbericht*, Grüne und Alternative in den Räten Nordrhein-Westfalen, Frauenreferat, Düsseldorf

Mez, L. (1987) 'Von den Bürgerinitiativen zu den GRÜNEN. Zur Entstehungsgeschichte der "Wahlalternativen" in der Bundesrepublik Deutschland', in R. Roth and D. Rucht (eds) *Neue Soziale Bewegungen in der Bundesrepublik Deutschland*:263–76

——, and Wolter, U. (1980) 'Wer sind die Grünen?', in L. Mez and U. Wolter (eds) *Die Qual der Wahl. Ein Wegweiser durch die Parteienlandschaft zur Bundestagswahl 1980*, Olle und Wolter, Berlin:6–54

Mickel, W. (ed.) (1986) *Handlexikon zur Politikwissenschaft*, Schriftenreihe der Bundeszentrale für politische Bildung 237, Franz Ehrenwirth, Munich

Müller, F. (1979) 'Das Wählerpotential', in D. Murphy *et al.* (eds) *Protest. Grüne, Bunte und Steuerrebellen*:138–55

Müller-Rommel, F. (1982) '"Parteien neuen Typs" in Westeuropa: eine vergleichende Analyse', *Zeitschrift für Parlamentsfragen* 13, No. 3:369–90

——, (1983a) 'Die Grünen – künftig ein fester Bestandteil unseres Parteiensystems?', *Der Bürger im Staat* 33, No. 1:17–20

——, (1983b) 'Die Wahl zur Hamburger Bürgerschaft vom 19. Dezember 1982: Die neue Alte Mehrheit', *Zeitschrift für Parlamentsfragen* 14, No. 1:96–109

——, (1985) 'The Greens in Western Europe: similar but different', *International Political Science Review* 6, No. 4:483–99

——, (1989) 'The German Greens in the 1980s: Short-term Cyclical Protest or Indicator of Transformation?' *Political Studies* 37, No. 1:114–22

——, (1991) 'Stabilität durch Wandel: DIE GRÜNEN vor und nach der Bundestagswahl 1990', in R. Roth and D. Rucht (eds) *Neue soziale Bewegungen in der Bundesrepublik Deutschland*:441–57

——, and Poguntke, T. (1989) 'The Unharmonious Family: Green Parties in Western Europe', in E. Kolinsky (ed.) *The Greens in West Germany*:11–29

——, and Wilke, H. (1981) 'Sozialstruktur und "postmaterialistische" Wertorientierungen von Ökologisten. Eine empirische Analyse am Beispiel Frankreichs', *Politische Vierteljahresschrift* 22, No. 4:383–97

Murphy, D. (1979) 'Der Grüne und Bunte Protest', in D. Murphy *et al.* (eds) *Protest. Grüne, Bunte und Steuerrebellen*:12–68

——, (1983) '"Alternative" Politik und "sozialdemokratische" Kritik. Einige Anmerkungen zum Beitrag von Scharping und Hoffmann-Göttig', *Zeitschrift für Parlamentsfragen* 14, No. 1:146–53

——, and Roth, R. (1987) 'In viele Richtungen zugleich. DIE GRÜNEN – ein Artefakt der Fünf-Prozent-Klausel?', in R. Roth and D. Rucht (eds) *Neue soziale Bewegungen in der Bundesrepublik Deutschland*:303–24

——, Rubart, F., Müller, F. and Raschke, J. (eds) (1979) *Protest. Grüne, Bunte und Steuerrebellen. Ursachen und Perspektiven*, Rowohlt, Hamburg

Naßmacher, K.-H. (1986) 'Kommunalpolitik', in W. Mickel (ed.) *Handlexikon zur Politikwissenschaft*:244–9

Naßmacher, H. (1989) 'Die Aufgaben, die Organisation und die Arbeitsweise der kommunalen Vertretungskörperschaft', in O.W. Gabriel (ed.) *Kommunale Demokratie zwischen Politik und Verwaltung*:179–96

Nessel, R. and Nowack, C. (1982) *Startbahn 18 West. Voraussetzungen und Folgen des Bürgerengagements gegen den Ausbau des Frankfurter Flughafens*, Haag and Herchen, Frankfurt

Nimsch, M. (1989) 'Mainz bleibt Mainz – und Frankfurt?' *Stichwort GRÜN*, No. 10:20-1

Nippkau, F. (1986) 'Die Systemfrage stellt sich nicht', *Alternative Kommunalpolitik* 6, No. 3:30–1

Noeske, W. (1985) 'Junge und ältere Wähler – Unterschiede im Wahlverhalten anhand städtischer Wahlstatistiken', in Ausschuß Wahlforschung (ed.) *Beiträge zur kommunalen Wahlforschung*, Statistische Woche 1985 in Bonn, Arbeitsheft 5, Ausschuß Wahlforschung, Verband Deutscher Städtestatistiker, Duisburg:19–56

Noll, W. and Rechmann, B. (1991) *Strukturwandel im Ruhrgebiet*, Kommunalverband Ruhrgebiet, Abteilung Öffentlichkeitsarbeit/Wirtschaft, 2nd edn, Essen

Novy-Huy, R. (1988) 'Debatte im Rundbrief', letter published in *Kommunard/innen/en Rundbrief* 3/88, Grüne und Alternative in den Kommunalvertretungen Hessen e.V., Fulda:6

ÖSS (Ökologische und soziale Studien) (1988) *Wer wählt grün und warum nicht? Analysen und Thesen zu Wahlergebnissen und Wählerpotentialen der GRÜNEN. Eine Untersuchung im Auftrag des Landesvorstandes der*

References

GRÜNEN Nordrhein-Westfalen. Zusammenfassung der Ergebnisse, Ökologische und soziale Studien, Bochum

Pagenkopf, H. (1975) *Kommunalwahlrecht, Vol. 1: Verfassungsrecht*, 2nd edn, Heymann, Cologne

Papadakis, E. (1984) *The Green Movement in West Germany*, Croom Helm, London

Pappermann, E. (1984) 'Die kommunale Selbstverwaltung in Nordrhein-Westfalen', in Landeszentrale für politische Bildung Nordrhein-Westfalen (ed.) *Nordrhein-Westfalen: eine politische Landeskunde*, Kohlhammer, Cologne, Stuttgart, Berlin and Mainz:180–209

——, Roters, W. and Theisen, R.-D. (1981) *Kommunalrecht in Nordrhein-Westfalen*, Verwaltung in Praxis und Wissenschaft 8, Deutscher Gemeindeverlag, Cologne

Pappi, F.U. (1973) 'Parteiensystem und Sozialstruktur in der Bundesrepublik', *Politische Vierteljahresschrift* 14, No. 2:191–213

——, (1984) 'The West German Party System', in S. Bartolini and P. Mair (eds) *Politics in Contemporary Western Europe*, Frank Cass, London:7–26

——, and Terwey, M. (1982) 'The German Electorate: Old Cleavages and New Political Conflicts', in H. Döring and G. Smith (eds) *Party Government and Political Culture in Western Germany*, Macmillan, London and Basingstoke:174–96

Pelinka, A. (1986) 'Bürgerinitiativen', in W. Mickel (ed.) *Handlexikon zur Politikwissenschaft*:45–7

Pflaum, R. (1954) 'Politische Führung und politische Beteiligung als Ausdruck gemeindlicher Selbstgestaltung', in G. Wurzbacher (ed.) *Das Dorf im Spannungsfeld industrieller Entwicklung. Untersuchungen an den 45 Dörfern und Weilern einer westdeutschen ländlichen Gemeinde*, Kohlhammer, Stuttgart

Plöhn, J. and Barz, A. (1990) 'Saarland', in F. Esche and J. Hartmann (eds.) *Handbuch der deutschen Bundesländer*:383–416

Poguntke, T. (1987a) 'Grün-alternative Parteien: Eine neue Farbe in westlichen Parteiensystemen', *Zeitschrift für Parlamentsfragen* 18, No. 3:368–82

——, (1987b) 'New politics and party systems. The emergence of a new type of party?' *West European Politics* 10, No. 1:76–88

——, (1987c) 'The organization of a participatory party – the German Greens', *European Journal of Political Research* 15, No. 6:609–33

——, (1989) 'The "new politics" and Green Parties in Western Europe: a typological analysis', Paper presented at Annual Conference of the Political Science Association of the UK, University of Warwick, 4–6 April 1989

Pohl, W., Burmeister, U., Friedrich, M., Klemisch, H. and Lommer, H. (eds) (1985) *Handbuch für alternative Kommunalpolitik*, Informationsdienst Alternative Kommunalpolitik, AJZ, Bielefeld

Pridham, G. (1978) 'Ecologists in politics: the West German case', *Parliamentary Affairs* 31, No. 4:436–44

Prinz, H. (1984) 'Organisation, Personal, Datenschutz bei den Gemeinden', in SGK Nordrhein-Westfalen (ed.) *Der kommunale Wirkungskreis, Handbuch für die Arbeit in Rat und Ausschüssen*, SGK Nordrhein-Westfalen, Düsseldorf

Rammstedt, O. (ed.) *Bürgerinitiativen in der Gesellschaft. Politische Dimensionen und Reaktionen*, Argumente in der Energiediskussion 9, Neckar-Verlag, Villingen-Schwenningen

Raschke, J. (1979) 'Ursachen und Perspektiven des Protests', in D. Murphy *et al.* (eds) *Protest. Grüne, Bunte und Steuerrebellen*:156–88

——, (1991) *Krise der Grünen: Bilanz und Neubeginn*, Forschungsgruppe Neue Soziale Bewegungen, Schüren, Marburg

Rehrmann, N. (ed.) (1985) *Rot-Grünes "Modell Kassel"? Eine Bilanz nach vier Jahren*, Kasseler Verlag and Werkstatt Verlag, Kassel

Reichel, P. (1981) *Politische Kultur der Bundesrepublik*, Leske, Opladen

Reidegeld, E. (1985) 'Bürgerbeteiligung', in W. Pohl *et al.* (eds) *Handbuch für alternative Kommunalpolitik*:47–55

Richter, B. (1987) 'Die nordrhein-westfälische Gemeindeordnung – Entwicklung und Vergleich mit anderen deutschen Kommunalverfassungen', in U. Andersen (ed.) *Kommunale Selbstverwaltung und Kommunalpolitik in Nordrhein-Westfalen*:53–77

Rieß, J. (1985) 'Möglicher Zielorientierungen grüner Politik', in W. Pohl *et al.* (eds) *Handbuch für alternative Kommunalpolitik*:37–8

Rönsch, H.-D. (1980a) 'Grüne Listen – Vorläufer oder Katalysatoren einer neuen Protestbewegung? Zum Problem von "postindustriellen" Protestpotentialen', in O. Rammstedt (ed.) *Bürgerinitiativen in der Gesellschaft. Politische Dimensionen und Reaktionen*:375–434

——, (1983) 'Die Grünen: Wählerbasis, politische Entwicklung, Programmatik', *Gewerkschaftliche Monatshefte* 34, No. 2:98–111

Rohr, R. and Hau, W. (eds) (1985) *Grüne und andere Listen. "Es geht voran. Erfahrung wird gemacht". Eine kommunalpolitische Alternative*, az-Verlag, Frankfurt

Rohrbacher-List, G. (1984) '"Grüner" als "Grün" oder alle "GRÜNE" sind gleich?' *Grüne Rheinland/Pfälzer* 2, No. 6/7:10–11

Roth, R. (1988) 'Local Green politics in West German cities', Manuscript, Berlin

——, and Rucht, D. (eds) (1987) *Neue soziale Bewegungen in der Bundesrepublik Deutschland*, Studien zur Geschichte und Politik 252, Bundeszentrale für politische Bildung, Bonn

——, and Rucht, D. (eds) (1991) *Neue soziale Bewegungen in der Bundesrepublik Deutschland*, Studien zur Geschichte und Politik 252, 2nd edn, Bundeszentrale für politische Bildung, Bonn

References

Roth, W. (ed.) (1972) *Kommunalpolitik – für wen? Arbeitsprogramm der Jungsozialisten*, Rowohlt, Hamburg

——, and Edelhoff, D. (1983) 'Kommunalpolitik für wen? Das Juso-Kommunalprogramm 1971 - 12 Jahre danach', in P. Klein (ed.) *Sozialdemokratische Kommunalpolitik im Schatten Bonns*:74–88

Rucht, D. (1980) *Von Whyl nach Gorleben. Bürger gegen Atomprogramm und nukleare Entsorgung*, Munich

——, (1987) 'Zum Verhältnis von sozialen Bewegungen und politischen Parteien', *Journal für Sozialforschung* 27, No. 3/4:297–313

Rudnick, A. and Goltermann, W. (1981) '1,500 Grüne Parlamentarier in Niedersachsen!' *Moderne Zeiten* 1, No. 10:58–61

Rüdig, W. (1980) 'Bürgerinitiativen und Umweltschutz. Eine Bestandsaufnahme empirischer Befunde', in O. Rammstedt (ed.) *Bürgerinitiativen in der Gesellschaft. Politische Dimensionen und Reaktionen*:119–84

——, and Lowe, P.D. (1986) 'Political Ecology and the Social Sciences – The State of the Art', *British Journal of Political Science* 16, No. 4:513–50

Samtlebe, G. (1983) 'Die Verluste des kommunalen Einflusses in der Bundes-SPD', in P. Klein (ed.) *Sozialdemokratische Kommunalpolitik im Schatten Bonns*:7–23

Sarcinelli, U. (ed.) (1984) *Wahlen und Wahlkampf in Rheinland-Pfalz. Beiträge für die politische Bildungsarbeit aus Anlaß der Landtags- und Bundestagswahlen am 6. März 1983*, Leske and Budrich, Opladen

Schacht, K. (1985) 'Kommunales Wahlverhalten – Zum Stand der Forschung', in W. Bick (ed.) *Städtestatistik und kommunale Wahlforschung*:9–36

——, (1986) *Wahlentscheidung im Diensleistungszentrum. Analyse zur Frankfurter Kommunalwahl vom 22. März 1981*, Beiträge zur sozialwissenschaftlichen Forschung 91, Westdeutscher Verlag, Opladen

——, (1987) 'Politische Kultur, sozialer Wandel und Wahlverhalten im Dienstleistungszentrum Frankfurt', in D. Berg-Schlosser and J. Schissler (eds) *Politische Kultur in Deutschland*:275–81

Schäfer, R. and Stricker, H.-J. (1989) 'Die Aufgaben der Gemeinden und ihre Entwicklung', in O.W. Gabriel (ed.) *Kommunale Demokratie zwischen Politik und Verwaltung*:35-58

Scharf, T. (1989) 'Red-Green coalitions at local level in Hesse', in E. Kolinsky (ed.) *The Greens in West Germany*:159–87

Scharping, R. and Hoffmann-Göttig, J. (1982) '"Alternative" Politik in den Landesparlamenten? Ideologiekritische Inhaltsanalyse von 300 Redebeiträgen "grüner" Parlamentarier', *Zeitschrift für Parlamentsfragen* 13, No. 3:391–416

Scheffler, M. (1987) 'Städtepartnerschaften mit Nicaragua: Entwicklungspolitik in der Kommune – klein aber oho!' *Alternative Kommunalpolitik* 7, No. 1:19–21

Scheytt, O. (1991) 'Verwaltungshilfe für die Kommunen in den neuen

Ländern der Bundesrepublik Deutschland', *Archiv für Kommunalwissenschaften* 30, No. 1:3–16

Schiller, T. and von Winter, T. (1990) 'Hessen', in F. Esche and J. Hartmann (eds) *Handbuch der deutschen Bundesländer*:237–72

Schiller-Dickhut, R., Winter, M., Hoplitschek, E., Czymek, H., *et al.* (eds) (1981) *Alternative Stadtpolitik. Grüne, rote und bunte Arbeit in den Rathäusern*, VSA, Hamburg

Schmidt-Eichstaedt, G. (1989) 'Grundformen der inneren Gemeindefassung in der Bundesrepublik Deutschland', in O.W. Gabriel (ed.) *Kommunale Demokratie zwischen Politik und Verwaltung*:17–33

Schmidt-Jorzig, E. (1982) *Kommunalrecht*, Kohlhammer, Stuttgart

Schmitt, H. (1987) *Neue Politik in alten Parteien. Zum Verhältnis von Gesellschaft und Partei in der Bundesrepublik*, Westdeutscher Verlag, Opladen

——, (1989) 'On Party Attachment in Western Europe and the Utility of Eurobarometer Data', *West European Politics* 12, No. 2:122–39

——, Niedermayer, O. and Menke, K. (1981) 'Etablierte und Grüne. Zur Verankerung der ökologischen Bewegung in den Parteiorganisationen von SPD, FDP, CDU und CSU', *Zeitschrift für Parlamentsfragen* 12, No. 4:516–40

Schneider, G. and Ramb, H. (1988) *Hessische Kommunalverfassung. Gemeindeordnung. Landkreisordnung*, 9th edn, Hessische Landeszentrale für politische Bildung, Wiesbaden

Schneider, H. (1990) 'Baden-Württemberg', in F. Esche and J. Hartmann (eds) *Handbuch der deutschen Bundesländer*:53–90

Schomaker, H. (1986) 'Nachlese zur Kommunalwahl in Schleswig-Holstein: Derbe Wahlschlappe der CDU', *Alternative Kommunalpolitik* 6, No. 3:24–7

Schultze, R.-O. (1980) 'Nur Parteienverdrossenheit und diffuser Protest? Systemfunktionale Fehlinterpretationen der grünen Wahlerfolge', *Politische Vierteljahresschrift* 11, No. 2:292–313

——, (1987) 'Die Bundestagswahl 1987 – eine Bestätigung des Wandels', *Aus Politik und Zeitgeschichte*, No. 12/87:3–17

Schulz, A. and Schmitz, A. (1985) 'Rot-grünes "Modell-Kassel": Ein Trauerspiel mit magerem Ergebnis', in N. Rehrmann (ed.) *Rot-Grünes "Modell Kassel"*:61–70

Schuster, F., Zender, M., Niemann, B., von Wersebe, H., Kanitz, H. and Kramer, C. (1985) *DIE GRÜNEN in der Kommunalpolitik. Erste Erfahrungen und Konsequenzen*, Institut für Kommunalwissenschaften, Konrad-Adenauer-Stiftung, Kommunal-Verlag, Recklinghausen

Simon, K. (1987) 'Kommunale Demokratie – eine Politikvermittlungs-Idylle?', in U. Sarcinelli (ed.) *Politikvermittlung. Beiträge zur politischen Kommunikationskultur*, Bonn Aktuell, Stuttgart:232–47

References

Simon, T. (1984) '"Da müssen wir nochmals 'ran". Weshalb es für viele Grüne und Alternative Gemeinderäte in Kleinstädten die Möglichkeit des Ausscheidens bzw. der Rotation nicht gibt', *Alternative Kommunalpolitik* 4, No. 4:54

——, (1986) 'Mit der Einsamkeit eines Langstreckenläufers konfrontiert', *Alternative Kommunalpolitik* 6, No. 3:32–4

Smith, G. (1986) *Democracy in Western Germany: Parties and Politics in the Federal Republic*, 3rd edn, Gower, Aldershot

Sokol, B. (1985) 'Die Selbstverwaltungsgarantie: Aufgaben und Kompetenzen der Gemeinden', in W. Pohl *et al.* (eds) *Handbuch für alternative Kommunalpolitik*:29-38

Sontheimer, K. (1979) *Grundzüge des politischen Systems der Bundesrepublik Deutschland*, 7th edn, Piper, Munich

Sozialbericht 1987 (1988) *Sozialbericht 1987: Arbeitslosigkeit und Sozialhilfe in Mainz -Dokumentation*, Sozialdezernat der Stadt Mainz, Mainz

Sozialbericht 1988 (1989) *Sozialbericht 1988: Solidarität und Gerechtigkeit*, Sozialdezernat der Stadt Mainz, Mainz

Spretnak, C. and Capra, F. (1985) *Green Politics. The Global Promise*, Paladin, London

Städtetag (1991) 'Kreisfreie Städte und Landkreise in den neuen Bundesländern am 31.12.1989', *Der Städtetag* 44, No. 7:517–22

Stammen, T. (1977) 'Die Erneuerung der kommunalen Selbstverwaltung in Deutschland nach 1945', in T. Stammen and H. Rausch (eds) *Aspekte und Probleme der Kommunalpolitik*, 3rd edn, Ernst Vögel, Munich:10–32

Stinchcombe, A. (1975) 'Social Structure and Politics', in F. Greenstein and N.W. Polsby (eds) *Macropolitical Theory. Handbook of Political Science*, Vol. 3, Addison-Wesley, Reading MA:557–622

Stober, R. (1986) 'Alternative in der Verantwortung – Rechtsfragen alternativer Politik', *Der Städte- und Gemeinderat*, No. 1:3–8

Stöss, R. (1984a) 'Sollen die Grünen verboten werden? Zur Kritik konservativer Staatsrechtler an der Verfassungsmäßigkeit der Grünen/Alternativen', *Politische Vierteljahresschrift* 25, No. 4:403–24

——, (1984b) 'Im Visier des Staatsschutzes. Zu den juristischen Schikanen gegen den Grünen/Alternativen unterhalb der Verbotsschwelle', *Vorgänge* 23, No. 4:30–6

——, (ed.) (1986a) *Das Parteien-Handbuch: die Parteien der Bundesrepublik Deutschland 1945–1980*, Sonderausgabe, Westdeutscher Verlag, Opladen

——, (1986b) 'Wählergemeinschaften', in R. Stöss (ed.) *Das Parteien-Handbuch*: 2392-428

——, (1987) 'Parteien und soziale Bewegungen', in R. Roth and D. Rucht (eds) *Neue soziale Bewegungen in der Bundesrepublik Deutschland*:277–302

Strauß, F.J. (1984) *Bericht zur politischen Lage beim 4. Konferenz der*

References

Landräte und Oberbürgermeister der CSU, 6 October 1984, Nuremberg, Dokumentation, CSU, Munich

Swatzina, K. (1987) *Perspektiven grüner Kommunalpolitik*, Grüne und Alternative in den Räten Nordrhein-Westfalen, Düsseldorf

Thyerlei, M. (1986) 'Kommunalwahlen in Niedersachsen am 5. Oktober 1986', *Statistische Monatshefte Niedersachsen*, No. 12:382–90

Tolmein, O. (1986) *Ökorepublik Deutschland. Erfahrungen und Perspektiven rot-grüner Zusammenarbeit*, VSA, Hamburg

Traunsberger, E. and Klemisch, H. (1986) 'Zum Wesen der kommunalen Selbstverwaltung', paper presented at first national meeting of green and alternative local politicians, Haus Wittgenstein, Bonn, 19–20 April 1986

Troitzsch, K.G. (1976) *Sozialstruktur und Wählerverhalten. Möglichkeiten und Grenzen ökologischer Wahlanalysen, dargestellt am Beispiel der Wahlen in Hamburg von 1949–1974*, Anton Hain, Meisenheim am Glan

Unglaub, M. (1988) 'Das neue Wahlsystem bei Kommunalwahlen in Rheinland-Pfalz', Sonderdruck, *Statistische Monatshefte Rheinland-Pfalz* 41, No. 7:1–14

Veen, H.-J. (1984) 'Wer wählt grün? Zum Profil der neuen Linken in der Wohlstandsgesellschaft', *Aus Politik und Zeitgeschichte*, No. 35–36/1984:3–17

——, (1986) 'Lebensperspektiven, Arbeitsorientierungen und politische Kultur Jugendlicher in der Mitte der 80er Jahre', in R. von Voss and K. Friedrich (eds) *Die Jungwähler. Was sie denken und wie sie entscheiden*, Bonn Aktuell, Stuttgart:35–72

——, (1987) 'Die Anhänger der GRÜNEN – Ausprägungen einer neuen linken Milieupartei', in M. Langner (ed.) *Die Grünen auf dem Prüfstand, Analyse einer Partei*, Lübbe, Bergisch Gladbeck:60–127

——, (1989) 'The Greens as a Milieu Party', in E. Kolinsky (ed.) *The Greens in West Germany*:31–59

——, and Gluchowski, P. (1983) 'Tendenzen der Nivellierung und Polarisierung in den Wählerschaften von CDU/CSU und SPD von 1959 bis 1983 – eine Fortschreibung', *Zeitschrift für Parlamentsfragen* 14, No. 4:545–55

——, and Gluchowski, P. (1988) 'Sozialstrukturelle Nivellierung bei politischer Polarisierung - Wandlungen und Konstanten in den Wählerstrukturen der Parteien 1953–1987', *Zeitschrift für Parlamentsfragen* 19, No. 2:225–48

——, and Hoffmann, J. (1990) *Lage und Einschätzung der Grünen-Hessen im Vorfeld der Landtagswahl am 20. Januar 1991*, Forschungsinstitut der Konrad-Adenauer-Stiftung, Sankt Augustin

Voigt, R. (1981) 'Zur politischen Kultur der Landbevölkerung', *Sozialwissenschaftliche Informationen für Unterricht und Studium* 10, No. 1:28–31

References

——, (1986) 'Kommunalpolitik im ländlichen Raum. Ein Plädoyer für die Wiederbelebung der lokalen Politik', *Aus Politik und Zeitgeschichte*, No. 46–47/86:3–13

——, (1987) 'Finanzierung kommunaler Aufgaben', in U. Andersen (ed.) *Kommunale Selbstverwaltung und Kommunalpolitik in Nordrhein-Westfalen*:144–160

Weber, K. (1987) *Siedlungsflächenentwicklung im nördlichen Rheinhessen von 1950 bis 1983*, Informationen No. 15, Planungsgemeinschaft Rheinhessen-Nahe, Neustadt and Mainz

Wehling, H.-G. (1981) 'Parteien auf dem Dorf – Didaktische Orientierung', *Sozialwissenschaftliche Informationen für Unterricht und Studium* 10, No. 1:25–8

——, (1986) *Kommunalpolitik in der Bundesrepublik Deutschland*, Colloquium, Berlin

——, (1989) 'Rechtsstellung, Rolle und Sozialprofil der Bürgermeister', in O.W. Gabriel (ed.) *Kommunale Demokratie zwischen Politik und Verwaltung*:221–35

——, (1991) 'Elemente direkter Demokratie: Bürgerbegehren, Bürgerentscheid, Gemeinderats-und Bürgermeisterwahl als Chancen politischer Partizipation', in T. Pfizer and H.-G. Wehling (eds) *Kommunalpolitik in Baden-Württemberg*:125–35

——, and Pfizer, T. (eds) (1985) *Kommunalpolitik in Baden-Württemberg*, Landeszentrale für politische Bildung Baden-Württemberg, Stuttgart

——, and Pfizer, T. (eds) (1991) *Kommunalpolitik in Baden-Württemberg*, 2nd edn, Landeszentrale für politische Bildung Baden-Württemberg, Stuttgart

Weinberger, M.-L. (1984) *Aufbruch zu neuen Ufern? Grün-Alternative zwischen Anspruch und Wirklichkeit*, Neue Gesellschaft, Bonn

Weiß, F. (1986) 'Giftalarm nach Brand in Rösrather PVC-Werk: Grüne Panikmache?' *Alternative Kommunalpolitik* 6, No. 3:36–8

Werle, R. (1981) 'Die Grünen im Parteienwettbewerb auf der lokalen Ebene. Kandidaten und Wahlerfolge im nordbadischen Raum', *Sociologia Internationalis* 19, No. 2:175–93

Wiesenthal, H. (1985) 'Die Grünen in Nordrhein-Westfalen. Geschichte, Bedeutung, Programm und Willensbildung', in U. von Alemann (ed.) *Parteien und Wahlen in Nordrhein-Westfalen*, Schriften zur politischen Landeskunde Nordrhein-Westfalens 2, Landeszentrale für politische Bildung Nordrhein-Westfalen, Kohlhammer, Cologne

Woyke, W. and Steffens, U. (1987) *Stichwort: Wahlen. Ein Ratgeber für Wähler, Wahlhelfer und Kandidaten*, 5th edn, Leske and Budrich, Leverkusen

——, and Steffens, U. (1990) *Stichwort: Wahlen. Ein Ratgeber für Wähler, Wahlhelfer und Kandidaten*, 6th edn, Leske and Budrich, Leverkusen

Zeuner, B. (1983) 'Aktuelle Anmerkungen zum Postulat der "Basisdemokratie" bei den Grünen/Alternativen', *Prokla* 13, No. 51:106–17

Statistical Sources

Baden-Württemberg (1985) *Gemeindestatistik 1985, No. 2, Wahl der Gemeinderäte, Ortschaftsräte und Kreisräte am 28. Oktober 1984, Parts A and B*, Statistisches Landesamt Baden-Württemberg, Stuttgart
———, (1990) *Gemeindestatistik 1990, No. 2, Wahl der Gemeinderäte, Ortschaftsräte und Kreisräte am 22. Oktober 1989, Parts A and B*, Statistisches Landesamt Baden-Württemberg, Stuttgart
Bavaria (1985) *Kommunalwahlen in Bayern am 18. März 1984*, Beiträge zur Statistik Bayerns, No. 407, Bayerisches Landesamt für Statistik und Datenverarbeitung, Munich
———, (1990) *Statistischer Bericht: Kommunalwahl 1990, No. 7*, Bayerisches Landesamt für Statistik und Datenverarbeitung, Munich
Bielefeld (1989) *Kommunalwahl am 1. Oktober 1989: Analysen, Ergebniss*, Statistisches Amt und Wahlamt, Bielefeld
———, (1990) *Volkszählung 1987, Teil 1, Ergebnisse der Volks- und Berufszählung*, Statistisches Amt und Wahlamt, Bielefeld
Bonn (1985) *Kommunalwahl in der Stadt Bonn am 30. September 1984 – eine wahlstatistische Analyse*, Amt für Statistik und Einwohnerwesen, Bonn
Cologne (1984) *Kommunalwahl am 30. September 1984 in Köln. Ergebnisse und Kurzanalyse*, Kölner Statistische Nachrichten, Amt für Statistik und Einwohnerwesen, Cologne
———, (1987) *Statistisches Jahrbuch 1986*, No. 72, Amt für Statistik und Einwohnerwesen der Stadt Köln, Cologne
Darmstadt (1985) *Kommunalwahl 10.3.1985. Endgültiges Ergebnis. Repräsentative Wahlstatistik*, Statistische Mitteilungen des Magistrats der Stadt Darmstadt, Amt für Statistik und Einwohnerwesen, Darmstadt
Duisburg (1984) *Kommunalwahl 1984, Duisburger Wahlstatistik*, Amt für Statistik und Stadtforschung, Duisburg
———, (1988) *Duisburger Handbuch gesellschaftlicher Daten 1987, Städtische Bürgerbefragungen 1981–1987*, Daten und Information 20, Amt für Statistik und Stadtforschung, Duisburg
———, (1989) *Kommunalwahl 1989: Erste Analyse der Ergebnisse in Duisburg im Städte- und Regionalvergleich*, Amt für Statistik und Stadtforschung, Duisburg
Düsseldorf (1989) *Volkszählung 1987: Stadtteilergebnisse*, Statistische Informationen, No. 234, Amt für Statistik und Wahlen, Düsseldorf
Frankfurt (1985) 'Das Wahlverhalten nach Geschlecht und Altersgruppen bei der Wahl zur Stadtverordnetenversammlung am 10. März 1985 – Ergebnisse der repräsentativen Wahlstatistik', *Frankfurter Statistische Berichte*, No. 1, Amt für Statistik, Wahlen und Einwohnerwesen, Frankfurt:5–13

References

——, (1986) *Die Kommunalwahlen am 10. März 1985 in Frankfurt a.M.. Rechtsgrundlagen, Organisation, Wahlergebnisse*, Frankfurter Statistische Berichte 48, Sonderheft 46, Amt für Statistik, Wahlen und Einwohnerwesen, Frankfurt

——, (1988) 'Erste Ergebnisse der Volkszählung 1987', *Frankfurter Statistische Berichte* 50, No. 4:77–97

——, (1989a) *Strukturdaten der Frankfurter Wirtschaft. Ergebnisse der Arbeitsstättenzählung vom 25. Mai 1987*, Frankfurter Statistische Berichte, Sonderheft 51, Amt für Statistik, Wahlen und Einwohnerwesen, Frankfurt

——, (1989b) *Kommunalwahlen am 12. März 1989 in Frankfurt am Main: Vorläufige Ergebnisse*, Frankfurter Statistische Berichte, Sonderausgabe, Amt für Statistik, Wahlen und Einwohnerwesen, Frankfurt

——, (1989c) 'Das Wahlverhalten nach Geschlecht und Alter bei der Wahl zur Stadtverordnetenversammlung am 12. März 1989: Ergebnisse der repräsentativen Wahlstatistik', *Frankfurter Statistische Berichte* 51, No. 1, Amt für Statistik, Wahlen und Einwohnerwesen, Frankfurt:19–31

Heidelberg (1989) *Volkszählung 1987: Stadtteilergebnisse der Volks- und Berufszählung. Tabellenband 1: Strukturdaten zur Bevölkerung und Erwerbstätigkeit*, Stadtplanungs-und Vermessungsamt, Heidelberg

——, (1990) *Gemeinderatswahl in Heidelberg am 22. Oktober 1989: Ergebnisse und Kurzanalyse*, Stadtplanungsamt, Heidelberg

Hesse (1982) *Die Kommunalwahlen am 22. März 1981*, Beiträge zur Statistik Hessens, No. 127 Neue Folge, Hessisches Statistisches Landesamt, Wiesbaden

——, (1986) *Die Kommunalwahlen am 10. März 1985*, Beiträge zur Statistik Hessens, No. 184 Neue Folge, Hessisches Statistisches Landesamt, Wiesbaden

——, (1990) *Die Kommunalwahlen am 12. März 1989*, Beiträge zur Statistik Hessens, No. 230 Neue Folge, Hessisches Statistisches Landesamt, Wiesbaden

Kiel (1987) *Die Gemeindewahl am 2. März 1986 in Kiel. Auswertung der Ergebnisse*, Statistische Berichte, No. 130, Statistisches Amt, Kiel

Krefeld (1984) *Kommunalwahl 1984. Ergebnisse – Vergleiche – Analysen*, Amt für Statistik und Stadtentwicklung, Krefeld

Leverkusen (1985) *Kommunalwahl am 30. September 1984 in Leverkusen*, Berichte zur Stadtforschung, No. 4, Amt für Wahlen und Meldewesen, Leverkusen:2–35

Lübeck (1986) 'Die Wahl zur Bürgerschaft der Hansestadt Lübeck am 2. März 1986', *Hansestadt Lübeck, Beiträge und Zahlen aus Wirtschaft und Leben*, Statistisches Amt und Wahlamt, Lübeck

——, (1989) 'Ergebnisse der Volkszählung 1987 für die Hansestadt Lübeck und ihre Stadtteile', *Lübecker Zahlen*, No. 2, Statistisches Amt,

References

Lübeck
Mainz (1984a) *Kommunalwahl 1984: Gesamtstadt, Stadtteile, Stimmbezirke*, Hauptamt, Mainz
——, (1984b) *Europawahl 1984. Kommunalwahl 1984. Repräsentative Wahlstatistik der Stadt Mainz*, Hauptamt, Mainz
——, (1987a) *Mainz im Städtevergleich*, Beiträge zur Statistik und Stadtentwicklung, Amt für Umwelt und Stadtentwicklung, Mainz
——, (1987b) *Entwicklungen 1970-1985 im Spiegel der Zahlen*, Amt für Statistik und Stadtentwicklung in Zusammenarbeit mit dem Hauptamt, Mainz
——, (1988) *Der Arbeitsmarkt im Bezirk des Arbeitsamtes Mainz. Jahresbericht 1987*, Arbeitsamt Mainz, Statistisches Büro, Mainz
——, (1989) *Vorläufige Ergebnisse der Volkszählung vom 25. Mai 1987. Eckdaten der Stadt Mainz im Vergleich mit der Volkszählung 1970 und mit den Werten von Rheinland-Pfalz sowie der Bundesrepublik Deutschland*, Stadtverwaltung Mainz and Geographisches Institut, Johannes Gutenberg Universität, Mainz
Mannheim (1989) 'Ausgewählte Ergebnisse der Volkszählung 1987 nach den 17 Mannheimer Stadtbezirken', *Vierteljahresbericht*, No. 1/89, Amt für Statistik und Wahlen, Mannheim
Munich (1984) 'Die Ergebnisse der Stadtratswahlen am 18. März 1984', *Münchener Statistik*, No. 4, Munich:99–110
Münster (1989) *Wahlen 1989: Europawahl 18.06.89; Kommunalwahl 01.10.89*, Beiträge zur Statistik 50, Statistisches Amt, Münster
Neuss (1984) *Ergebnisse der Kommunalwahl am 30. September 1984*, Statistische Informationen, Amt für Wirtschaftsförderung und Stadtentwicklung, Neuss
——, (1989a) *Volkszählung 1987: Erste Ergebnisse*, Statistische Informationen, Amt für Wirtschaftsförderung und Stadtforschung, Neuss
——, (1989b) *Kommunalwahl 1989: Ergebnisse und Kurzanalyse*, Statistische Informationen, Amt für Wirtschaftsförderung und Stadtforschung, Neuss
——, (1990) *Volkszählung 1987: Ergebnisse für statistische Bezirke*, Statistische Informationen, Amt für Wirtschaftsförderung und Stadtforschung, Neuss
North Rhine Westphalia (1984) *Kommunalwahlen in Nordrhein-Westfalen 1984, No. 4, Ergebnisse nach Gemeinden*, Landesamt für Datenverarbeitung und Statistik Nordrhein-Westfalen, Düsseldorf
——, (1989) *Kommunalwahlen in Nordrhein-Westfalen 1989, No. 4, Ergebnisse nach Gemeinden*, Landesamt für Datenverarbeitung und Statistik Nordrhein-Westfalen, Düsseldorf
Nuremberg (1991) *Ergebnis der Kommunalwahl 1990*, Statistische Nachrichten der Stadt Nürnberg, Amt für Stadtforschung und Statistik, Nuremberg
Oberhausen (1985a) *Kommunalwahl am 30. September 1984. Ergebnisse der*

269

References

repräsentativen Wahlstatistik und endgültige Wahlergebnisse, Beiträge zum Wahlgeschehen, No. 10, Amt für Statistik und Wahlen, Oberhausen

——, (1985b) *Kommunalwahlen am 30. September 1984. Statistische Wahlresultate und weitere Analysen*, Beiträge zum Wahlgeschehen, No. 11, Amt für Statistik und Wahlen, Oberhausen

——, (1989) *Kommunalwahl am 1 Oktober 1989. Ergebnisse und Kurzanalyse: vorläufiges Wahlergebnis*, Beiträge zum Wahlgeschehen, No. 18, Amt für Statistik und Wahlen, Oberhausen

Rhineland Palatinate (1985) *Die Kommunalwahlen in Rheinland-Pfalz am 17. Juni 1984. Ergebnisse nach Verwaltungskreisen, Verbandsgemeinden und Gemeinden mit Vergleichszahlen der Kommunalwahlen 1979*, No. 312, Statistisches Landesamt Rheinland-Pfalz, Bad Ems

——, (1990) *Die Kommunalwahlen in Rheinland-Pfalz am 18. Juni 1989. Ergebnisse nach Verwaltungskreisen, Verbandsgemeinden und Gemeinden mit Vergleichszahlen der Kommunalwahlen 1979*, No. 340, Statistisches Landesamt Rheinland-Pfalz, Bad Ems

Saarland (1984) *Kommunal- und Europawahl am 17. Juni 1984*, Einzelschriften zur Statistik des Saarlandes, No. 67, Statistisches Amt des Saarlandes, Saarbrücken

——, (1989) *Europa- und Kommunalwahl am 18. Juni 1989*, Einzelschriften zur Statistik des Saarlandes, No. 74, Statistisches Amt des Saarlandes, Saarbrücken

Salzgitter (1987) *Die Kommunalwahlen 1986 in der Stadt Salzgitter*, Salzgitter in Zahlen, Amt für Wirtschaftsförderung, Statistik und Wahlen, Salzgitter

Schleswig-Holstein (1978) *Die Kreis- und Gemeindewahl am 5. März 1978*, Statistische Monatshefte Schleswig-Holstein, Statistisches Landesamt Schleswig-Holstein:110-36

——, (1986) *Die Kreis- und Gemeindewahl am 2. März 1986 in Schleswig-Holstein. Endgültiges Ergebnis*, Statistische Berichte des Statistischen Landesamtes Schleswig-Holstein, No. 3–5, Statistisches Landesamt Schleswig-Holstein, Kiel

——, (1990) *Kommunalwahl am 25. März 1990 in Schleswig-Holstein. Endgültiges Ergebnis*, Statistische Berichte des Statistischen Landesamtes Schleswig-Holstein, No. 3-5, Statistisches Landesamt Schleswig-Holstein, Kiel

Stuttgart (1985) *Gemeinderatswahl 1984*, Statistische Blätter Sonderbeiträge, No. 41d, Statistisches Amt der Landeshauptstadt Stuttgart, Stuttgart

Wiesbaden (1983) *Analysen zum politischen Verhalten in Wiesbaden*, Planungsgruppe beim Oberbürgermeister, Wiesbaden

——, (1984) *Materialien zum Wahlverhalten seit der Kommunalwahl 1981*, Planungsgruppe beim Oberbürgermeister, Wiesbaden

Wuppertal (1984) *Kommunalwahl am 30. September 1984*, Wuppertaler Statistik, Sonderheft 17, Amt für Stadtentwicklung und Stadtforschung, Wuppertal

Documents, Reports and Other Publications

ALK (1985) 'Aktionsgemeinschaft Lebenswertes Königstein (ALK): Kommunalpolitik in der Provinz', in R. Rohr and W. Hau (eds) *Grüne und andere Listen*:61–77

AKP (Alternative Kommunalpolitik), Informationsdienst Alternative Kommunalpolitik, Fachzeitschrift für Grüne und Alternative Politik, Vols. 1–10, 1980–1990

Augsburg (1984) 'Warum wollen die Grünen in das Augsburger Rathaus? Kurzprogramm', DIE GRÜNEN im Kreisverband Augsburg, Augsburg

Bochum (1987) '2 Jahre Ratsarbeit', DIE GRÜNEN im Rat, Bochum

Bonn (1984) 'DIE GRÜNEN: Ein Lichtblick. Programm für Bonn', DIE GRÜNEN Kreisverband Bonn, Bonn

——, (1985) 'Ein Jahr im Rat ... wir lernen fliegen', FRAKTION DIE GRÜNEN im Rat der Stadt Bonn, Bonn

——, (1988) 'Rechenschaftsbericht der GRÜNEN IM RAT der Stadt Bonn', Bonn

——, (1989) 'Alternativen sind machbar, Frau Nachbar! Aus der Haushaltsrede der Stadtverordneten Edith Kühnle', *Grünphase*, Informationen aus der grünen Ratsfraktion, Bonn, No. 18, February/March 1989:7

Cologne (1989) '4 Jahre 1984–1988. Nachrichten, Polemiken, Dokumente der GRÜNEN im Kölner Rat, Ausgewählte Werke', DIE GRÜNEN im Kölner Rat, Cologne

Dortmund (1987) 'DIE GRÜNEN im Rathaus 1984–86. Ein Bericht', DIE GRÜNEN im Rathaus, Dortmund

Erklärung (1984) 'Kommunalpolitische Erklärung', verabschiedet auf der Landesdelegiertenversammlung der GRÜNEN in Marl am 18.3.1984, DIE GRÜNEN, Landesverband Nordrhein-Westfalen, Düsseldorf

Geseke (1984) 'Kommunalpolitisches Grundsatzprogramm', Ortsverband der GRÜNEN, Geseke

——, (1987) 'Zur Lage der Fraktion. Drei Jahre GRÜNE im Rat der Stadt Geseke – Eine Bilanz', Fraktion DIE GRÜNEN im Rat, Geseke

Grüne Hessenzeitung, unofficial publication of the Hesse Green Party: various issues from each of years of publication

Grüne und Alternative in den Räten Nordrhein-Westfalen (1988) 'Zur Situation in den Fraktionen', Fragebogen-Auswertung, 1.3.88, Düsseldorf

References

Kassel (1985) 'Kommunal', DIE GRÜNEN Kassel, Kassel
Krefeld (1988) 'Kommunalwahlen 1989', Blattgrün, Zeitung der Krefelder Grünen, No. 21, September/October 88:6
Leverkusen (1988) 'Umweltschutzbericht Januar 1988 der Fraktion DIE GRÜNEN im Rat der Stadt Leverkusen', Leverkusen
Lippstadt (1984) 'Kommunalpolitische Alternativen', DIE GRÜNEN – Ortsverband Lippstadt, Lippstadt
——, (1986) 'DIE GRÜNEN im Rat der Stadt Lippstadt: eine Bürgerinformation', No. 3, November '86, Ratsfraktion "DIE GRÜNEN", Lippstadt
——, (1988) 'DIE GRÜNEN im Rat der Stadt Lippstadt: eine Bürgerinformation', No. 4, March '88, Ratsfraktion "DIE GRÜNEN", Lippstadt
LWL (1987) *Rundbrief*, December '87, DIE GRÜNEN im Landschaftsverband Westfalen-Lippe, Münster
Marburg (1985) 'Kommunalwahl '85: Ein Programm für Marburg, Kurzfassung', DIE GRÜNEN, Ortsverband Marburg, Marburg
Munich (1984) 'DIE GRÜNEN in den Kreistag!' Die Grünen im Landkreis München, Garching
——, (undated) '100 Tage GRÜNE und Alternative Liste München im Münchener Rathaus', GRÜNE und Alternative Liste München, Munich
Nuremberg (1985) 'Solidarität mit Nicaragua', Verein zur Förderung der Städtepartnerschaft Nürnberg/San Carlos und Region in Nicaragua, Nuremberg
Paderborn (1988) 'GRÜNE Ratspost – eine Bilanz, 3 Jahre GRÜNE im Rathaus', DIE GRÜNEN im Rathaus, Paderborn
Pantheon (1987) 'Diskussionsbeiträge, Beschlüsse, Stellungnahmen zum Treffen der Landesverbände, Bundestagsfraktion DIE GRÜNEN, Bundesvorstand, Bundeshauptausschuß und Mitglieder VertreterInnen aus Orts- und Kreisverbänden der GRÜNEN am 12. Dezember 1987', Pantheon, Bonn, Bundesgeschäftsstelle DIE GRÜNEN, 11 December 1987, Bonn
Pulheim (1984) 'DIE GRÜNEN ins Rathaus, Kommunalwahl '84', Ortsverband der GRÜNEN Pulheim, Pulheim
——, (1986) 'Stattzeitung. Informationsblatt der GRÜNEN in Pulheim' 2, No. 1, January/February 1986, Fraktion "DIE GRÜNEN" im Rat der Stadt Pulheim, Pulheim
——, (1987) 'Stattzeitung. Informationsblatt der GRÜNEN in Pulheim' 3, No. 1, January 1987, Fraktion "DIE GRÜNEN" im Rat der Stadt Pulheim, Pulheim
Römerfraktion (1983) 'Was machen DIE GRÜNEN im Parlament? Haushaltsdokumentation 1983 der GRÜNEN IM RÖMER – Beispiele aus zwei Jahren GRÜNER Kommunalpolitik in Frankfurt', DIE GRÜ-

NEN IM RÖMER, Frankfurt
——, (1984) 'Verzeichnis aller Anträge und Anfragen vom 1. April bis 31. August 1984', Grüne Römerpost, Berichte aus der Arbeit der GRÜNEN IM RÖMER, Sonderheft, October 1984, Frankfurt
——, (1985) 'Konzeptionen für die Veränderung einer Stadt', Grüne Römerpost, Berichte aus der Arbeit der GRÜNEN IM RÖMER, January 1985, Frankfurt
Soest (1987) 'DIE GRÜNEN – eine Herausforderung', DIE GRÜNEN im Kreistag, Kreis Soest, Wurfsendung, Lippstadt
——, (1988) 'Themen, Positionen, Initiativen 1987', DIE GRÜNEN im Kreistag, Kreis Soest, Lippstadt
Taxi (1985) 'Aufstieg und Fall des Frauentaxi-Projekts in Tübingen. Eine Dokumentation', die Taxi-Frauen im Frauenzentrum, Tübingen
Wiesbaden (1985) 'Kommunalprogramm Wiesbaden', Die GRÜNEN Wiesbaden, Wiesbaden

Additional Mainz Sources

In addition to the published and unpublished sources stated above, reference was also made to the following materials:

The minutes of the Mainz city council: July 1984 to June 1987.
The minutes of the *Fraktionsgruppe* of the Mainz Greens: July 1984 to December 1988
Grüne Seiten, newspaper of the Mainz Green *Fraktion*, 1985–7
Bulletäng, publication of the Mainz Green *Fraktion*, 1988–9
The minutes of selected meetings of the Mainz Green Party: 1984–7
Mainzer Allgemeine Zeitung
Mainzer Rhein Zeitung

Index

Index

276

Index